THE ARTFUL VEGAN

THE ARTFUL VEGAN

FRESH FLAVORS FROM THE MILLENNIUM RESTAURANT

ERIC TUCKER *with* BRUCE ENLOE

DESSERT RECIPES *by* AMY PEARCE

PHOTOGRAPHY *by* RENÉE COMET

NUTRITIONAL INFORMATION *by* PAUL ROSE

TEN SPEED PRESS
Berkeley & Toronto

Ten Speed Press
P.O. Box 7123
Berkeley, California 94707
www.tenspeed.com

Distributed in Australia by Simon & Schuster Australia, in Canada by Ten Speed Press
Canada, in New Zealand by Southern Publishers Group, in South Africa by Real Books, and
in the United Kingdom and Europe by Airlift Book Company.

Cover and book design by Betsy Stromberg
Photography by Renée Comet except bottom photograph on page 202, by Tom Erikson
Food and prop styling by Pouké
Photo assistance by Tom Hood

Library of Congress Cataloging-in-Publication Data

Tucker, Eric, 1965–
 The artful vegan : fresh flavors from the Millennium Restaurant / Eric Tucker with Bruce
Enloe ; dessert recipes by Amy Pearce ; photography by Renée Comet.
     p. cm.
Includes index.
 ISBN 1-58008-207-6 (paper) — ISBN 1-58008-538-5 (hardcover)
 1. Cookery, Vegan. 2. Cookery, International. 3. Millennium (Restaurant :
San Francisco, Calif.) I. Enloe, Bruce. II. Pearce, Amy. III. Title.
 TX837 .T82 2003
 641.5'636—dc21
                    2003004082
Printed in China
First printing, 2003

1 2 3 4 5 6 7 8 9 10 — 07 06 05 04 03

ACKNOWLEDGMENTS

I would like to thank Ann and Larry Wheat, Chip Conley, and Joie de Vivre Hospitality for making Millennium possible and for their unwavering support. I also want to thank the folks who really make it all happen: Millennium's kitchen crew and support staff. Words can't express my love, respect, and gratitude for you guys and gals. I would also like to thank Damon Eckard and David Corley for all of their outstanding work. Specials thanks to Bruce and Amy for sharing the vision, for creative inspiration, and for being all-around good friends. Thanks to Margret Malone for the grand vision of taking Milly's to San Francisco. Thanks to Kirsty Melville, Brie Mazurek, Betsy Stromberg, and Renée Comet for their patience and dedication to this book, and to everyone who helped create the text, from testing recipes to calculating nutritional information to giving me a kick in the pants when needed. Thanks to all of Millennium's purveyors, who provide us with fresh, seasonal ingredients on a daily basis. Thanks to Doris and Richie Chan at Eurasia in New Jersey. Finally, thank you to Joan and Gerald Tucker. *E.T.*

I would like to thank Eric for being a mentor, friend, and an incredible creative collaborator. Thanks to the gang at Millennium, especially the greatest kitchen crew in the world, past and present. Thanks to Ann Wheat, Larry Wheat, and Chip Conley for keeping a great idea alive. Thanks to Ten Speed Press for their interest and patience. Thanks to Veritable Vegetables, Terra Sonoma, Star Route Farms, Little Farms, Laguna Farms, Green Hill Farms, Mariquita Farms, Wine Forest Wild Mushrooms, Rei de Fungi, and all of the other folks who bring the food that makes all this possible and real. Thanks to the winemakers and importers mentioned in the wine introduction, plus any that may have been overlooked. Thanks to Mother's Café & Garden in Austin. Thanks to Ruby Goins, for her inspiration. Thanks to my family: Carol, Sam, Travis, and Tracy Enloe; Sarah and Ben Kent; Dorothy and Edgar LeBlanc; and Steve and Denise Busby. And in memory of Loretta Girlinghouse, Christine Ogg, and Ruby Enloe, some other great chefs to whom I owe much. The biggest thanks go to Nicole LeBlanc for her patience, quiet collaboration, and love. *B.E.*

I would like to thank Mom Pearce for having me in the kitchen when I was very young and always teaching me to be creative, and Danner Pearce; Kris Jensen for artful encouragement; The Natural Gourmet Cookery School, Sascha Weiss, and everyone in New York who helped get me started; James Foran, Verite Mazzola, Andrew Field, and everyone else who taught me the *other* way of baking (with eggs and butter); Eric Tucker for teaching me to use exotic ingredients and for giving me creative freedom and inspiration; Anna Eyre and Jo Defazio for being star pastry assistants; all my friends in Humboldt County and Alabama for eating my creations; and the loyal clientele of Millennium Restaurant especially: without you this wouldn't be possible. *A.P.*

CONTENTS

INTRODUCTION

What do we have here? Another Millennium cookbook. Another body of work spanning the past four years. What we have here is a literary piece that chronicles a moment in time—and more important, a moment in mind. It is the distillate, the end result, and the means to that result (the recipes) of our thoughts, inspirations, and relationships to food and food products—and not just from myself and the chefs at Millennium, but from our purveyors, from the folks growing the tomatoes, from the forager gathering the chanterelles, and from the miller grinding the corn polenta. This book, like most cookbooks, is a written account of the end result of their labor, both physical and cerebral: from the hands of the grower to the hands of the chef to the hands of the server to your dinner table.

Where have we been in the few years since we published our last book, *The Millennium Cookbook*? We have been right here in the kitchen, now on the bottom floor of San Francisco's Savoy Hotel, at 580 Geary Street. Through our food, we have been across the globe doing what we do best, extrapolating elements of the cuisines of different cultures, making them our own, and presenting them to you at the dinner table. Fusion cuisine, California cuisine, or nouvelle cuisine? Pacific Rim, Nuevo Latino, Pan Asian, or Mediterranean Basin cuisine? Multilatitudinal or multilongitudinal cuisine? Save the labeling for the folks in offices on Madison Avenue. How about *inspired cuisine,* which should be the basis for all chefs worth their Britanny sea salt, whether they cook classic Escoffier or are the vanguard of the latest and greatest culinary movement of the month.

Inspiration comes from our surroundings: we get excited when we see Mariquita Farm's broccoli di ciccio at the farmers' market; awestruck when Connie Green brings us our first Alaskan Blue chanterelle; floored by dozens of different kimchee when we wander into a Korean market on Geary and say, "Hey, we could make these!"; or get drawn into the Food Network at 2 A.M. as we sit watching with a beer and a bag of potato chips and think, "Hmm, that's a good idea. Of course we would have to lose the pork, butter, and veal stock—but I like the way that guy on TV presents that thing." Inspiration, in many respects, is the goal of this book. For those who look at it, we want you to be inspired to cook from it. We want to pass along our knowledge, our experiences, and our joys, to have you make these recipes your own and add them to your culinary vocabulary.

Where else have we been? We have brought the farmers' market to you with our Farmers' Market Dinners, arranging the upstairs of our dining room as a market and cooking a dinner with each course based on the produce of one farm. We've been outdoors gathering mushrooms, miner's lettuce, sagebrush, and nepita for our Exotic Mushroom and Wild Foods Dinners. We've been standing in the field cooking for and serving 130 guests at Mariquita Farm in Watsonville, California. We've brought the wineries into the restaurant, with amazing dinners that showcase organic wines from Coturri, Topolos, Chateau Bousqette, and Punset, to name a few. We've explored convincing vegan adaptations of down-home Americana cuisine in our Southern

Comfort Dinners (with a little bit of New Jersey thrown in as well), and we've challenged your taste buds and sinus cavities with our annual Chile Dinner, when we literally handpick each chile in the fields at Tierra Vegetables.

So what is Millennium? In many respects, Millennium is nothing more than the sum total of all the folks involved in running the restaurant, from chef to server to busser to the janitorial crew; we're all interrelated. When it comes directly to the food, two folks in particular stand out in their contributions to Millennium: former Sous-Chef Bruce Enloe and Pastry Chef Amy Pearce. Bruce came to Millennium by way of Austin, Texas. Texas-vegetarian . . . sounds incongruent? Not in the slightest. Think big flavor. You don't need a big slab of steer for big flavor. And Bruce is just the chef to show you what Texas-vegetarian is all about. His roots and—more important, I think, judging from his family stories—his family heritage came to us through his cooking. Think chiles, smoke, and dark roux, and you start to get the picture. Like myself, Bruce was extremely influenced by our local surroundings, the ethnic cuisines and food products available to us in the San Francisco Bay Area. In 2003, Bruce left us to travel, with the goal of starting up his own organic restaurant, but his dishes will continue to be offered on Millennium's menu. His interest and commitment to organic wines is still evident in our wine list, which he was instrumental in establishing; as of this writing, it is probably the strongest and most in-depth organic wine list in the country.

Amy is also a southerner, from Alabama to be exact, and she too lets her roots shine in her work. She has a knack for transposing down-home favorites into strictly vegan desserts that are sexy and elegant. Amy graduated from the Natural Gourmet Cooking School in New York City and has worked at some of the finer restaurants in San Francisco, doing classic dessert cookery (think eggs, butter, white sugar). The combination of

backgrounds—the more natural foods vegan coupled with the classic foundation—has allowed her to raise the bar on what vegan desserts can be: innovative, artful, and elegant, ranging from ultradecadent to light, ethereal, and refreshing. Amy's desserts can hold their own against any classic dessert anywhere.

Others on the staff have also brought their influences to the table in the Millennium kitchen. From her experience living in Japan, former Chef Elisha Trotter brought new ideas and methods for pickling vegetables. From Vince Peterson's year in Italy we got a shaved porcini mushroom salad. Louisa Shafia's Persian heritage, Stuart Rieter's time in the Peace Corps in Ghana . . . each staff member brings his or her background to Millennium, and our cuisine reflects their firsthand takes on dishes from around the world.

How does it happen in the Millennium kitchen? If you have ever had a chance to work, hang out, or get to know people who work in restaurant kitchens, you know that a high percentage of them are or were musicians. Such is the case with me. Such was also the case for Bruce and, through the years, probably more than half of the Millennium kitchen and wait staff. Somewhere someone once said, Never marry a musician or a chef. What if you are both? Is that the worst of all realities? I don't know about that, but creating a dish is very much like composing a song. We always make musical references when tasting a dish. It needs more of a top note, maybe something bright and acidic or tongue-tingling spicy to cut through the richness of the mix. It needs more bottom end, more bass, more body or backbone from, say, earthy roasted garlic or the warmth and depth of caramelized onions.

Bruce, Amy, and I compose dishes by literally riffing off each other. Half of this is done through "virtual cooking." We sit down at a table, for example, with some white beans. What are we going to do with them? One of us might suggest a ragoût with fennel and mushrooms. Another thinks we should wrap it in phyllo dough and give it a shot of truffle oil so the diner who cracks it open will be treated to that intense truffle effluvium melding with the fennel. Great! Sounds like we're heading to the north of Italy. Let's serve it over some roasted garlic soft polenta enhanced with a bit of cashew cream for contrasting texture. Let's maintain the theme, keep up the intensity, and serve the whole thing over a wine-porcini reduction. How about Zinfandel instead of an Italian varietal, being that we are here in California. Cool. Now we need something green and something pungent to cut through all that richness. How about grilled broccoli rabe? Excellent! It's September, and figs are at their prime, so let's garnish the dish with roasted figs to mirror some of the elements of the sauce and a few capers to contrast with the overall lushness of

the dish. Sold! It's on tomorrow's menu. Riffing, jamming, whatever you want to call it: that is how it happens in our kitchen.

We try not to be overt about our politics, but every bite of food and every sip of wine or coffee makes a statement at our restaurant. Whether you like it or not, you also make a statement every time you dine at Millennium: you support organic and sustainable agriculture from predominantly small local growers and purveyors. Sure, we have fantastic organic wine from France, some of it produced by the family of our San Francisco distributor, Véronique Raskin, of Organic Wine Company. We have amazing grits and corn products freshly milled for us from South Carolina (thanks very much to Anson Mills) and even Bulgarian chanterelles imported by the King of Mushrooms, Todd Spanier. But the brunt and the core of our produce and products are local or relatively locally grown or produced. I can hop in my car and visit almost every major farm and purveyor within a couple of hours' drive or, better yet, visit them at one of our local farmers' markets. We are lucky and blessed with an abundance of organic farming in northern California.

But it's not just happening here. It is happening all across the country, even if not to this extent in some places. Small independent farms and product suppliers are incorporating sustainable agriculture practices, keeping heirloom produce alive, selling only locally at markets and farm stands and farmers' markets, and generally caring about their product and their environment. You may have to look a bit harder to find organic produce in some areas, but it's out there.

One of the things I enjoy most about utilizing small local farms and purveyors is that I can have direct contact with the person who is growing our kale or pressing our olive oil. I can talk produce with these people, I can talk soil, I can talk weather, I can talk food. I can understand their passions, and they can understand mine. I can get the kale directly from their hands, try to do it justice in my kitchen, and get it onto your plate. And you can do this, too. If you have a passion for food, and especially for fruits and vegetables, you can seek out your local growers and foster relationships with them. It can and does make a difference.

One of our favorite purveyors is Terra Sonoma of Sebastopol. Susan Stover and Tony Sadoti left San Francisco for Sonoma County to start Animalitos Farm in 1990. This was no small feat; it was a lot of work in the beginning. In 1994 they took over the reigns of a small company that specialized in bringing cut flowers and produce to accounts in San Francisco. They expanded on that original concept to become a clearinghouse of sorts for a dozen or so small farms from their neck of western Sonoma County. They fax us information about produce available from their farm and from the other farms they deal with. We order what we need, and Tony jumps in the truck and transports the food down to us, as well as to many other fine restaurants in the Bay Area.

What makes this so great is the sense of community it fosters. Some of the farms are literally a couple of Meyer lemon trees in Susan and Tony's neighbor's backyard; wild blackberry brambles growing between the vineyards next door; Indian red peaches from a lady Susan met in the parking lot of a local produce market. We're not talking about companies with semis rolling down their driveways to drop off pallets of produce; we're talking about people from down the street in their station wagons, with kids in tow, dropping off two cases of kabocha squash. I've been lucky to have a chance to spend some time with Susan and Tony at their house, which is their farm, and at their loading and receiving dock. It's the closest thing we have to a neighbor up the street with a vegetable garden.

Where does this lead us? Back into the kitchen, of course—where we turn our inspiration into the best food we can possibly prepare. Through this book and our first book, we want to share this wealth of produce and possibility with you, and we hope that you, too, will be inspired.

See you in the kitchen.

WINE AT MILLENNIUM

My first glass of wine was a Guinness. That is to say, tasting Guinness was the first time I realized there was a world of alcohol beyond Budweiser. I remember being shocked and alarmed by the intensity of flavor. I had to put it down and sit for ten minutes before taking another sip. This reaction has recurred several times over the years: my first snifter of hot Frangelico (liqueur), my first a glass of Patron Reposado (tequila), my first Islay (single-malt) scotch, and—more recently and with great passion—my introduction to wine.

As a chef, I'm constantly barraged with information about wine in cookbooks and magazines and at events. Wine is mentioned and talked about with that knowing smile, with a sigh and a faraway wistful look—an attitude to which most of the world responds with, "Geez, what an irritating snob." I include myself in this excluded world and do believe that most wine lovers have achieved their insight not by some higher vision but as a lucky addendum to their birth.

But let's face it, wine families produce wine lovers. The greatest winemakers in the world were weaned on the juice. There are a million bottles of wine in the world, and one does not become an expert by starting at the age of thirty (which is, unfortunately, usually the age at which one not brought up in the wine world can actually start to afford median to higher quality wines). Good wine is expensive. There may be more exceptions to that statement than there are grapes in California, but let's be honest with ourselves: you can't achieve enough knowledge about good, inexpensive wines without spending some serious money in the learning process. It takes commitment. Commitment means time, and time, as we all know, is money.

I began exploring the world of wine many years ago, drinking Chiantis in wicker baskets at the various Italian restaurants where I worked in Texas. Most French and California wines that came my way were of the mass-produced and generic styles. My luckiest early wine experience was with a local winery, Messina Hof, which produced excellent, reasonably priced wines designed for, and succeeding at, quenching local thirst. They produce a white Cabernet that should be drunk only on a hot Texas day, about mid-afternoon. The effect, I assure you, is pure synergy of time and place.

To me, wine is fig preserves. My grandmother made good fig preserves, and she probably learned how to make them from her mother or grandmother (although she may have just learned from a book). Every year, a few more jars of fig preserves would show up in the pantry, usually because the fig tree had started dropping more fruit than we could eat before it rotted, and definitely because the figs were just too good to throw away. I can still taste those figs; they taste like summer.

I moved to California several years ago and began my learning in earnest. When I began tasting wine in the company of more experienced tasters, I discovered that I have a good palate and began to trust my instincts. I am not an expert. I am not even a novice. I love wine and am passionate about good wine and good food. Anyone with this attitude can educate themselves about wine.

In my first year in California I learned more about good wine than ever before—that is to say, I finally *got it.* It helps that living in San Francisco one can be in Napa or Sonoma in an hour, visiting friends and tasting wine. Wine-tasting rooms are God's gift to poor chefs. It's a single school with a thousand classrooms, each one interesting and exciting to explore. I learn as much from bad wine as I do from good wine as I come to understand how they earn their definition.

ORGANIC AGRICULTURE

Humans and dirt have produced wine for five thousand years. About fifty years ago, chemicals were added to the process. We've recently learned that chemicals do not improve wine and probably destroy both humans and dirt. This seems simple and easy to fix; however, unfortunately, chemical agriculture, like many bad ideas, has a great deal of momentum.

The arguments against organic agriculture usually follow two lines. The first insists that those who don't like chemical agriculture are Luddites and fear science. To that I argue that organic agriculture *is* a science. Biodiversity is consistently more effective than any other method at reducing infestation in the long term. Pests do not develop a tolerance for diversity. Monoculture (the process of planting one crop over a vast area) is a system that inevitably ends in infestation or plant disease because it requires farmers to constantly be on the defensive: farmers are so busy fighting symptoms they never get to fight the disease. The truth is that nature is diverse. The science of diversity allows for the natural processes of infestation or disease by providing relief in the form of *beneficials.* Beneficials are plants, insects, and other life forms that are intentionally introduced into the farm or vineyard to help create a diverse environment. It's not being defensive, it's being harmonic. This is only one good example of how organic agriculture is a lucid, even scientific, approach to farming.

The second argument against organic agriculture claims that it's just not economically feasible. However, a little research into the devastating effects of current monoculture-based chemical farming suggests that organic farming is more cost-efficient in the long run. According to John Robbins, in his book *Diet for a New America,* topsoil depletion from our current mishandling of our natural resources is topping 4 million acres a year—an area the size of Connecticut. This land had previously been fertile for generations. Destroying land is shortsighted and economically draining; if land is the prime capital in farming, it's bad capitalism.

Life is short. Organic food and wine are made with love and care. They taste better, smell better, and *are* better. I am a firm believer that people can often vote more effectively with their wallets than at the ballot box. This is why we serve only wine made from organically grown grapes at Millennium.

Michael Topolos, of Topolos at Russian River Vineyards, believes that farming organically is a "mingling of accountability, responsibility, and reverence for our living environment." His first organic vineyard was the one closest to his home, where his children played. Many organic growers the world over (and organic winemaking *is* a worldwide movement) acknowledge that early experiments were intuitive reactions to the presence of poisons in the field. I personally like the assessment of Sante Losio, of Fiume Wines, who describes organic winemakers as people "who are dedicated to making grapes happy."

When choosing your wine, consider where the grapes are grown. Organic wine suffered some blows when consumers first encountered the juvenile efforts of the early producers, so much so that many organic growers became reluctant to advertise the pedigree of their grapes. Organic winemakers may be the only artisans who are afraid to advertise the quality of their raw ingredients. I'd like to join the growing group of those who call for an end to this stigma. Organically grown grapes are right, they are natural, and they make better wine.

WINE AND FOOD

I'm accustomed to a couple of approaches to pairing wine and food. The first I call the **taste and plan** method. In my second month or so at Millennium, I came in to work to find half the kitchen staff sitting in the dining room at a table full of wine. It was a wine meeting for an upcoming wine dinner, something we do two or three times a year. Sascha Weiss, our pastry chef at that time, tasted a wine and said, "I think it would be good with something grilled." There were murmurs of assent or dissent, and then someone else made a suggestion, perhaps, "I smell cloves"—or blueberries, or horse poop. What a joy, to taste and talk! I've come to discover that this creative approach to wine pairing is my favorite method for coming up with ideas.

The second method is **classic pairings,** about which there has been plenty written. You might already be familiar with this method (Zinfandel with grilled meat, Champagne with caviar, and so on). I have chosen to share the benefits of my experience in the form of advice for the cook who already has some knowledge of classic wine pairings but who seeks advice in the translation to the world of vegetable-based cuisine. That's also why it may sound like it's written in a dialect of Klingon, if you are new to wine.

TASTE AND PLAN

Eric always sets aside time before a dinner to taste the wine. We bring in the produce availability sheets from our purveyors and take extensive notes with our ideas. It is the burden of chefs to guess with precision. This challenge has its great rewards when the guesses become real plates going to real customers during our wine events. It also has its scary moments and disappointments. But thinking, planning, and some basic guidelines can help to make the rewarding times outnumber the scary ones.

There are two basic ways to pair wines: either complement them with the flavors they lack to create a complete palate experience, or mirror the flavors

they contain to isolate or feature an unusual or exceptional quality. Examples of complementary pairings include serving rich foods with acidic wines, such as pasta with Chianti; or matching a wine that has a mild nose and full body with an aromatic dish (with, say, rosemary or lavender) and a lighter prime component, such as a salad or a mildly seasoned mash of potatoes or celeriac. A favorite pairing for us is to select an aromatic, slightly sweet wine to complement a spicy and acidic dish, usually a Riesling or Gerwürztraminer with a tamale or Southeast Asian–inspired spring roll.

Mirroring the flavors is often more fun, as it can really draw attention to specific wines. Some of the more unusual connections Eric and I have discovered while spelunking the caverns of wine flavor include epazote, Lapsang tea (to accent a resinous pine quality), hazelnuts, chocolate, and oak (we smoked mushrooms over oak chips). We especially enjoy finding unusual spice qualities, like Szechuan pepper, ancho chile, or ginger reflected in unusual places, such as Italian wines. These discoveries have led to exciting ideas for foods and food combinations we might never have approached before tasting the wine. This sense of fun and exploration is incredibly important for pairing wines, and in my mind, for any creative pursuit.

CLASSIC PAIRINGS

Traditional meat-wine pairings translate well into vegan dishes. To go with classic meat-pairing wines such as Cabernet, Zinfandel, and Syrah, we like to prepare fresh or dried porcini mushrooms, maybe in a reduction sauce of the wine that is served; black chanterelles; *Agaricus* mushrooms (such as cremini, button, or portobello); marinated seitan or tempeh in roasted vegetable stock; caramelized onions; and dark roux. These rich wines also benefit from the presence of seasonings such as black pepper, nutmeg, and clove, and herbs such as thyme, rosemary, and parsley. Hearty wines go well with foods that are grilled, smoked, or roasted.

Dishes usually prepared with poultry are classically paired with lighter reds, such as some Merlot, Pinot Noir, Sangiovese, or even Spanish Rioja. Rich white wines like Chardonnay and Sauvignon Blanc are also often appropriate. With these wines we pair lighter, more delicate mushrooms, such as chanterelles or hedgehogs; bean-based dishes; grain-based dishes; and seitan or tempeh marinated in light vegetable stock. Recommended seasonings include white pepper, nutritional yeast, fennel, paprika, and garlic, and herbs such as sage, bay, oregano, and marjoram.

For classic wine pairings usually made with fish dishes, we use oyster, king pleurotus, honshimeji, and even matsutake mushrooms; dishes featuring sea vegetables or saffron; and meat analogs (seitan, tempeh, and mushrooms) in light stocks made with kombu. Seasonings to consider include lemon, coriander, curry, saffron, and white pepper, and herbs such as lavender or dill. Wines for these include dry, minerally whites such as Viognier, Sancerre, Pinot Gris, and Alsatian whites. Champagne is often lumped in this group, but it honestly deserves its own category, sitting appropriately at any stage of a well-prepared meal.

In general, in pairing food and wine, pour the same wine you are using in the sauce or marinade of a dish. The recommended serving order of wines is lightest to most full-bodied and youngest to oldest, the rationale being that a lighter-bodied wine is more difficult to taste after a fuller one, but you can get around it if sufficient time passes between wines or if you serve a palate-cleansing intermezzo.

Vinegar competes with wine, but when used with a light hand as a seasoning rather than as a primary component, it can be quite nice. Our food tends to be about seasoning, and therefore, many of the recipes in this book are better paired with spicier, less delicate wines, such as Italian reds like Sangiovese or Nebbiolo, and California Zinfandels.

I sent an early draft of this piece to my parents and my father made a suggestion. He said I should put the bit about organics at the end as the subject was obviously important to me and should be the last thing that people read so they remember it. My mom liked it where it was so people would come across it quickly if they were only browsing. When I was in high school, my parents didn't even know what organic agriculture was.

Learning about organic wine and meeting people like Bob Blue of Bonterra Vineyards, Michael Topolos, and Tony Coturri, and import industry pioneers like Sante Losio, of Fiume Wines, and Véronique Raskin, of Organic Wine Company, has been rewarding beyond measure. These are people who live and breathe (and drink) organics. They spend their life talking about it, promoting it, and sharing it. It is because of people like them that my mother and father can argue over the best way to help me share a message that would have once sounded like so much New Age psychobabble. So, if you don't mind, I'd like to propose a toast . . .

—B.E.

APPETIZERS

Our starters invigorate the palate. Whether it's the super-intense mushroom flavors of our Morel–Caramelized Onion Roll or the hot hot heat of our sweet-and-spicy Sweet Mango, Mustard, and Habanero Sauce complementing our Yuca–Black Bean Cakes, expect bold flavors. Even our delicate corn flan captures the intensity of summer with sweet corn, a full-flavored tomato compote, and spicy grilled nectarines. Dishes such as the Blue Corn Empanadas make great entrées in their own right, perhaps paired with a simple salad. Our butternut squash cakes and beet-coriander cakes would make great side dishes and are open for interpretation using other shredded root vegetables. Throw an appetizers-only party with some of these offerings, and you will wow your guests with a globetrotting diversity of culinary styles, tastes, and textures. There is something here for everyone.

Crisp Yuba Rolls with Nori, Shiitakes, Hijiki, and Barley ៛ 11

Crisp Shredded Vegetable Rolls with Tamarind Sauce,
Coconut Curry, and Chile Oil ៛ 12

Morel–Caramelized Onion Rolls with Truffled Beet Salad
and Pinot Noir Reduction ៛ 14

Roasted Baby Artichokes in Moroccan Glaze
with Meyer Lemon Aïoli ៛ 16

Miso-Broiled Japanese Eggplant over Noodle Cakes
with Walnut-Miso Sauce and Wasabi Cream ៛ 18

Asian Eggplant Caviar with Black Sesame Buns
and Saffron–Lotus Root Pickles ៛ 20

Black Rice Cakes and Grilled Oyster Mushrooms and Pineapple ៛ 22

Black Olive, Eggplant, and Black Beluga Lentil Caviar ៛ 23

Blue Corn Empanadas Filled with Smoked Tempeh–Root Vegetable
Picadillo, Mint Mojo, and Strawberry-Papaya Salsa ៛ 24

Sesame-Crusted Oyster Mushroom Calamari
over Burdock Kimpira ⚡ 26

Grilled Vegetable Terrine with Arugula–Toasted Almond Pesto ⚡ 28

Corn Flan over Tomato Compote with Spicy Grilled Nectarine ⚡ 30

Seitan Saté Skewers with Spicy Peanut-Coconut Sauce ⚡ 32

Israeli Couscous and Buckwheat–Filled Dolmas
with Zaatar Dipping Sauce ⚡ 34

Exotic Mushroom Ceviche ⚡ 35

Cumin-Balsamic Roasted Mushrooms ⚡ 36

Roasted Porcini Mushrooms with Shaved Porcini Salad
and Jellied Porcini Stock ⚡ 37

Yuca–Black Bean Cakes with Sweet Mango, Mustard,
and Habanero Sauce ⚡ 38

Ancho Chile–Black Bean Cakes with Uncle
Junior's Hemp Seed Mole ⚡ 40

Butternut Squash Cakes with Roasted Chanterelles
and Pink Pearl Apples ⚡ 41

Buster's Potato Torte with Rosemary-Pistachio Pesto
and Cashew "Gruyère" ⚡ 42

Stuffed Squash Blossoms with Sweet Corn Tofu Cheese
and Cilantro Pesto ⚡ 44

Beet-Coriander Cakes with Red Lentil Dal
and Pomegranate-Glazed Eggplant ⚡ 47

Crisp Yuba Rolls *with* Nori, Shiitakes, Hijiki, *and* Barley

SERVES 4

Yuba is dried tofu skin sold in flat sheets. We reconstitute the yuba and roll it around nori, mushrooms, and barley. The rolls bake up crisp and crunchy with that subtle sea "twang" of the nori and hijiki. We serve them with our Spicy, Sweet, and Sour Kumquat-Lime Dressing, which you can make ahead and refrigerate until ready to serve. E.T.

CRISP YUBA ROLLS

2 teaspoons canola oil

3 teaspoons toasted sesame oil

2 cloves garlic, minced

1 bunch scallions, white and light green parts only, thinly sliced

2 teaspoons peeled and minced fresh ginger

1/2 teaspoon shichimi togarashi (Japanese seven-spice powder), or 1/4 teaspoon crushed red pepper flakes

1/2 ounce hijiki sea vegetable, reconstituted (see page 223)

1 cup thinly sliced fresh shiitake mushrooms

11/2 cups cooked hulled or pearled barley, or 1/4 cup cooked barley and 1/4 cup cooked black barley

3 teaspoons tamari

4 sheets yuba, reconstituted according to package directions and drained

4 (8 by 7-inch) sheets nori

SPROUT SALAD

1 cup mung bean sprouts

1/4 cup onion sprouts

1/4 cup daikon, clover, or radish sprouts

1 carrot, peeled and grated

2 tablespoons finely shredded mint leaves

1 tablespoon fresh lime juice

Salt

1/2 cup Spicy, Sweet, and Sour Kumquat-Lime Dressing (page 53)

4 teaspoons coarsely chopped peanuts, toasted (see page 222), for garnish

To make the filling, place a sauté pan over high heat and add 1 tablespoon of the canola oil and 1 teaspoon of the toasted sesame oil. Add the garlic, scallions, and ginger, and sauté for 1 minute. Add the shichimi togarashi, hijiki, and mushrooms, and sauté for 3 minutes, or until the mushrooms are wilted. Add the barley and 2 teaspoons of the tamari, and toss well with the mushroom mixture. Remove from the heat and let cool to room temperature.

To make the rolls, preheat the oven to 350°F. Line a baking sheet with parchment paper. In a small bowl, mix together the remaining 1 teaspoon canola oil, 2 teaspoons toasted sesame oil, and 1 teaspoon tamari.

Lay 1 piece of the yuba on either a sushi rolling mat or a piece of plastic wrap on a flat, dry surface. Place 1 piece of the nori over the yuba. Spread 1/2 cup of the filling along the bottom one-third of the yuba-nori sheet. Roll into a tight cylinder and transfer onto the baking sheet. Brush the roll with the tamari mixture.

Repeat the rolling procedure with the remaining yuba, nori, and filling to make 3 more rolls. Bake for 20 minutes, or until the rolls are light brown with a lacquered look.

To make the salad, toss all of the ingredients together in a bowl.

To serve, thinly coat the bottom of each plate with 2 tablespoons of the kumquat-lime dressing. Place about 1/3 cup of the sprout salad in the center of the plate. Cut 1 roll in half diagonally and lean each piece against the salad. Sprinkle chopped peanuts around the plate.

NUTRITIONAL INFORMATION

PER ROLL: 349 calories (38% from fat), 23 g protein, 31 g carbohydrate, 15 g fat, 0 mg cholesterol, 276 mg sodium, 5 g fiber

PER 1/3 CUP SPROUT SALAD: 22 calories (4% from fat), 1.3 g protein, 5 g carbohydrate, 0.1 g fat, 0 mg cholesterol, 12 mg sodium, 1.5 g fiber

CRISP SHREDDED VEGETABLE ROLLS *with* TAMARIND SAUCE, COCONUT CURRY, *and* CHILE OIL

SERVES 4

We paired this appetizer with Pacific Rim Riesling at one of our Bonny Doon Vineyards Dinners. The oil, curry, and tarmarind sauce combine on the plate into a complex yet harmonious mix of flavors—but feel free to serve the rolls with just one of them or with your favorite dipping sauce. The tamarind sauce calls for tamarind pulp, which includes the seeds; it's available in Asian and East Indian markets. Garnish the rolls with a simple sprout salad, if desired.

Our Seven-Secret Chile Oil actually has more than seven ingredients in it, but the extra ingredients make for a complex, toasty, spicy flavoring oil well worth the effort to assemble. Feel free to improvise on this recipe. At home I have made it with fresh chiles and with cumin and fennel seeds for an even more complex flavor. E.T.

MILLENNIUM SEVEN-SECRET CHILE OIL

1 cup canola oil or grapeseed oil
1/4 cup dark sesame oil
1/4 cup raw peanuts
1 dried ancho chile, torn open
8 dried chiles de árbol or Chinese red chiles
1 teaspoon Spanish paprika
1/2 teaspoon Szechuan peppercorns
2 quarter-sized pieces peeled fresh ginger
6 shallots, peeled and halved
Grated zest of 1 orange
1 tablespoon Chinese fermented black beans
1 lemongrass stalk, bottom half crushed with the back of a knife
1 1/2 teaspoons salt

SWEET TAMARIND SAUCE

1/4 cup tamarind pulp
1/2 cup plus 2 tablespoons water
Juice of 1/2 orange
1/2 teaspoon grated orange zest
2 teaspoons peeled and minced fresh ginger
2 tablespoons Florida Crystals (see page 224)
3 tablespoons tamari

YELLOW COCONUT CURRY

4 shallots, peeled
2 dried chiles de árbol
2 teaspoons coarsely chopped fresh galangal
1 lemongrass stalk, bottom half only, coarsely chopped
1 teaspoon grated lime zest
Juice of 1 lime
1 teaspoon coriander seeds, toasted (see page 223)
1/2 teaspoon caraway seeds, toasted (see page 223)
1/4 teaspoon freshly ground black pepper
1 teaspoon minced fresh turmeric root, or
   1/3 teaspoon dried turmeric
2 teaspoons light miso
1 cup coconut milk
1 teaspoon cornstarch, dissolved in 2 tablespoons water
Salt

CRISP SHREDDED VEGETABLE ROLLS

1 leek, white part only, julienne
2 teaspoons peeled and minced fresh ginger
1 carrot, peeled and shredded
1 yellow summer squash, julienne
1 red bell pepper, julienne
1 fennel bulb, shredded
1 teaspoon canola oil, plus additional for brushing
2 teaspoons sesame seeds
1 tablespoon umeboshi vinegar
2 tablespoons mint chiffonade
2 tablespoons firmly packed cilantro leaves
2 tablespoons Thai basil chiffonade
8 brick pastry sheets
1/4 cup mung bean sprouts

To make the chile oil, combine all of the ingredients in a saucepan over low heat, and heat until the oil is just simmering. Simmer for 30 minutes, or until chiles are crisp and brown. Remove from the heat and let sit overnight at room temperature. Strain the oil through a fine-mesh strainer. (Store refrigerated, in a glass container, for up to 6 months.)

To make the tamarind sauce, heat the tamarind pulp with 1/2 cup of the water in a saucepan over medium heat, breaking up the tamarind with a whisk. When the pulp resembles a thick purée, remove it from the heat and press through a fine-mesh strainer into a blender container. Add the orange juice, orange zest, ginger, sugar, tamari, and remaining 2 tablespoons water. Blend until smooth. (Store refrigerated, in an airtight container, indefinitely. Warm to room temperature before serving.)

To make the coconut curry, in a blender, blend the shallots, chiles, galangal, lemongrass, lime zest, lime juice, coriander seeds, caraway seeds, black pepper, turmeric, and miso until the mixture is a coarse paste. Combine with the coconut milk in a saucepan over low heat and simmer for 15 minutes, or until reduced by one-third. Slowly whisk in the cornstarch slurry until the sauce is thick enough to coat the back of a spoon. Add salt to taste. Remove from the heat and strain the sauce through a fine-mesh strainer. (Store refrigerated, in an airtight container, for up to 5 days. Warm to room temperature before serving.)

To make the filling, preheat the oven to 450°F. Combine the leek, ginger, carrot, summer squash, bell pepper, and fennel in a bowl. Toss with the canola oil, sesame seeds, and vinegar.

Heat a very large sauté pan or wok over high heat until very hot. Add half the vegetables and sear them, stirring constantly, for 1 minute, so they remain crisp yet pick up a bit of a charred flavor from hitting the red-hot pan. When done, transfer the vegetables to a bowl.

Dry and reheat the pan, and then repeat with the remaining vegetables. Let cool to room temperature. Toss the seared vegetables with the mint, cilantro, and basil.

To make the rolls, line a baking sheet with parchment paper. Place 1 brick pastry sheet on a flat surface. Brush with the canola oil. Place another sheet overlapping one-third of the first sheet, and brush with more oil. Spread $1/2$ cup of the filling and 1 tablespoon of the bean sprouts over the bottom of the first sheet. Fold over the edges and roll tightly together. Place on the baking sheet. Repeat with the remaining pastry sheets and filling to make 3 more rolls. Bake for 10 minutes, or until lightly golden in color.

To serve, place 2 tablespoons of the tamarind sauce and 2 tablespoons of the yellow curry on the bottom of each plate. Drizzle 1 teaspoon of the chile oil over the plate. Cut 1 roll in half diagonally and lean the halves against each other in the center of the plate.

NUTRITIONAL INFORMATION

PER ROLL: 255 calories (51% from fat), 4.3 g protein, 21 g carbohydrate, 12 g fat, 0 mg cholesterol, 848 mg sodium, 5.7 g fiber

PER TEASPOON CHILE OIL: 39 calories (90% from fat), 0.3 g protein, 0.7 g carbohydrate, 4 g fat, 0 mg cholesterol, 40 mg sodium, 0.2 g fiber

PER 2 TABLESPOONS TAMARIND SAUCE: 28 calories (1% from fat), 0.8 g protein, 6.6 g carbohydrate, 0.1 g fat, 0 mg cholesterol, 378 mg sodium, 1.2 g fiber

PER 2 TABLESPOONS COCONUT CURRY: 84 calories (72% from fat), 1.2 g protein, 5 g carbohydrate, 7.4 g fat, 0 mg cholesterol, 58 mg sodium, 0.6 g fiber

MOREL–CARAMELIZED ONION ROLLS *with* TRUFFLED BEET SALAD *and* PINOT NOIR REDUCTION

SERVES 6

Here's a recipe for late spring, when morels are in season and when local beets come to the market. If you cannot get fresh morels, try making this with some meaty portobellos and, if you are extremely lucky, fresh porcini; dry morels will also do nicely. Fill the rolls with extra filling to make an elegant and satisfying entrée. An earthy Pinot Noir will pair perfectly with this dish. E.T.

HORSERADISH TOFU CREAM

6 ounces silken tofu
2 tablespoons prepared white horseradish, plus more
  as needed, or 1 tablespoon freshly grated horseradish
  plus 1 teaspoon rice vinegar
1 tablespoon light miso
Juice of 1 lemon

MOREL–CARAMELIZED ONION ROLLS

2 large Yukon Gold or yellow Finn potatoes, quartered
1 tablespoon extra virgin olive oil, plus more as needed
1 clove garlic, minced
Salt and freshly ground black pepper
1 tablespoon extra virgin olive oil
2 red onions, sliced into thin crescents
2 cloves garlic, minced
1/2 teaspoon Sucanat (see page 224)
1/2 teaspoon dried thyme
8 ounces fresh morels, cleaned and halved
Salt and freshly ground black pepper
9 (13 by 18-inch) sheets phyllo dough
Canola oil for brushing

TRUFFLED BEET SALAD

1 carrot, peeled
1 red beet, peeled
1/4 red onion, sliced into very thin crescents
2 tablespoons balsamic vinegar
1 tablespoon extra virgin olive oil
1 teaspoon white truffle oil
Salt and freshly ground black pepper

BEET–PINOT NOIR REDUCTION

1 1/2 cups Pinot Noir
1 cup vegetable stock (page 205)
1 clove garlic
4 fresh morels, portobellos, or porcini, or an equiva-
  lent amount of dried morels, portobellos, or porcini
3 tablespoons balsamic vinegar
1 tablespoon Sucanat (see page 224)
1 red beet, peeled and cut into small dice
1/4 teaspoon salt
4 whole black peppercorns

Chopped chives, for garnish

To make the horseradish cream, combine all of the ingredients in a blender and blend until smooth. (Store refrigerated for up to 1 week.)

To make the rolls, bring 4 cups of salted water to a boil. Add the potatoes and decrease the heat to medium. Simmer for 20 minutes, or until al dente. Remove from the heat and let sit for 5 to 7 minutes, until soft. Drain the potatoes and place in a bowl. Heat the olive oil in a sauté pan over medium heat. Add the garlic and sauté for 3 minutes, or until lightly browned. Pour the garlic and oil over the potatoes. Mash the potatoes, adding another teaspoon of oil if desired. Add salt and pepper to taste.

Heat the olive oil in a large skillet over medium heat. Add the onions and the garlic and sauté, stirring often, for 7 minutes, or until very soft. Add the Sucanat and thyme, and continue to sauté for 5 to 7 minutes, until brown and caramelized. Add the morels and sauté for 2 minutes to soften the morels. Season with salt and pepper to taste.

Preheat the oven to 350°F. Line a baking sheet with parchment paper.

Spread 1 sheet of phyllo dough on a flat, dry work surface. Place a second sheet over it. Brush the phyllo with oil, and then place another sheet over it. Brush the third sheet with oil. Place one-third of the mashed potatoes along the length of the bottom of the phyllo. Place one-third of the mushroom mixture along the length next to the mashed potatoes. Roll up the phyllo tightly and then cut in half. Cut each half in half again diagonally and place on the sheet pan. This makes 2 portions; repeat until you have 6 portions. Bake for 15 minutes, or until lightly browned.

To make the salad, grate or shred the carrot in a food processor fitted with the shredding attachment. Do the same with the beet. Rinse the beet in cold water for 30 seconds to remove some of the pigment and to keep the beet crisp. Let sit in a colander for about 5 minutes to drain off excess moisture.

In a bowl, combine the carrot, beet, onion, vinegar, olive oil, and white truffle oil. Toss well, and add salt and pepper to taste.

To make the reduction, combine all of the ingredients and bring to a boil in a saucepan over medium-high heat. Decrease the heat to low and simmer for 20 minutes, or until reduced by one-half. Remove from the heat and pour through a strainer into a second saucepan. Return to the heat and simmer over low for 15 to 20 minutes, until reduced to about $1/4$ cup and syrupy in consistency. Remove from the heat.

To serve, place $1/4$ cup of beet salad on each of 6 plates, with 2 rolls on top. Drizzle with 1 tablespoon of the beet reduction. Spoon 2 teaspoons of the horseradish cream around the plate, and garnish with chopped chives.

NUTRITIONAL INFORMATION

PER ROLL: 242 calories (36% from fat), 5 g protein, 34 g carbohydrate, 10 g fat, 0 mg cholesterol, 376 mg sodium, 4.6 g fiber

PER SERVING TRUFFLED BEET SALAD: 49 calories (53% from fat), 0.7 g protein, 5.3 g carbohydrate, 3 g fat, 0 mg cholesterol, 23 mg sodium, 1.4 g fiber

PER TABLESPOON REDUCTION: 103 calories (3.9% from fat), 1.6 g protein, 10 g carbohydrate, 0.2 g fat, 0 mg cholesterol, 200 mg sodium, 1.3 g fiber

PER TABLESPOON HORSERADISH CREAM: 8 calories (48% from fat), 0.9 g protein, 0.8 g carbohydrate, 0.7 g fat, 0 mg cholesterol, 49 mg sodium, 0.1 g fiber

Roasted Baby Artichokes *in* Moroccan Glaze *with* Meyer Lemon Aïoli

SERVES 4

This appetizer shows off baby artichokes, the small artichokes that grow at the base of the artichoke plant. Look for artichokes that are less than 2 inches long; the choke should not be developed, so they're 100 percent edible. The Moroccan glaze they're marinated in is a Millennium standard; we use it on everything. The recipe makes about 2¼ cups, much more than you'll need for the artichokes, but we're sure you'll put the leftovers to use. (For a simpler version of this glaze, just combine ¼ cup freshly squeezed orange juice and 2 teaspoons tamari.)

If you think all lemons are created equal, then you haven't tried a Meyer lemon. Its juice is slightly sweeter than a standard lemon, and this rich aïoli highlights its floral quality.

This recipe can be served hot either as a plated appetizer or at room temperature as part of an antipasto display. Serve it with wedges of our focaccia (page 217) and some pungent olives, such as little niçoise. E.T.

MOROCCAN GLAZE

1½ cups tomato sauce or tomato purée
½ cup freshly squeezed orange juice
½ cup freshly squeezed lemon juice
½ cup tamari
4 cloves garlic
¼ cup pure maple syrup or Sucanat (see page 224)
½ teaspoon crushed red pepper flakes
1 teaspoon ground coriander
½ teaspoon ground cinnamon
2 teaspoons ground cumin
1 teaspoon fennel seeds, ground
2 teaspoons peeled and minced fresh ginger
1 tablespoon balsamic vinegar

MEYER LEMON AÏOLI

½ cup plus 2 tablespoons extra virgin olive oil
2 cloves garlic, minced
Juice of 2 Meyer lemons

1 teaspoon grated Meyer lemon zest
2 ounces silken tofu
1 teaspoon nutritional yeast (see page 224)
1 teaspoon Dijon mustard
Salt and freshly ground black pepper

ROASTED BABY ARTICHOKES

1 fresh lemon, halved
2 bay leaves
1¼ teaspoons salt
24 baby artichokes, prepared (see page 222) and halved
6 cloves garlic, minced
4 bay leaves
1 orange, peeled and segments separated
¼ teaspoon crushed red pepper flakes
2 tablespoons extra virgin olive oil

To make the glaze, combine all of the ingredients in a blender and blend until smooth. (Store refrigerated, in an airtight container, for up to 2 weeks.)

To make the aïoli, heat 2 tablespoons of the olive oil in a sauté pan over medium heat. Add the garlic and sauté for 5 minutes, or until lightly browned. Let cool to room temperature. Combine the sautéed garlic and oil with the lemon juice and zest, tofu, yeast, and mustard, and blend with either a handheld immersion blender or a conventional blender. Slowly add the remaining ½ cup oil and blend until emulsified. Season with salt and pepper to taste. (Store refrigerated, in an airtight container, for up to 1 week.)

To make the artichokes, preheat the broiler or the oven to 450°F. Bring 2 quarts of water to a boil, and add the lemon, bay leaves, and 1 teaspoon of the salt, followed by the artichokes. Simmer for 7 to 10 minutes, until the artichokes are tender. Drain well in a colander. If not roasting immediately, cool with ice water to stop the cooking process.

In a bowl, toss the artichokes with ¼ cup of the Moroccan glaze, the garlic, bay leaves, orange, pepper flakes, olive oil, and the remaining salt. Place the mixture on a baking sheet and broil or roast in the oven for 10 minutes, turning after 5 minutes, or until the liquid reduces and glazes onto the artichokes. Remove from the heat. Remove and discard the bay leaves.

To serve, place 6 artichokes on each plate and top with 2 tablespoons of the aïoli, or serve on a platter with the aïoli on the side.

NUTRITIONAL INFORMATION

PER 6 GLAZED ARTICHOKES: 166 calories (34% from fat), 5.8 g protein, 24 g carbohydrate, 7 g fat, 0 mg cholesterol, 415 mg sodium, 8.5 g fiber

PER 2 TABLESPOONS AÏOLI: 157 calories (95% from fat), 8 g protein, 1.2 g carbohydrate, 17 g fat, 0 mg cholesterol, 15 mg sodium, 0.1 g fiber

MISO-BROILED JAPANESE EGGPLANT *over* NOODLE CAKES *with* WALNUT-MISO SAUCE *and* WASABI CREAM

SERVES 6

I have been a fan of eggplant broiled with sweet miso since I discovered it on my first visit to San Francisco. Since then, I have come up with numerous variations on that theme here at the restaurant and at home. If you want to make things simple, try just the miso-eggplant part of the recipe as a side dish, or broil miso-marinated tofu for an entrée. E.T.

WALNUT-MISO SAUCE

1/2 cup walnuts, toasted (see page 223)
2 tablespoons white miso
1 tablespoon tamari
1 scallion, green part only, minced
1/2 cup water or vegetable stock (page 205)

WASABI CREAM

1 tablespoon dried wasabi powder, reconstituted
    with enough water to form a thick paste, plus more
    as needed
2 ounces silken tofu
2 teaspoons rice vinegar
1/4 cup water
2 tablespoons canola oil (optional)
1/2 teaspoon salt

MISO-BROILED EGGPLANT

1 clove garlic, minced
2 teaspoons peeled and grated fresh ginger
2 scallions, green part only, minced
3 tablespoons white miso or any light miso
3 tablespoons mirin (sweet rice wine)
1 tablespoon sesame seeds, toasted (see page 223;
    optional)
1 tablespoon toasted sesame oil
6 Japanese eggplants, halved lengthwise

NOODLE CAKES

1/4 pound dried thin rice noodles, reconstituted
    according to package directions and drained
1 ounce dried arame sea vegetable, reconstituted
    (see page 223)

2 scallions, white part only, minced
1 teaspoon black sesame seeds (optional)
1/2 teaspoon toasted sesame oil
1/4 teaspoon salt
1 1/2 teaspoons cornstarch or arrowroot
Canola oil for sautéing

Black and white sesame seeds, toasted (see page 223),
    for garnish

To make the walnut-miso sauce, combine the walnuts, miso, tamari, scallions, and $1/4$ cup of the water in a blender and blend until the mixture is a coarse purée. Slowly add the remaining water until the mixture is the thickness of heavy cream.

To make the wasabi cream, combine all of the ingredients in a blender and blend until smooth.

To make the eggplant, in a shallow baking dish, whisk together the garlic, ginger, scallions, miso, mirin, sesame seeds, and sesame oil. Add water as needed to make a thin paste. Place the eggplant halves cut side down in the miso mixture, and marinate for 30 minutes.

Preheat the broiler. Place the eggplant cut side up on a baking dish or baking sheet. Spoon some of the marinade over the eggplant and broil for 5 to 7 minutes, until the eggplant flesh is soft and the top is browned. (Keep your broiler rack as low as possible to prevent burning.) Remove from the heat, and keep warm.

To make the noodle cakes, mix the noodles, arame, scallions, black sesame seeds, sesame oil, and salt together in a bowl. Add the cornstarch, working it in with your hands until the mixture holds together.

In a nonstick sauté pan, heat about $1/2$ teaspoon of canola oil over medium-high heat. Divide the noodle mixture into 6 portions. Place a portion in the heated sauté pan and press it down with a spatula until it is 3 to 4 inches in diameter and about $1/2$ inch thick. Sauté for 2 to 3 minutes per side, until light brown and crisp. Transfer to a plate. Repeat with the 5 portions. If your pan size allows, sauté more than 1 cake at a time.

To serve, place 1 noodle cake in the center of each plate. Place 2 broiled eggplant halves overlapping each other on top of the cake. Spoon 2 tablespoons of the walnut sauce and 2 tablespoons of the wasabi cream around the plate. Sprinkle toasted sesame seeds around the dish.

NUTRITIONAL INFORMATION

PER NOODLE CAKE: 214 calories (62% from fat), 1.9 g protein, 17 g carbohydrate, 14 g fat, 0 mg cholesterol, 81 mg sodium, 1.9 g fiber

PER EGGPLANT: 110 calories (29% from fat), 3.8 g protein, 17 g carbohydrate, 4 g fat, 0 mg cholesterol, 739 mg sodium, 6.5 g fiber

PER 2 TABLESPOONS WALNUT SAUCE: 77 calories (67% from fat), 3.6 g protein, 3.3 g carbohydrate, 6 g fat, 0 mg cholesterol, 378 mg sodium, 0.8 g fiber

PER 2 TABLESPOONS WASABI CREAM: 56 calories (75% from fat), 1 g protein, 2 g carbohydrate, 5 g fat, 0 mg cholesterol, 165 mg sodium, 0 g fiber

ASIAN EGGPLANT CAVIAR *with* BLACK SESAME BUNS *and* SAFFRON–LOTUS ROOT PICKLES

SERVES 6

There are many versions and variations of eggplant caviar. This is one I had at Barbara Tropp's China Moon Café when I first visited San Francisco back in 1989. We serve this with a yeasted sesame bun and our pungent Saffron–Lotus Root Pickles. Our version of a sesame bun is both chewy and somewhat flaky, like a croissant; it goes great with almost any spread.
E.T.

SAFFRON–LOTUS ROOT PICKLES

1 lotus root, cut into 10 to 12 (1/4-inch-thick) slices
1 cup rice vinegar or white wine vinegar
1 cup water
1 tablespoon sea salt
2 cloves garlic

ASIAN EGGPLANT CAVIAR

2 large globe eggplants
1 tablespoon plus 1 teaspoon toasted sesame oil
1/2 teaspoon salt
2 cloves garlic, minced
2 tablespoons peeled and minced fresh ginger
1/4 teaspoon crushed red pepper flakes
1 teaspoon Szechuan peppercorns, toasted (see page 223) and ground
2 tablespoons Sucanat (see page 224)
2 teaspoons balsamic vinegar
2 teaspoons tamari

SESAME BUNS

1 cup warm water (105° to 110°F)
1/2 (1/4-ounce) package active dry yeast
1/4 teaspoon Florida Crystals (see page 224)
2 teaspoons toasted sesame oil, plus more as needed
2 teaspoons olive oil
2 scallions, white and green parts, minced
2 tablespoons black sesame seeds, plus more as needed
1 teaspoon salt
1/4 teaspoon freshly ground black pepper
2 1/4 cups unbleached all-purpose flour

To make the pickles, combine all of the ingredients in a saucepan over medium heat. Bring to a boil and boil for 15 minutes, or until the roots are yellow in color. Refrigerate for 2 hours, or until chilled. (Store refrigerated, in an airtight container with the brine, for up to 2 weeks.)

To make the caviar, preheat the oven to 450°F. Slice the eggplants in half lengthwise. Score the cut sides and rub in 1 teaspoon of the sesame oil. Season with salt. Place the eggplant halves cut side down on a baking sheet. Roast in the oven for 40 to 45 minutes, until the eggplants are very soft. Remove and let cool to room temperature. Purée the roasted eggplants in a food processor fitted with the metal blade.

Put the remaining 1 tablespoon sesame oil in a sauté pan over medium heat. Add the garlic and ginger, and sauté for 1 minute. Decrease the heat to low, and add the pepper flakes and the Szechuan peppercorns, followed by the Sucanat, vinegar, tamari, and eggplant purée. Sauté, stirring often, for 10 minutes, or until the mixture tightens up and turns a couple shades darker. (Store refrigerated, in an airtight container, for up to 4 days.)

To make the buns, in a large bowl, combine the water, yeast, and sugar. Let sit for 10 minutes, or until bubbly.

Whisk in the sesame oil, olive oil, scallions, sesame seeds, salt, and pepper. Slowly whisk in the flour, switching to a wooden spoon when too thick for a whisk, until 1 3/4 cups of the flour has been used. Reserve the remaining 1/2 cup flour to dust the work surface when kneading the dough.

Preheat the oven to 450°F. Line a baking sheet with parchment paper. Turn the dough out onto a floured surface and knead for 5 minutes. Place in a large oiled bowl and let rise for 1 hour, or until doubled in size. Punch the dough down, turn out onto a floured surface, and cut into 6 pieces. Roll each piece into a long strip about 8 inches long by 3 inches wide. Brush the surface with sesame oil. Starting at one end, fold the dough over 1 inch and continue down, folding the dough into a tight coil. Flatten and lengthen the dough with a rolling pin until about 4 inches long by 2 inches wide. Place on the baking sheet. Brush the top with sesame oil and sprinkle with black sesame seeds. Repeat with the remaining dough to make 5 more buns. Bake for 15 minutes, or until the buns are lightly browned and crisp on the bottom.

To serve, place 1 bun, 1/4 cup of the caviar, and 2 pieces of root pickles on each plate.

NUTRITIONAL INFORMATION

PER 1/4 CUP CAVIAR: 109 calories (25% from fat), 3 g protein, 19 g carbohydrate, 3.4 g fat, 0 mg cholesterol, 276 mg sodium, 4 g fiber

PER BUN: 198 calories (32% from fat), 4.7 g protein, 29 g carbohydrate, 7.2 g fat, 0 mg cholesterol, 3 mg sodium, 1.8 g fiber

PER 2 PIECES ROOT PICKLE: 8 calories (0% from fat), 0.1 g protein, 2 g carbohydrate, 0 g fat, 0 mg cholesterol, 62 mg sodium, 0 g fiber

Black Rice Cakes *and* Grilled Oyster Mushrooms *and* Pineapple

SERVES 6

This is an appetizer for when you want to pull out all the stops. It is exotic in flavor and exotic in appearance, with its purple-black rice, orange sauce, and tuft of enoki mushrooms. This appetizer is so good, in fact, that you might want to make it an entrée with some baby bok choy and a glass of dry Riesling.

The Thai purple-black hulled rice cooks up sticky instead of mushy, and once the starches cool, it forms a firm rice cake. We also like Chinese forbidden black rice, which has a smaller grain and also cooks up firm yet glutinous. It is called "forbidden" because it was once off limits to commoners and only consumed by the emperor (thanks to Lotus Foods, a Bay Area–based importer, you can now find it in most specialty food stores). E.T.

BLACK RICE CAKES

1/4 teaspoon salt, plus more as needed
1/2 cup Thai purple rice or forbidden black rice
1/2 cup jasmine rice
1/2 cup minced red onion
2 teaspoons peeled and minced fresh ginger
1 tablespoon sesame seeds, toasted (see page 223)
2 teaspoons toasted sesame oil
2 teaspoons canola oil

GRILLED OYSTER MUSHROOMS AND PINEAPPLE

3/4 cup Sweet Tamarind Sauce (page 12)
1 clove garlic, minced
1 teaspoon toasted sesame oil
1 teaspoon canola oil
6 fresh pineapple slices, cored
18 oyster mushrooms

6 to 8 tablespoons Asian Eggplant Caviar (page 20), for garnish
1 (4-ounce) package enoki mushrooms, for garnish
1 scallion, white part only, cut into thin 2-inch-long chiffonade, for garnish
2 tablespoons Thai basil chiffonade, for garnish

To make the rice cakes, bring 2 cups of water to a boil in a 2-quart saucepan. Add the salt, followed by the Thai and jasmine rice. Decrease the heat to medium-low. Cover and simmer for 25 minutes, or until tender and fluffy. Remove from the heat, and let sit, still covered, for 15 minutes, or until cool enough to handle.

Preheat the oven to 400°F. Coarsely purée one-third of the cooked rice in a food processor fitted with the metal blade, or mash it by hand. Add it to a mixing bowl with the remaining rice, the onion, ginger, and sesame seeds. Add salt to taste.

Line a baking sheet with parchment paper and brush with 1 teaspoon of the sesame oil and 1 teaspoon of the canola oil. Shape the rice mixture into six 1/2-inch-thick round patties. Place on the baking sheet and brush with the remaining 1 teaspoon sesame oil and 1 teaspoon canola oil. Bake for 25 minutes, or until firm and crisp around the edges.

To grill the mushrooms and pineapple, preheat the grill or broiler. In a bowl, combine the tamarind sauce with the garlic and the sesame and canola oils. Dip the pineapple slices into the marinade and grill or broil for 2 minutes per side, or until lightly charred or browned. Set aside. Dip the oyster mushrooms in the marinade and grill or broil for 1 minute, or until heated through. Grill the other side for about 30 seconds.

To serve, place 1 rice cake in the center of each plate. Top with 1 slice of grilled pineapple, then 1 heaping tablespoon of eggplant caviar. Arrange the grilled oyster mushrooms around the caviar, and drizzle 2 tablespoons of the tamarind sauce around the plate. Plant 1 small bundle of enoki mushrooms in the caviar. Sprinkle scallions and basil around the plate.

NUTRITIONAL INFORMATION

PER CAKE: 112 calories (26% from fat), 2.4 g protein, 18.7 g carbohydrate, 3.3 g fat, 0 mg cholesterol, 62 mg sodium, .8 g fiber

PER SERVING MUSHROOMS AND PINEAPPLE: 34 calories (38% from fat), 1.7 g protein, 4 g carbohydrate, 1.5 g fat, 0 mg cholesterol, 2 mg sodium, 0.7 g fiber

BLACK OLIVE, EGGPLANT, *and* BLACK BELUGA LENTIL CAVIAR

SERVES 8

The caviar reference here is more a play on "beluga" than a description of an attempt to mimic real fish eggs. The tiny, firm black beluga lentils may hint at what their name implies, but really they make a rich, smoky, pungent tapenade just waiting to be spooned onto some toasted crostini. A grill works best for preparing this dish, but a broiler will also do the trick of charring the onions and eggplant. This caviar goes especially well with these toasted crostini, Millennium Focaccia (page 217), or any crusty hearth bread. E.T.

LENTIL CAVIAR

1/4 cup extra virgin olive oil

1/4 cup balsamic vinegar

6 cloves garlic, unpeeled, and 2 cloves garlic, minced

3/4 teaspoon salt

1/2 teaspoon freshly ground black pepper

1 globe eggplant, halved and flesh scored with a knife

1 red onion, sliced into 1/2-inch-thick rings

1/2 red bell pepper or fresh pimiento-type pepper

1 teaspoon grated lemon zest

2 tablespoons minced fresh parsley (optional)

1/2 teaspoon dried Mexican oregano

1/4 cup pitted kalamata olives

2/3 cup cooked black beluga lentils or French lentils (see page 220)

TOASTED CROSTINI

1 sweet or sour baguette

1 clove garlic, peeled and halved

1 tablespoon extra virgin olive oil

1 teaspoon Spanish paprika (optional)

Salt and freshly ground black pepper

To make the caviar, preheat the grill or broiler. In a bowl, combine 2 tablespoons of the oil with the vinegar, minced garlic, 1/4 teaspoon of the salt, and 1/4 teaspoon of the black pepper. Coat the eggplant halves, onion slices, and red pepper in the marinade.

Place the eggplant halves on the grill cut side down or, if using a broiler, toward the flame. Grill or broil for 2 minutes, or until the grill marks are seared into the flesh or the eggplant browns slightly. Flip the eggplant over and cook the skin side for 5 to 7 minutes, until it blisters and chars and the eggplant is very soft overall. Remove from the heat, and when cool enough to handle, scrape off some of the char. Grill or broil the onion slices and pepper half for 5 minutes, or until both are lightly charred on each side and very soft. Grill or broil the garlic cloves for 5 minutes, or until the skins are charred. Remove from the heat, and peel when the garlic is cool enough to handle.

Place the eggplant, onion, red pepper, garlic, remaining 2 tablespoons olive oil, lemon zest, parsley, oregano, remaining 1/4 teaspoon black pepper, and remaining marinade in a food processor fitted with the metal blade, and pulse until it resembles a coarse paste. Add the olives and pulse until the olives are chopped and the mixture looks like a coarse purée. Transfer to a mixing bowl and fold in the lentils and 1/2 teaspoon salt or more to taste. (Store, covered, in the refrigerator for up to 4 days. Warm to room temperature before serving.)

To make the crostini, preheat the oven to 350°F. Cut the baguette on a slight diagonal into thirty-two 1/3-inch-thick slices. Rub each slice with the cut side of the garlic clove. Place the slices on a baking sheet (use two, if needed). Brush or dab each slice with the oil and sprinkle with the paprika and salt and pepper to taste. Bake for 10 to 12 minutes, until the crostini are brown around the edges and only slightly brown in the center. Let cool before serving.

To serve, place the caviar on or beside the crostini.

NUTRITIONAL INFORMATION

PER 6 TABLESPOONS CAVIAR: 117 calories (52% from fat), 2.8 g protein, 12 g carbohydrate, 7.3 g fat, 0 mg cholesterol, 85 mg sodium, 3.3 g fiber

PER 4 CROSTINI: 181 calories (17% from fat), 5.5 g protein, 31 g carbohydrate, 3.5 g fat, 0 mg cholesterol, 347 mg sodium, 1.8 g fiber

BLUE CORN EMPANADAS *with* SMOKED TEMPEH–ROOT VEGETABLE PICADILLO, MINT MOJO, *and* STRAWBERRY-PAPAYA SALSA

SERVES 6

This Latin-American appetizer really shines with its intense sweet, sour, and spicy flavor combinations and its crisp cumin-flecked empanada crust. It also makes a great entrée when served with red rice and maybe some braised greens. A mojo is a Latin-American sauce similar to salsa but usually thinner. Mojos usually contain garlic and citrus juice, and they can be used as marinades, dipping sauces, or dressings for fruits and vegetables. We make a lot of mojos at Millennium. E.T.

MINT MOJO

2 tablespoons extra virgin olive oil
2 tablespoons canola oil
4 cloves garlic, minced
1/2 bunch mint leaves, coarsely chopped
1/2 bunch parsley, stemmed and coarsely chopped
1 serrano chile, seeded
Juice of 4 limes
Salt

STRAWBERRY-PAPAYA SALSA

1/2 strawberry papaya or regular papaya, seeded
2 oranges, peeled and supremed (see page 222)
1/2 red onion, cut into small dice
1/2 serrano or jalapeño chile, minced
Juice of 1 lime
2 tablespoons minced chopped cilantro
Salt

EMPANADA DOUGH

11/2 cups all-purpose flour
2/3 cup blue cornmeal
1 teaspoon whole cumin seeds, toasted (see page 223)
1/2 teaspoon salt
1/4 cup unrefined corn oil or canola oil
1/4 cup water, plus more as needed

SMOKED TEMPEH–ROOT VEGETABLE PICADILLO

2 teaspoons canola oil
1/2 yellow onion, cut into small dice
2 cloves garlic, minced
1 cup small-diced parsnip or turnip
1 cup small-diced peeled carrot
2 teaspoons ancho chile powder or other mild chile powder
1/2 teaspoon ground cinnamon
Juice of 1 blood orange or 1 regular orange
1 tablespoon tomato paste
2 tablespoons Sucanat (see page 224)
3 tablespoons golden raisins
3 tablespoons chopped pitted green olives
1/2 pound smoked tempeh (see page 219), crumbled
1 cup vegetable stock (page 205) or water
Salt and freshly ground black pepper
Flour for dusting

To make the mojo, heat the olive oil and canola oil in a pan over medium heat. Add the garlic and sauté for 3 to 5 minutes, until lightly browned. Remove from the heat and let cool to room temperature. Combine with the mint, parsley, serrano, lime juice, and salt in a blender and blend until smooth. (Store refrigerated for up to 2 days.)

To make the salsa, scoop out the flesh of the papaya and cut into small dice. Toss in a bowl with the oranges, onion, pepper, lime juice, and cilantro. Add salt to taste. (Store refrigerated for up to 2 days.)

To make the empanada dough, place the flour, cornmeal, cumin seeds, and salt in a mixing bowl. Toss together. Slowly add the oil, working into the flour mixture with a fork or your hands until evenly distributed. Slowly add the water until the mixture holds together as a soft dough. Wrap the dough in plastic wrap and refrigerate for 1 hour before using.

To make the picadillo, heat the canola oil in a large skillet over medium-high heat. Add the onion and garlic and sauté for 2 minutes, or until just starting to brown. Add the parsnip, carrot, chile powder, and cinnamon, and sauté for another 2 minutes, stirring often. Add the orange, tomato paste, Sucanat, raisins, olives, tempeh, stock, and salt and black pepper to taste. Cover, and decrease the heat to medium-low. Simmer for 10 minutes, or until the root vegetables are just soft. Remove the lid and continue to simmer for 15 minutes, or until most of the liquid evaporates. Remove from the heat, adjust the salt and pepper, and let cool to room temperature.

To make the empanadas, preheat the oven to 400°F. Line a baking sheet with parchment paper. Flour a surface, and roll out one-sixth of the dough about 7 inches square and 1/4 inch thick. Cut a 6-inch circle out of the dough. Repeat with the remaining dough, making 5 more empanadas.

For each empanada, place 1/2 cup of the picadillo filling on the bottom half of the dough, leaving a 1/2-inch lip.

Brush the 1/2-inch perimeter with water. Fold the top half of the dough over the filling. Crimp the edges with a fork. Bake the empanadas on the baking sheet for 12 to 15 minutes, until the crusts are slightly brown and dry.

To serve, cut each empanada in half diagonally and stack one half over the other in the middle of each plate. Spoon 3 tablespoons of the mojo around the plate. Place 2 heaping tablespoons of the salsa next to the empanada.

NUTRITIONAL INFORMATION

PER EMPANADA: 375 calories (32% from fat), 11 g protein, 51 g carbohydrate, 14.4 g fat, 0 mg cholesterol, 82 mg sodium, 5.5 g fiber

PER 3 TABLESPOONS MOJO: 150 calories (78% from fat), 1.7 g protein, 7.2 g carbohydrate, 13 g fat, 0 mg cholesterol, 17 mg sodium, 2.2 g fiber

PER 2 TABLESPOONS SALSA: 6 calories (4% from fat), 0.1 g protein, 1.4 g carbohydrate, 0.1 g fat, 0 mg cholesterol, 0.0 mg sodium, 0.2 g fiber

SESAME-CRUSTED OYSTER MUSHROOM CALAMARI
over BURDOCK KIMPIRA

SERVES 4

These succulent "calamari" have become a favorite at Millennium. Mark and Laura Segelman, two of our regular customers, liked this dish so much that Mark had it specially prepared for their wedding.

This dish works well with many mushrooms, including honshimeji, clamshell, and king trumpet mushrooms. The mushrooms are arranged over a mound of kimpira (Japanese stir-fried burdock and carrots). B.E.

KIMPIRA

2 teaspoons sesame oil

2 (12- to 16-inch-long) burdock roots, peeled and sliced diagonally into thin, 2-inch-long sticks

2 carrots, peeled and sliced diagonally into thin, 2-inch-long sticks

1 teaspoon peeled and minced fresh ginger

1 teaspoon minced garlic

2 teaspoons Florida Crystals (see page 224)

1 tablespoon tamari

2 teaspoons sesame seeds, toasted (see page 223)

OYSTER MUSHROOM CALAMARI

1/2 cup rice flour

1/2 cup corn flour

1/4 cup sesame seeds

1 tablespoon black sesame seeds

2 teaspoons Japanese or Korean chile powder, or 1 1/2 teaspoons sweet paprika plus 1/2 teaspoon cayenne pepper

1 1/2 teaspoons salt

16 oyster mushrooms

1 cup soy milk

1 to 2 cups canola or light vegetable oil, for frying

1/2 cup Wasabi Cream (page 18)

1/2 cup kecap manis (page 215)

1/4 cup thinly sliced scallions, green parts only, or chives, for garnish

2 teaspoons sesame seeds, toasted (see page 223), for garnish

2 teaspoons black sesame seeds, toasted (see page 223), for garnish

4 teaspoons Sea Vegetable Salad (page 109) or reconstituted seaweed (see page 223), for garnish

1/2 lime, cut into 4 wedges, for garnish

To make the kimpira, heat the sesame oil in a wok or skillet over high heat. Add the burdock roots and carrots and stir-fry for 1 minute, or until crisp-tender. Add the ginger, garlic, Florida Crystals, and tamari, and cook for 1 minute, or until a nice glaze has formed. Remove from the heat and let cool. Sprinkle with the sesame seeds and set aside.

To make the oyster mushrooms, set up a dredging station by combining the flours, sesame seeds, chile powder, and salt in one bowl and placing the soy milk in a second bowl. Fill a wok or skillet with 1/2 inch canola oil and heat over medium-high heat until shimmering but not smoking (about 350°F). Test the oil with a piece of bread; it is hot enough when the bread floats to the surface and becomes golden brown in 30 seconds or less. Dredge each mushroom in the soy milk, and then in the flour mixture, and fry in batches of 6 to 8 mushrooms for 1 1/2 minutes, or until the mushrooms are golden brown and float to the surface. Be careful not to crowd the pan. Flip the mushrooms after about 45 seconds, midway through the cooking. Drain well on paper towels.

To serve, place 1/4 cup of the kimpira in the center of each plate and stack about 4 mushrooms on top of the kimpira. Drizzle 2 tablespoons of the wasabi cream and 2 tablespoons of the kecap manis around the stack, and sprinkle with scallions and sesame seeds. Place 1 teaspoon of sea vegetable salad on top of the stack and garnish with a wedge of lime.

NUTRITIONAL INFORMATION

PER 4 MUSHROOMS: 339 calories (46% from fat), 9.3 g protein, 37 g carbohydrate, 18 g fat, 0 mg cholesterol, 739 mg sodium, 6.5 g fiber

PER 1/4 CUP KIMPIRA: 45 calories (8% from fat), 1.2 g protein, 9 g carbohydrate, 0.5 g fat, 0 mg cholesterol, 137 mg sodium, 1.9 g fiber

GRILLED VEGETABLE TERRINE *with* ARUGULA–TOASTED ALMOND PESTO

SERVES 8

This recipe takes some advance planning because the terrine needs to be refrigerated overnight to set, but the results are impressive. The finished dish is a firm, layered vegetable torte. If you don't want to fire up a grill, you can roast the vegetables in a broiler. For a variation on this summer recipe, use roasted root vegetables.

The simple pesto is given a slight Latin-American spin with the addition of charred onion and chile, and it makes a great dip in itself or blended with white beans or silken tofu. Serve the entire dish with some chickpea socca (page 134), as an appetizer or as a light entrée. E.T.

ARUGULA PESTO

1/2 yellow onion, cut into 1/4-inch-thick rings
1 jalapeño chile, seeded
2 bunches arugula, stemmed
1 cup almonds, toasted (see page 222)
2 cloves garlic, peeled
4 tablespoons extra virgin olive oil
Juice of 1/2 lemon
2 tablespoons water
1/2 teaspoon salt, plus more as needed

VEGETABLE TERRINE

1/2 cup balsamic vinegar
1/4 cup plus 1 teaspoon extra virgin olive oil
1/2 teaspoon dried oregano
1/2 teaspoon dried basil
4 cloves garlic, minced
1 teaspoon salt, plus more as needed
1/4 teaspoon freshly ground black pepper
1 red onion, sliced into 1/3-inch-thick rounds
1 small globe eggplant, sliced into 1/3-inch-thick rounds
2 gold zucchini, sliced lengthwise into 1/3-inch-thick strips
2 green zucchini, sliced lengthwise into 1/3-inch-thick strips
6 plum tomatoes, halved
2 red bell peppers, seeded

2 yellow bell peppers, seeded
2 teaspoons agar powder (see page 224), dissolved in 1/2 cup boiling water

Millennium Focaccia (page 217), toasted
4 teaspoons capers, for garnish
Basil leaves or arugula leaves, for garnish

To make the pesto, preheat the broiler. Place the onion rings and jalapeño on a baking sheet. Broil for 5 to 7 minutes, until half the surface area is lightly charred. Remove and let cool to room temperature. Transfer to a food processor fitted with the metal blade, and add the arugula, almonds, and garlic. Process, slowly adding the oil and lemon juice, followed by the water, until smooth. Add the salt, plus more to taste. (Store in an airtight container, with a coating of oil on top, for up to 4 days.)

To prepare the vegetables, preheat the grill or broiler. In a bowl, combine the vinegar, 1/4 cup of the olive oil, the oregano, basil, garlic, salt, and black pepper. Add the red onion and eggplant to the marinade. Toss well. Grill or broil the red onion and eggplant for 2 minutes per side, or until lightly charred and still slightly al dente. Remove from the grill or broiler.

Place the gold and green zucchini, tomatoes, and red and yellow bell peppers in the marinade and toss well. Grill or broil the zucchini for 2 minutes per side, or until lightly charred and still slightly al dente. Grill the plum tomatoes for 30 seconds to 1 minute per side, until moisture is released and the tomatoes begin to char. Grill the bell peppers for 3 to 4 minutes, until the skins are slightly charred. Remove from the heat. Scrape the charred skin off the bell peppers.

Preheat the oven to 350°F. Line an 8 by 5-inch loaf pan or terrine with aluminum foil. Brush the foil lightly with the remaining 1 teaspoon olive oil. Spread an even layer of onions onto the bottom of the loaf pan, followed by alternating layers of green zucchini, eggplant, plum tomatoes, yellow bell pepper, red bell pepper, and gold zucchini until all of the vegetables are used. Add salt to taste. Pour the dissolved agar over the layered vegetables. Cover the terrine with foil and bake for 1 hour, or until set.

Remove the pan from the oven. Place a heavy object, such as a brick or a heavy can, over the top of the terrine. Let sit at room temperature for 4 hours. Refrigerate overnight.

To unmold the terrine, remove the foil from the top, invert onto a plate, and tap the edges. The terrine should come free. Remove any attached foil.

To serve, slice the vegetable terrine into 8 servings. Place 1 serving on the center of each plate. Place a dollop of the arugula pesto on the corner of the serving. Sprinkle with $1/2$ teaspoon capers. Place 2 wedges of toasted focaccia at the edges of the plate. Garnish with basil leaves.

NUTRITIONAL INFORMATION

PER SLICE TERRINE: 177 calories (15% from fat), 4 g protein, 22 g carbohydrate, 2.2 g fat, 0 mg cholesterol, 260 mg sodium, 5.9 g fiber

PER 2 TABLESPOONS PESTO: 52 calories (85% from fat), 0.7 g protein, 1.3 g carbohydrate, 5 g fat, 0 mg cholesterol, 127 mg sodium, 0 g fiber

CORN FLAN *over* TOMATO COMPOTE *with* SPICY GRILLED NECTARINE

SERVES 6

Here is an elegant appetizer for a summer meal. The flan has an amazing silken custard texture. The tomato compote is so good you'll want to keep some on hand to brush on bruschetta or perhaps spread on a grilled eggplant sandwich. Note that the flan needs to be made in advance so it can set up properly. E.T.

CORN FLAN

2 teaspoons agar powder (see page 224), dissolved in 1 cup boiling water
Kernels from 2 ears sweet corn
14 ounces silken firm tofu
1 cup soy or rice milk
1 tablespoon light miso
1 teaspoon nutritional yeast (see page 224)
2 scallions, green part only, minced
1/2 teaspoon ground nutmeg
Salt and freshly ground black pepper

TOMATO COMPOTE

1 tablespoon extra virgin olive oil
2 cloves garlic, minced
1/3 teaspoon fennel seeds
1/2 teaspoon crushed red pepper flakes
4 very ripe Early Girl or Celebrity tomatoes or plum tomatoes, seeded and chopped into 1/2-inch dice
1 teaspoon Sucanat (see page 224)
1 tablespoon sherry
1 teaspoon sherry vinegar
1 teaspoon cornstarch or arrowroot, dissolved in 2 tablespoons water
Salt

FRIED LEEK HAIR (OPTIONAL)

Canola oil for frying
1 leek, white part only, cleaned well, patted dry, cut in half, and julienne

SPICY GRILLED NECTARINE

1 teaspoon canola oil
1 teaspoon sherry vinegar

1/3 teaspoon cayenne pepper
2 firm yellow nectarines

2 tablespoons basil chiffonade, for garnish
1/4 cup basil oil (page 215), for garnish

To make the flan, preheat the oven to 350°F. Place the agar slurry, half of the corn, the tofu, soy milk, miso, and yeast in a blender. Blend until smooth. Transfer to a bowl and fold in the remaining corn, the scallions, and nutmeg. Season with salt and pepper to taste.

Pour the mixture into six 6-ounce custard cups or teacups. Place the filled cups in a deep baking dish. Fill the baking dish with water until it comes halfway up the sides of the cups. Bake in the oven for 1 hour, or until nearly set; it will seem loose when removed from the oven. Let cool to room temperature, and then refrigerate for at least 6 hours, until set. Remove from the refrigerator and let sit at room temperature for 1 hour before serving. At serving time, dip a knife in hot water, run it around the edge of the cup, and invert the flan onto a plate, tapping the bottom if it sticks.

To make the compote, heat the olive oil in a skillet over medium-high heat. Add the garlic and sauté for 30 seconds, or until translucent. Add the fennel seeds and pepper flakes and sauté for another 30 seconds. Add the tomatoes, Sucanat, sherry, and vinegar. Bring to a boil and then stir in the cornstarch. Simmer for 1 minute to thicken. Add salt to taste. Let cool. (Store refrigerated, in an airtight container, for up to 4 days. Warm to room temperature before serving.)

To make the leek hair, heat at least 1 inch of oil in a deep wok or saucepan over high heat until very hot. Fry a test leek; it should immediately start to fry and float at the surface of the oil. Slowly add half of the leeks to the oil. Fry for 30 to 45 seconds, until just starting to turn light brown. Transfer with a slotted spoon or wire skimmer to a paper or a kitchen towel to drain. The leeks should be crisp seconds after cooling.

Repeat with the remaining leeks. (Store in an airtight container at room temperature for up to 1 day.)

To make the nectarine, preheat the grill or broiler. In a mixing bowl, combine the oil, vinegar, and cayenne pepper. Slice each nectarine into thirds, and then cut two slices two-thirds of the way through each piece so it can be fanned out after grilling. Toss the nectarines with the marinade, and grill or broil for 1 minute per side, or until lightly browned.

To serve, spoon ¼ cup of the tomato compote in the center of each plate. Place 1 flan on top of the compote. Fan 1 piece of the sliced nectarine around the plate. Sprinkle some of the basil chiffonade and drizzle 2 teaspoons of the basil oil around the plate. Place a tuft of fried leek hair on top of the flan.

NUTRITIONAL INFORMATION

PER FLAN: 90 calories (34% from fat), 7.4 g protein, 13 g carbohydrate, 4.8 g fat, 0 mg cholesterol, 158 mg sodium, 2 g fiber

PER ¼ CUP COMPOTE: 33 calories (46% from fat), 0.6 g protein, 4.3 g carbohydrate, 1.9 g fat, 0 mg cholesterol, 7 mg sodium, 0.8 g fiber

PER SLICE NECTARINE: 29 calories (27% from fat), 0.4 g protein, 5.5 g carbohydrate, 1 g fat, 0 mg cholesterol, 0 mg sodium, 0.7 g fiber

PER 2 TABLESPOONS LEEK HAIR: 17 calories (88% from fat), 0.1 g protein, 0.4 g carbohydrate, 1.7 g fat, 0 mg cholesterol, 1 mg sodium, 0.1 g fiber

Seitan Saté Skewers *with* Spicy Peanut-Coconut Sauce

SERVES 6

This is one of our versions of the Indonesian classic. We make our own seitan nuggets simmered in a flavorful lemongrass-infused marinade. This version of peanut sauce is enhanced with coconut milk and pungent Szechuan peppercorns. We use pineapple here, but feel free to try just about any firm-fleshed fruit, such as nectarines, apricots, Asian pears, or other stone fruits. To make this appetizer, you will need twelve 4- to 5-inch wooden skewers soaked in water for 1 hour. E.T.

SPICY PEANUT-COCONUT SAUCE

- $1/2$ teaspoon Szechuan peppercorns, toasted (see page 223) and ground
- $1/2$ teaspoon coriander seeds, toasted (see page 223) and ground
- 3 tablespoons tightly packed cilantro leaves
- 2 cloves garlic, minced
- 1 serrano or Thai chile, seeded and minced
- 1 tablespoon peeled and minced fresh ginger
- 2 teaspoons Sucanat or agave nectar (see page 224)
- $1/2$ (14-ounce) can of coconut milk
- $1/2$ cup peanut butter
- 3 tablespoons tamari, plus more as needed
- 1 tablespoon toasted sesame oil
- Juice of 1 lime
- Water or vegetable stock (page 205) as needed
- 2 scallions, white part only, chopped
- $1/4$ cup chopped toasted peanuts (see page 222; optional)

SEITAN SATÉ NUGGETS

- $1/2$ (14-ounce) can coconut milk
- 1 lemongrass stalk, coarsely chopped
- $1/4$ cup peeled and coarsely chopped fresh ginger
- 1 fresh lime, halved
- 4 cloves garlic, minced
- $1/2$ teaspoon crushed red pepper flakes
- $1/2$ yellow onion, coarsely chopped
- $1/4$ bunch cilantro
- $1/4$ bunch mint

- $1/4$ cup tamari
- 12 cups vegetable stock (page 205)
- $1 1/2$ cups gluten flour
- $1/6$ cup unbleached white flour
- $2/3$ cup warm water (90° to 100°F)

BEAN SPROUT SALAD

- 1 cup fresh mung bean sprouts
- $1/2$ cup daikon or radish sprouts
- $1/2$ cup shredded peeled carrot
- 2 scallions, green part only, chopped
- 1 teaspoon fresh ginger juice (see page 222) or peeled and grated fresh ginger
- 1 teaspoon agave nectar (see page 224)
- 2 teaspoons rice vinegar
- Salt

- 24 mint leaves, plus $1/2$ cup fresh mint leaves, chiffonade, for garnish
- 24 (1-inch) pieces fresh pineapple
- $1/2$ cup chopped toasted peanuts (see page 222), for garnish
- $1/2$ cup fresh cilantro leaves, chiffonade, for garnish

To make the peanut-coconut sauce, in a blender, combine the Szechuan peppercorns, coriander seeds, cilantro, garlic, chile, ginger, Sucanat, coconut milk, peanut butter, tamari, sesame oil, and lime juice. Blend until smooth, slowly adding water to thin to the consistency of heavy cream. Add the tamari to taste, transfer from the blender to a bowl, and fold in the scallions and peanuts. (Store, covered, in the refrigerator for up to 4 days.)

To make the nuggets, combine the coconut milk, lemongrass, ginger, lime, garlic, pepper flakes, onion, cilantro, and mint in a large stock or soup pot. Set aside until the seitan is prepared.

Place the gluten flour and unbleached white flour in a mixing bowl. Mix together. Slowly add the water, kneading it in with your hands until you have a firm dough. Let rest for 10 minutes. Cut the dough into 4 to 6 pieces. Coat your cutting board and hands with water to prevent the dough from sticking and then roll each piece out into a cigar shape. Using kitchen shears, scissors, or a knife, cut 1-inch pieces of dough from each dough cigar, to make about 24 nuggets.

Bring the marinade to a boil over medium-high heat, and then add the seitan nuggets. Decrease the heat to medium-low and simmer for 40 minutes, or until the seitan is firm. Drain the seitan and let cool to room temperature before serving. (Store refrigerated in the marinade and covered for up to 4 days.)

To make the salad, blanch the bean sprouts for 10 seconds (see page 223). Shock in ice water, drain, and let cool.

Combine the bean sproats, daikon, carrot, scallions, ginger juice, agave nectar, rice vinegar, and salt in a mixing bowl. Toss well.

To assemble the skewers, preheat the grill or broiler. Skewer 1 piece of the seitan followed by a mint leaf, followed by a piece of pineapple. Repeat until each skewer has 2 pieces each of seitan, mint, and pineapple. Brush the skewers with the peanut sauce and marinate for 15 minutes. Grill or broil the skewers for 2 minutes per side, or until charred or browned.

To serve, mound 1/4 cup of the sprout salad in the center of each plate and crisscross 2 skewers over the salad. Spoon 1/4 cup of the peanut sauce over and around the skewers. Sprinkle with the chopped peanuts, mint, and cilantro.

NUTRITIONAL INFORMATION

PER 4 NUGGETS: 131 calories (24% from fat), 21.8 g protein, 3.7 g carbohydrate, 3.2 g fat, 0 mg cholesterol, 152 mg sodium, 0.2 g fiber

PER 1/4 CUP PEANUT-COCONUT SAUCE: 159 calories (73% from fat), 4.7 g protein, 6.7 g carbohydrate, 14 g fat, 0 mg cholesterol, 82 mg sodium, 1.3 g fiber

PER 1/4 CUP SALAD: 16 calories (6% from fat), 0.9 g protein, 3.7 g carbohydrate, 0.2 g fat, 0 mg cholesterol, 6 mg sodium, 0.8 g fiber

ISRAELI COUSCOUS *and* BUCKWHEAT—FILLED DOLMAS *with* ZAATAR DIPPING SAUCE

MAKES 24 TO 30 DOLMAS

Our version of dolmas combines nutty toasted buckwheat and saffron-hued Israeli couscous with pungent preserved oranges and dried cranberries. If grape leaves are not available, try rolling the filling in blanched red or green chard leaves. The filling also makes a great salad on its own. This recipe makes enough for a small to medium dinner party. Serve with cucumber raita (page 214) or just some wedges of lemon. E.T.

ZAATAR DIPPING SAUCE

2 tablespoons sesame seeds, toasted (see page 223)
2 tablespoons dried sumac powder (see page 126)
1 teaspoon dried thyme
Juice of 1 lemon
1/3 cup extra virgin olive oil
Salt

COUSCOUS AND BUCKWHEAT SALAD

1/4 teaspoon saffron threads
1/2 teaspoon salt
1/2 cup whole buckwheat groats
1 cup Israeli couscous
2 tablespoons extra virgin olive oil
1/2 red onion, cut into small dice
1/2 teaspoon dried oregano
1/2 teaspoon ground cinnamon
1/4 teaspoon crushed red pepper flakes
1/2 cup pine nuts, toasted (see page 222)
1/2 cup dried cranberries or dried cherries
1/3 cup Millennium Preserved Oranges (page 216),
  cut into small dice
1/4 cup fresh mint leaves, coarsely chopped
Salt and freshly ground black pepper

24 to 30 brine-packed large grape leaves, drained and
  rinsed well to remove excess salt (more leaves are
  needed if smaller)
Juice of 3 lemons
2 tablespoons extra virgin olive oil
Salt and freshly ground black pepper

To make the zaatar sauce, combine the sesame seeds, sumac powder, thyme, lemon juice, and olive oil in a mixing bowl and whisk until emulsified. Add salt to taste. (Store, covered, in the refrigerator indefinitely.)

To make the couscous salad, in a saucepan, bring 2 1/2 cups water, saffron, and salt to a boil. Decrease the heat to low and simmer. Meanwhile, in a second saucepan, toast the buckwheat over medium-high heat, stirring constantly for 2 to 3 minutes, until fragrant and darker in color. Add the couscous, followed by the saffron water. Bring back to a boil, decrease the heat to a simmer, and cook for 7 to 10 minutes, until the couscous is cooked through yet al dente. Remove from the heat and let sit for 10 minutes. Drain in a colander.

Heat the olive oil in a sauté pan over medium heat. Add the onion and sauté for 5 minutes, or until just soft. Add the oregano, cinnamon, and pepper flakes. Sauté for an additional 30 seconds, or until aromatic. Transfer to a large mixing bowl. Add the pine nuts, cranberries, oranges, buckwheat, and couscous. Add the mint, and season with salt and pepper to taste.

To make the dolmas, preheat the oven to 350°F. Place a large grape leaf on a flat surface. Put 2 tablespoons of the filling in the center, fold the outside edges over the filling, and roll away from you to form a tight cylinder. Repeat with the remaining grape leaves. Place the finished grape leaves in a shallow baking pan and sprinkle with lemon juice, olive oil, and salt and pepper to taste. Cover the pan with aluminum foil and bake for 20 minutes, or until heated through. Let cool to room temperature. (Alternatively, grill the dolmas for 2 minutes per side, or until grill marks form.)

To serve, place the dolmas on a platter and serve with the dipping sauce on the side.

NUTRITIONAL INFORMATION

PER DOLMA: 72 calories (34% from fat), 2 g protein, 10 g carbohydrate, 2.5 g fat, 0 mg cholesterol, 322 mg sodium, 3.4 g fiber

PER TABLESPOON ZAATAR SAUCE: 94 calories (93% from fat), 0.4 g protein, 1 g carbohydrate, 10 g fat, 0 mg cholesterol, 1 mg sodium, 0.2 g fiber

EXOTIC MUSHROOM CEVICHE

SERVES 8

If you are a mushroom head like I am, our version of the traditional seafood-based ceviche—using maitake, oyster, and cremini mushrooms—will prove just as satisfying as its seafood counterpart if not more so. The acid from the citrus "cooks" the mushrooms, although they are technically raw. Serve this as an appetizer in a martini glass with a wedge of lime and some toasted tortilla strips. This ceviche also makes a great side dish or salsa for any Latin American–inspired entrée. E.T.

8 ounces maitake mushrooms, cut into bite-sized pieces
8 ounces oyster mushrooms
4 ounces cremini or button mushrooms, cleaned with a damp kitchen towel and halved
Juice of 3 limes
2 tablespoons extra virgin olive oil
1/2 teaspoon salt, plus more as needed
1/2 red onion, diced
1 small cucumber, peeled, seeded, and diced
2 ripe tomatoes, seeded and diced
1 ripe avocado, peeled, pitted, and diced
1 clove garlic, minced
1 to 2 serrano or aji chiles, seeded and minced
Juice of 1 orange

1/2 teaspoon grated orange zest
2 teaspoons fresh oregano
2 tablespoons minced cilantro
Freshly ground black pepper
6 lime wedges, for garnish
32 toasted tortilla strips (see page 77), for garnish

To make the ceviche, place the maitake, oyster, and cremini mushrooms, two-thirds of the lime juice, the olive oil, and the salt in a mixing bowl. Toss well and cover. Marinate for 2 hours.

Place the onion, cucumber, tomatoes, avocado, garlic, chiles, orange juice, orange zest, oregano, cilantro, and remaining lime juice in a mixing bowl. Add salt and pepper to taste. Add the marinated mushrooms to the salsa mixture and combine.

To serve, divide the ceviche mixture among 8 martini glasses, and garnish with a wedge of lime and 4 toasted tortilla strips.

NUTRITIONAL INFORMATION

PER SERVING: 111 calories (52% from fat), 3.3 g protein, 11 g carbohydrate, 7.2 g fat, 0 mg cholesterol, 127 mg sodium, 2.5 g fiber

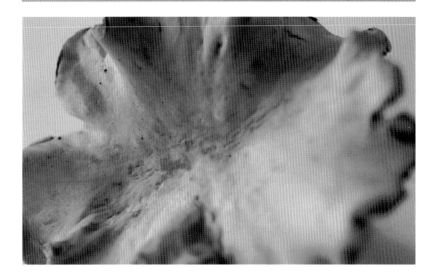

Cumin-Balsamic Roasted Mushrooms

SERVES 6

This tasty preparation of mushrooms is simple. Try it with any firm, fleshy mushrooms, such as cremini, button, portobello, or even porcini. The intense heat of the broiler intensifies the mushroom flavor and caramelizes the seasonings onto the mushrooms. These are delicious as part of an antipasto platter with seasonal grilled vegetables and focaccia (page 217). E.T.

4 cloves garlic, minced

1 teaspoon cumin seeds, toasted (see page 223) and coarsely ground

1/2 teaspoon ground ancho chile powder

1/4 teaspoon freshly ground black pepper

3 tablespoons balsamic vinegar

3 tablespoons tamari

2 tablespoons extra virgin olive oil

16 ounces cremini or button mushrooms, cleaned with a damp kitchen towel

To make the mushrooms, preheat the broiler. In a mixing bowl, combine the garlic, cumin, chile powder, black pepper, vinegar, tamari, and olive oil. Immerse the mushrooms completely in the marinade for 10 to 15 minutes.

Place the mushroom caps button side down on a baking dish. Brush marinade onto the mushrooms. Broil for 5 to 7 minutes, until the mushrooms are brown and dry. Serve warm, or let cool to room temperature.

NUTRITIONAL INFORMATION:

PER SERVING: 43 calories (62% from fat), 2 g protein, 6 g carbohydrate, 2.8 g fat, 0 mg cholesterol, 250 mg sodium, 1.2 g fiber

Roasted Porcini Mushrooms *with* Shaved Porcini Salad *and* Jellied Porcini Stock

SERVES 6

One morning in the fall of 1999, a few of our usually late-sleeping Millennium chefs agreed to wake up incredibly early and go on a mushroom foray with one of our wild mushroom purveyors, Connie Green. Thanks to a sleepy driver, our group showed up late and missed the main group. As a result, we ended up following a different trail than the rest of the foragers and returned with several pounds of fresh, wild porcini! It's a good thing I skipped coffee that morning, or we wouldn't have this recipe. This dish was inspired by the multiple preparations the other chefs and mycophiles suggested for this versatile, delicious, and magical giant mushroom. Only the most fresh and firm porcini should be used. B.E.

2 teaspoons olive oil, or dry sherry for oil free

2 small red onions, coarsely chopped

2 cloves garlic, minced

2 celery stalks, thinly sliced

1/4 teaspoon salt, plus 2 pinches

1/4 teaspoon freshly ground black pepper, plus
   2 pinches

6 porcini mushrooms (about 4 to 6 ounces each),
   gills removed and reserved

1 (12-ounce) bottle dark beer

1 tablespoon tamari

2 teaspoons dark molasses

2 teaspoons Sucanat (see page 224)

1 teaspoon nutritional yeast (see page 224)

2 cups vegetable stock (page 205) or water

2 tablespoons walnut oil

1/2 small celery root, peeled

1 teaspoon sherry vinegar

1/4 cup walnuts, toasted (see page 223), for garnish

6 rosemary sprigs, for garnish

To make the porcini stock, in a small saucepan, combine the olive oil, onion, garlic, celery, 1/4 teaspoon of the salt, and 1/4 teaspoon of the pepper. Sauté over medium-low heat, stirring often, for 45 minutes, or until the onions are caramelized. Add the mushroom gills and beer and simmer for 15 minutes, or until the beer reduces by half. Add the tamari, molasses, Sucanat, nutritional yeast, and stock and simmer slowly for 20 minutes, or until reduced by one-third. Pour through a fine-mesh strainer and return to the pan. Continue to simmer for 10 minutes, or until the sauce gels slightly, like consommé.

To roast the mushrooms, preheat the broiler. Combine 1 tablespoon of the walnut oil with 2 tablespoons of the porcini stock and a pinch each of salt and pepper. Cut the 3 largest porcini in half lengthwise and lay them out on a baking sheet with the insides facing up. Drizzle with the oil-stock mixture, and broil for 5 to 7 minutes, until brown. Keep warm.

To make the salad, using a vegetable peeler, shave the 3 remaining porcini and the celery root into a mixing bowl. Dress the salad with the remaining 1 tablespoon walnut oil, the sherry vinegar, and a pinch each of salt and pepper.

To serve, spoon some of the stock onto each plate, place one-sixth of the porcini salad on the stock and top with 1 roasted porcini half. Garnish with toasted walnuts and rosemary.

NUTRITIONAL INFORMATION

PER SERVING: 321 calories (49% from fat), 8.3 g protein, 54 g carbohydrate, 9.8 g fat, 0 mg cholesterol, 278 mg sodium, 8.1 g fiber

YUCA–BLACK BEAN CAKES *with* SWEET MANGO, MUSTARD, *and* HABANERO SAUCE

SERVES 6

These black bean cakes will prove addicting, especially if you like things spicy. Yuca, also known as cassava, is a slightly sweet root available in most Hispanic markets. If you cannot find fresh yuca—or if you find only yuca root weighing 10 pounds and have no clue what to do with the other 9 pounds—try substituting a sweet potato or any yellow-fleshed potato. The cakes are great with our Roasted Tomato Salsa, which calls for ripe, meaty tomatoes, or any salsa of your choice. E.T.

ROASTED TOMATO SALSA

2 large beefsteak tomatoes, cored, seeded, and cut into 1-inch dice
1/2 red onion, cut into small dice
2 cloves garlic, minced
1 dried ancho chile, toasted and coarsely ground
1/2 teaspoon dried Mexican oregano
Juice of 1 lime
1/2 teaspoon salt
1/4 cup chopped cilantro

MANGO, MUSTARD, AND HABANERO SAUCE

1/2 mango, pitted, peeled, and diced
2 tablespoons agave nectar (see page 224)
1/4 cup Dijon mustard
2 tablespoons water
1/2 habanero, Scotch bonnet, or aji chile, plus more if desired, seeded

YUCA–BLACK BEAN CAKES

2 teaspoons extra virgin olive oil
1/2 red onion, sliced in thin crescents
2 cloves garlic, minced
1 red bell pepper, cut in small dice
1 teaspoon ground cumin
1/2 teaspoon dried thyme
1/3 teaspoon ground allspice
2 cups cooked black beans
1 1/2 cups grated yuca root or sweet potato
1/4 cup coarsely chopped cilantro
1/2 teaspoon salt

2 tablespoons water, plus more as needed
1/2 cup dried corn masa flour
Canola oil for sautéing or baking

Chopped cilantro, for garnish

To make the salsa, preheat the broiler. Place the tomatoes in a mixing bowl and add the onion, garlic, chile, and oregano. Toss together, and then spread on a baking sheet. Place the mixture under the broiler, and broil for 3 to 5 minutes, until the tomato and onion start to char. Toss the mixture, and broil for another 3 to 5 minutes, until about half of the mixture is lightly charred.

Let the mixture cool to room temperature. Drain the excess liquid from the tomato mixture and transfer to a mixing bowl. Add the lime juice, salt, and cilantro and toss. (Store refrigerated for up to 2 days.)

To make the habanero sauce, place the mango, agave nectar, mustard, water, and chile in a blender. Blend until smooth. (Store refrigerated for up to 4 days.)

To make the cakes, heat the olive oil in a pan over medium heat. Add the onion and garlic and sauté for 5 to 7 minutes, until golden. Add the red bell pepper, followed by the cumin, thyme, and allspice. Sauté, stirring often, for 5 minutes, or until the bell pepper is tender. Remove from the heat and let cool to room temperature.

In a mixing bowl, combine the sautéed onion mixture with the black beans, yuca root, cilantro, salt, and water. Mix well with your hands or a spoon, lightly crushing some of the beans. Slowly add the corn masa and mix until all of it is incorporated and the mixture holds together as a firm dough. If the mixture is dry and crumbly, add more water until it holds together. Shape the mixture into 12 cakes, each about 3 inches in diameter and $1/2$ inch thick.

Heat a little canola oil in a nonstick skillet over medium-high heat. In batches, sauté the cakes for 3 minutes per side, or until browned and crisp. Drain on paper towels and keep warm. (Alternatively, for lower fat, preheat the broiler or the oven to 450°F. Brush the cakes with soy milk, and broil or bake on an oiled, parchment-lined pan for 12 to 15 minutes, until browned crisp.)

To serve, place 2 cakes on each plate with 3 tablespoons of the habanero sauce and $1/4$ cup of the salsa. Garnish with cilantro.

NUTRITIONAL INFORMATION

PER 2 CAKES: 195 calories (17% from fat), 7.3 g protein, 34 g carbohydrate, 4 g fat, 0 mg cholesterol, 165 mg sodium, 5.5 g fiber

PER TABLESPOON HABANERO SAUCE: 14 calories (10% from fat), 0.2 g protein, 3.6 g carbohydrate, 0.2 g fat, 0 mg cholesterol, 47 mg sodium, 0.2 g fiber

PER $1/4$ CUP SALSA: 28 calories (9% from fat), 1 g protein, 6.5 g carbohydrate, 0.4 g fat, 0 mg cholesterol, 164 mg sodium, 1.6 g fiber

ANCHO CHILE–BLACK BEAN CAKES *with* UNCLE JUNIOR'S HEMP SEED MOLE

SERVES 8

This variation on our black bean cakes has a warm, toasty quality from the ancho chile and the toasted pecans. These cakes also make a great veggie burger. The mole sauce is a tribute to Uncle Junior, famous Caribbean chef and subject of the reggae classic, "Let's Go Visit Uncle Junior," a song popular among denizens of San Francisco's Haight District. Look for the papaya juice and hemp seeds in health food stores. B.E.

UNCLE JUNIOR'S HEMP SEED MOLE

$1/2$ habanero chile
$1/2$ large sweet yellow pepper
$1/2$ large gold tomato
$1/2$ yellow onion
1 cup fresh papaya juice
$1^1/2$ tablespoons white vinegar
1 teaspoon salt
1 teaspoon agave nectar (see page 224)
$1/4$ cup hemp seeds, toasted (see page 223)

ANCHO CHILE–BLACK BEAN CAKES

1 teaspoon olive oil
1 small red onion, diced
2 cloves garlic, minced
2 cups packed black beans, cooked
$2/3$ cup pecans, toasted (see page 222)
2 ancho chiles, toasted, seeded, and ground
3 tablespoons tofu aïoli (page 213)
Juice of 1 lime
Grated zest of 1 lime
3 tablespoons corn flour
1 teaspoon cumin seeds, toasted (see page 223)
   and ground
$1/2$ teaspoon dried oregano
$1/2$ teaspoon salt
Canola oil or soy milk for frying

Sliced avocado, for garnish
Cilantro sprigs, for garnish

To make the mole, smoke the habanero, yellow pepper, tomato, and onion together for at least 1 hour (see page 219). Transfer to a blender and add the papaya juice, vinegar, salt, agave nectar, and hemp seeds. Blend until smooth. Strain through a fine-mesh strainer, if desired, to remove the chunks. (Store refrigerated for up to 1 week.)

To make the cakes, heat the olive oil in a sauté pan over medium-high heat. Add the onion and garlic, and sauté for 2 to 3 minutes, until soft. In a large bowl, combine the onions, garlic, beans, pecans, chiles, aïoli, lime juice and zest, flour, cumin seeds, oregano, and salt. Remove one-third of the mixture, and process in a food processor fitted with the metal blade or a blender until smooth. Return the processed portion to the bowl and fold in. Form the mixture into 8 cakes, about 3 inches in diameter and $1/2$ inch thick.

Heat a little canola oil in a nonstick skillet over medium-high heat. In batches, sauté the cakes for 2 minutes per side, or until browned and crisp. Drain on paper towels, and keep warm. (Alternatively, for lower fat, preheat the broiler or the oven to 500°F. Brush the cakes with soy milk and broil or bake on a baking sheet for 15 minutes, or until browned and crisp.)

To serve, place 1 cake on each plate, and garnish with $1/3$ cup of the mole and some of the avocado and cilantro.

NUTRITIONAL INFORMATION

PER CAKE: 155 calories (39% from fat), 6 g protein, 20 g carbohydrate, 7.5 g fat, 0 mg cholesterol, 155 mg sodium, 4.5 g fiber

PER $1/3$ CUP MOLE: 35 calories (51% from fat), 2 g protein, 3 g carbohydrate, 2.4 g fat, 0 mg cholesterol, 236 mg sodium, 0.7 g fiber

BUTTERNUT SQUASH CAKES *with* ROASTED CHANTERELLES *and* PINK PEARL APPLES

SERVES 6

Two of the most beautiful citizens of the vegetable kingdom appear together for a few weeks in late fall and early winter. By sheer coincidence, they complement each other brilliantly in flavor as well as in color. Chanterelle mushrooms provide an earthy quality heightened only by the tartness of beautiful pink pearl apples. Buttery butternut cakes with wild rice and scallions provide a stunning canvas, and horseradish wakes up the entire plate. Who says winter is dreary? B.E.

HORSERADISH CASHEW CREAM

1/2 cup plus 2 tablespoons unsalted raw cashews, or
  1/3 cup raw cashew butter
1 tablespoon grated fresh horseradish
2 teaspoons sherry vinegar
1 teaspoon nutritional yeast (see page 224)
3/4 cup water or vegetable stock (page 205)
1 teaspoon salt

ROASTED APPLES

2 pink pearl apples, cored and cut into 1/2-inch dice
1 1/2 cups button chanterelles, or large chanterelles
  torn into bite-sized pieces
1 teaspoon canola oil
1 tablespoon dry sherry
1/2 teaspoon salt
1/4 teaspoon freshly ground black pepper

BUTTERNUT SQUASH CAKES

1 (2-pound) butternut squash, peeled, seeded, grated,
  and pat dry (about 3 cups)
1 cup cooked wild rice
6 scallions, white and green parts, thinly sliced,
  1 tablespoon reserved for garnish
2 teaspoons salt
1 teaspoon ground cinnamon
1/2 teaspoon ground allspice
1/4 cup cornstarch, plus more as needed
1/2 cup canola or grapeseed oil for frying, plus more
  as needed

To make the cream, blend all of the ingredients in a blender for 3 to 5 minutes, until creamy.

To make the apples, preheat the oven 400°F. In an ovenproof pan, toss the apples, chanterelles, oil, sherry, salt, and pepper together. Place the pan in the oven and roast for 15 minutes, or until the chanterelles are cooked but before the apples begin to get too soft. Keep warm until ready to serve.

To make the squash cakes, in a mixing bowl, combine the squash, wild rice, scallions, salt, cinnamon, allspice, and cornstarch. Mix until the dough holds together in firm patties. If necessary, add cornstarch or a little bit of the canola oil to aid in the binding process. Form the dough into 6 patties about 3 inches across and 1/2 inch thick.

Heat a little canola oil in a nonstick skillet over medium-high heat. In batches, sauté the cakes for 3 minutes per side, or until browned and crisp. Drain on paper towels, and keep warm. (Alternatively, for lower fat, preheat the broiler or the oven to 500°F. Brush the cakes with soy milk and broil or bake on a baking sheet for 15 minutes, or until browned and crisp.)

To serve, place 1 cake in the center of each plate and spoon a little of the warm roasted apples and mushrooms over the cake. Drizzle 2 tablespoons of the horseradish cream over the whole assembly. Garnish with the reserved scallions.

NUTRITIONAL INFORMATION

PER CAKE: 224 calories (21% from fat), 4 g protein, 43 g carbohydrate, 5 g fat, 0 mg cholesterol, 793 mg sodium, 6.1 g fiber

PER SERVING APPLES: 181 calories (17% from fat), 5.5 g protein, 31 g carbohydrate, 3.5 g fat, 0 mg cholesterol, 347 mg sodium, 1.8 g fiber

PER 2 TABLESPOONS HORSERADISH CREAM: 62 calories (68% from fat), 1.9 g protein, 3 g carbohydrate, 4.9 g fat, 0 mg cholesterol, 237 mg sodium, 0.7 g fiber

BUSTER'S POTATO TORTE *with* ROSEMARY-PISTACHIO PESTO *and* CASHEW "GRUYÈRE"

SERVES 8

Buster (David) Little, from Little Organic Farms, has been bringing us his hand-picked specialty potatoes since the days of Milly's, our parent restaurant in San Rafael, California, before it closed in 1995. Sometimes we've even gotten a couple of free toys thrown in by his zealous children. Now that's a family business! We only wish that his potatoes grew year-round so we could keep this on the menu all the time. Enjoy this torte this fall with your favorite farmer's potatoes.

The Gruyère-style tofu cheese calls for fermented bean (also called lam yee, fu ye, or bean curd cheese), an unusual ingredient available in Asian markets. It is very pungent but an excellent source of what we call "funk"—that bizarre, musty flavor associated with ripe cheese or anchovies. If strong flavors terrify you, this dish will be fine without the fermented bean curd, but you'll be passing up a world of fun(k)!

At Millennium, we prepare the torte and let it cool overnight before slicing. This ensures that neat slices show off the layered colors of the potatoes. We gently reheat the individual slices in a 450°F oven for 10 minutes and brown slightly under a broiler. B.E.

GRUYÈRE-STYLE TOFU CHEESE

12 ounces firm tofu
1 teaspoon umeboshi vinegar
2 teaspoons nutritional yeast (see page 224)
1 cube white fermented bean curd (about 1 teaspoon)
1 teaspoon light miso

ROSEMARY-PISTACHIO PESTO

1/3 cup pistachios, toasted (see page 222)
1 cup loosely packed arugula
1/2 cup loosely packed fresh basil leaves
1 1/2 teaspoons minced fresh rosemary
2 cloves garlic, crushed
3 teaspoons salt
3 tablespoons olive oil or pistachio oil

3 Yukon Gold or yellow Finn potatoes, cut into 1/8-inch-thick slices
3 large All Red or Huckleberry potatoes, or other red-fleshed potatoes, cut into 1/8-inch-thick slices
3 large Peruvian purple potatoes, or other all-blue-fleshed potatoes, cut into 1/8-inch-thick slices
1 cup loosely packed arugula leaves
2 teaspoons olive or pistachio oil
2 to 3 teaspoons balsamic vinegar
Salt and freshly ground black pepper
2 tablespoons balsamic vinegar reduction (page 222), or 1 teaspoon truffle oil, for garnish

To make the tofu cheese, blend all of the ingredients in a food processor fitted with the metal blade or a blender for 6 to 10 minutes, until creamy.

To make the pesto, blend all of the ingredients in a food processor fitted with the metal blade or a blender for 1 to 3 minutes, until a paste is formed. Add a little water or more oil if the mixture is too dry.

To make the torte, bring 2 quarts salted water to a boil. Boil the yellow potatoes for 7 minutes, or until al dente. Transfer to ice water to stop the cooking process. Repeat with the red potatoes, and then the blue potatoes, keeping them separate.

Preheat the oven to 350°F. Lightly oil an 8-inch pie tin. Shingle the blue potatoes along the bottom and top with a layer of one-third of the pesto and then a layer of one-third of the tofu cheese. Repeat with the yellow potatoes, one-third of the pesto, and one-third of the tofu cheese, followed by the red potatoes and the remaining pesto and tofu cheese. Cover and bake the torte for 1 hour, or until set, removing the cover for the last 10 minutes of baking.

To serve, dress the arugula in the oil, vinegar, and salt and pepper to taste. Slice the torte into 8 slices and place each slice on a plate with some arugula. Drizzle some of the reduction on the plate.

NUTRITIONAL INFORMATION

PER SLICE TORTE: 193 calories (40% from fat), 7 g protein, 18.7 g carbohydrate, 10.5 g fat, 0 mg cholesterol, 870 mg sodium, 2.5 g fiber

PER 1/4 CUP TOFU CHEESE: 32 calories (48% from fat), 3.5 g protein, 1 g carbohydrate, 1.9 g fat, 0 mg cholesterol, 145 mg sodium, 0.5 g fiber

PER 2 TABLESPOONS PESTO: 79 calories (83% from fat), 1.4 g protein, 2.1 g carbohydrate, 7 g fat, 0 mg cholesterol, 708 mg sodium, 0.7 g fiber

STUFFED SQUASH BLOSSOMS *with* SWEET CORN TOFU CHEESE *and* CILANTRO PESTO

SERVES 6

Natives to the Americas have been cultivating squash for more than ten thousand years. I wonder if that means that thousands of years ago they were just as excited by that unmistakable sign of summer, the squash flower, as we are today. These edible blossoms can generally be found in Hispanic markets. In Mexico, they are traditionally eaten in quesadillas; in the United States, we latecomers are just beginning to appreciate this beautiful delicacy. In this recipe, we stuff the sturdy flowers with sweet corn, another exciting American summer crop. B.E.

CILANTRO PESTO

1 bulb garlic
1 tablespoon olive oil, plus more as needed
1/2 cup pecans, toasted (see page 222)
1 large bunch cilantro, chopped, large stems removed
2 teaspoons light miso
Pinch of salt
1/4 cup water or vegetable stock (page 205), as needed

TOFU CHEESE

6 ounces extra firm tofu, drained
1 tablespoon tahini (optional)
1 teaspoon nutritional yeast (see page 224)
1 teaspoon umeboshi vinegar

Kernels from 3 ears sweet white corn
2 teaspoons olive oil, plus more as needed
1 dried ancho chile, toasted (see page 222) and ground
2 teaspoons cumin seeds, toasted (see page 223) and ground
2 teaspoons Mexican oregano
2 teaspoons salt
12 large squash blossoms
3 large zucchini, pattypan, or other summer squash, cut into small dice
1 small white onion, minced
1 jalapeño chile, seeded and minced

2 teaspoons coriander seeds, toasted (see page 223) and ground
Juice of 1 lime
1 teaspoon tamari
6 avocado slices, for garnish
6 lime wedges, for garnish

To make the pesto, preheat the oven to 350°F. Roast the garlic (see page 222), reserving the oil. In a food processor fitted with the metal blade, combine the roasted garlic and its oil with the pecans, cilantro, miso, and salt. Process until a smooth paste is formed. If the pesto is too dry, add enough of the water to achieve the right consistency.

To make the tofu cheese, crumble the tofu well and mix by hand with the tahini, yeast, and vinegar in a bowl. Transfer half the mixture to a food processor fitted with the metal blade and process until creamy. Return to the bowl and combine with the unprocessed half.

To make the squash blossoms, preheat the broiler. Oil a baking sheet with a little oil. In a small mixing bowl, toss the corn, 1 teaspoon of the olive oil, the ancho chile, cumin seeds, oregano, and 1 teaspoon of the salt. Spread the mixture on the baking sheet and roast under the broiler for 7 to 10 minutes, until the corn starts to brown. Let cool.

When the corn mixture is cool enough to handle, combine with the tofu cheese. Spoon the mixture into the squash blossoms.

Preheat the broiler. In a bowl, combine the summer squash, onion, jalapeño, coriander seeds, lime juice, tamari, the remaining 1 teaspoon olive oil, and 1/2 teaspoon of the remaining salt. Spread the squash mixture on a small baking sheet and broil, rotating and stirring often, for 10 minutes, or until lightly browned. Keep warm.

Place the stuffed blossoms on the same baking sheet, brush with olive oil, and sprinkle with the remaining

$^1/_2$ teaspoon salt. Broil the blossoms for 4 minutes. Turn over and broil for 2 minutes, or until lightly blackened.

To serve, place 2 blossoms on each plate, and garnish with some of the roasted summer squash, a dollop of pesto, a slice of avocado, and a lime wedge.

NUTRITIONAL INFORMATION

PER 2 STUFFED BLOSSOMS: 149 calories (15% from fat), 6 g protein, 23 g carbohydrate, 5 g fat, 0 mg cholesterol, 800 mg sodium, 5 g fiber

PER 2 TABLESPOONS TOFU CHEESE: 15 calories (57% from fat), 1 g protein, 0.5 g carbohydrate, 1 g fat, 0 mg cholesterol, 59 mg sodium, 0.2 g fiber

PER TABLESPOON PESTO: 37 calories (72% from fat), 0.6 g protein, 2 g carbohydrate, 3 g fat, 0 mg cholesterol, 56 mg sodium, 0.4 g fiber

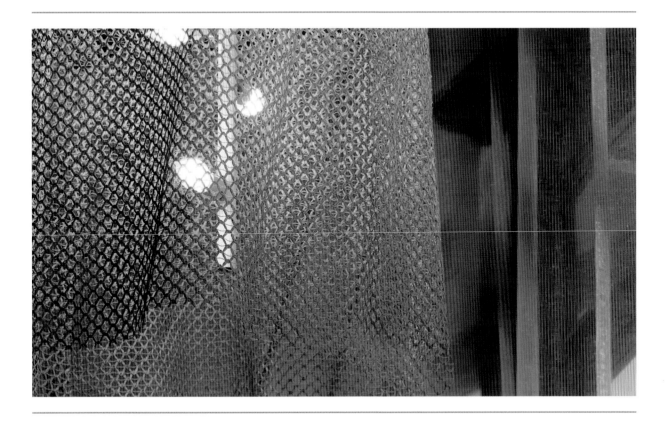

BEET-CORIANDER CAKES *with* RED LENTIL DAL *and* POMEGRANATE-GLAZED EGGPLANT

SERVES 6

Middle Eastern and Turkish flavor combinations inspire this appetizer. Because of the toasted lentils, this particular dal has a chunkier texture than the typical puréed consistency of most dals. Enjoy it with a cup of strong coffee and your favorite belly dancer! B.E.

SAFFRON CREAM

1/4 teaspoon saffron threads
1/4 cup hot water
2 tablespoons olive oil
2 cloves garlic, minced
1 teaspoon umeboshi vinegar
2 teaspoons Dijon mustard
6 ounces package extra firm silken tofu
1 teaspoon salt

RED LENTIL DAL

1/2 cup red lentils
1 teaspoon salt
1 small white or yellow onion
1 jalapeño chile, roasted (see page 222), seeded, and minced
1 teaspoon curry powder
1 teaspoon ground annatto seeds or Spanish paprika
1 1/2 cups water or vegetable stock (page 205)

GLAZED EGGPLANT

1 teaspoon whole mustard seeds
1 teaspoon whole fennel seeds
1/4 teaspoon ground cloves
1 teaspoon olive oil
1 tablespoon peeled and minced fresh ginger
1 clove garlic, minced
2 Asian or 1 large globe eggplant, halved lengthwise and cut diagonally into 1/4-inch-thick slices
2 teaspoons salt
1 cup fresh pomegranate juice (see page 224)
1 tablespoon balsamic vinegar
1 teaspoon Sucanat (see page 224)

BEET-CORIANDER CAKES

2 large red beets, peeled and grated
1 small red onion, thinly sliced
1/2 cup slivered almonds
1 cup garbanzo flour, plus more as needed
1 teaspoon coriander seeds, toasted (see page 223) and ground
1 teaspoon cumin seeds, toasted (see page 223) and ground
1 teaspoon mint tea
1 1/2 teaspoons salt
1/4 teaspoon crushed red pepper flakes
1 cup canola oil for frying (optional)

Seeds from 1 pomegranate, for garnish
2 tablespoons small fresh mint leaves, for garnish

To make the cream, infuse the saffron threads in the hot water for at least 30 minutes.

Heat the olive oil in a pan over medium heat. Add the garlic, and sauté for 2 to 5 minutes, until golden brown. Let cool. Combine the saffron, garlic, vinegar, mustard, tofu, and salt in a blender, and blend until smooth.

To make the dal, heat a heavy-bottomed saucepan over high heat. Dry-toast the lentils, stirring constantly, for 2 minutes, or until they give off a nutty aroma. Add the salt, onion, jalapeño, curry powder, and annatto seeds. Toast for 1 minute. Add the water, and bring to a boil. Decrease to a simmer and cook for 15 minutes, or until the dal is stew-like in consistency.

To make the glazed eggplant, heat a heavy-bottomed saucepan over medium-high heat. Add the mustard and fennel seeds and toast for 1 minute, shaking the pan to keep the seeds from burning. When the seeds are aromatic, add the cloves, olive oil, ginger, and garlic. When it sizzles, add the eggplant and salt, and cook for 5 to 7 minutes, until the eggplant starts to brown. Add the pomegranate juice, vinegar, and Sucanat, and bring to a boil. Decrease the heat to medium and

(continued)

BEET-CORIANDER CAKES, *continued*

simmer for 20 minutes, or until the liquid is absorbed. Keep warm.

To make the beet cakes, in a mixing bowl, combine the beets, onion, almonds, garbanzo flour, coriander seeds, cumin seeds, mint tea, salt, and pepper flakes. Mix until the dough holds together in firm patties, adding more flour or a little oil if needed to aid in the binding process. Form the beet mixture into 6 cakes about 3 inches across and $1/2$ inch thick.

Heat a little canola oil in a nonstick skillet over medium-high heat. One at a time, sauté the cakes for 3 minutes per side, or until browned and crisp. Drain on paper towels, and keep warm. (Alternatively, for lower fat, preheat the broiler or the oven to 500°F. Brush the cakes with soy milk, and broil or bake on a baking sheet for 20 minutes, or until browned and crisp.)

To serve, divide the dal evenly among the plates. Spoon some of the eggplant over the dal, and then top with a warm cake. Garnish with some of the saffron cream, pomegranate seeds, and fresh mint.

NUTRITIONAL INFORMATION

PER CAKE: 209 calories (4% from fat), 7 g protein, 22 g carbohydrate, 11 g fat, 0 mg cholesterol, 508 mg sodium, 3.5 g fiber

PER $1/4$ CUP DAL: 81 calories (3% from fat), 5.2 g protein, 14 g carbohydrate, 0.3 g fat, 0 mg cholesterol, 317 mg sodium, 6 g fiber

PER 2 TABLESPOONS EGGPLANT: 43 calories (16% from fat), 1 g protein, 9 g carbohydrate, 0.9 g fat, 0 mg cholesterol, 476 mg sodium, 1.4 g fiber

PER TABLESPOON SAFFRON CREAM: 20 calories (83% from fat), 0.8 g protein, 0.2 g carbohydrate, 2 g fat, 0 mg cholesterol, 199 mg sodium, 0 g fiber

SALADS

Salads have always been a strong part of the Millennium repertoire. Each season provides a diverse abundance of different fruits and vegetables to use in salads: rare white asparagus of spring; bountiful heirloom tomatoes of summer; figs and Asian pears of fall; beets, fennel, and citrus of winter.

Here, we have the much-asked-for classic, Milly's Warm Cabbage Salad, a Latin-American twist on an heirloom tomato stack with a hazelnut mojo, an addictive but simple creamy wasabi dressing paired with avocado, and many other fresh and elegant salads.

Milly's Warm Cabbage Salad for Shirley Ward ❧ 51

Avocado, Sea Vegetable, and Plum with Creamy Wasabi Dressing
and Spicy Candied Peanuts ❧ 52

Nori Salad Roll with Spicy, Sweet, and Sour
Kumquat-Lime Dressing ❧ 53

Southwest Salad Timbale with Nopal Cactus ❧ 54

Grilled Radicchio de Treviso with Pink Grapefruit,
Pink Peppercorns, and Garlic-Tarragon Ranch Dressing ❧ 56

Roasted Tomato Panzanella Salad with Braised Garlic
and Zinfandel Vinaigrette ❧ 57

White Nectarine and Canary Melon Salad with Gewürztraminer,
Pistachio, and Kaffir Lime Leaf Vinaigrette ❧ 58

Heirloom Tomato Stack with Bitter Greens, Avocado, Basil, and
Curried Hazelnut Mojo Dressing ❧ 59

Asian Guacamole Salad with Crisp Rice Noodles
and Mizuna Greens ❧ 60

Spanish Marble Potato Salad with Grilled Frisée,
and Creamy Sherry Vinaigrette ✤ 61

Grilled White Asparagus with Baby Lola Rosa Lettuce and
Vanilla-Lavender Aïoli ✤ 62

Indian Summer Grilled Fig and Radicchio on a Rosemary Skewer
with Cherry Tomato Salad ✤ 65

Bitter Greens with Fennel and Beets, Asian Pear, and Pomegranate
Vinaigrette with White Truffle Oil ✤ 66

MILLY'S WARM CABBAGE SALAD *for* SHIRLEY WARD

SERVES 6

Here's a favorite from Milly's (Millennium's parent restaurant in San Rafael), as requested by Santa Rosa's premier broccoli and baby carrot grower, Shirley Ward, from Stoney Farms. It seems that this salad has its own cult following—and for good reason: red cabbage marinated in umeboshi (tart Japanese plum) vinegar is sautéed with onions and caraway seeds, served over shredded spinach, and topped with toasted walnuts. This salad is simple—and addictively good! E.T.

1 head red cabbage, shredded

1/2 cup umeboshi vinegar

1/4 cup extra virgin olive oil, or water or vegetable stock (page 205) for oil free

1 red onion, halved crosswise and cut into 1/4-inch-thick crescents

2 cloves garlic, minced

1 teaspoon coarsely ground caraway seeds

2 tablespoons balsamic vinegar

1/2 teaspoon freshly ground black pepper

3 cups loosely packed fresh spinach chiffonade

3/4 cup coarsely chopped toasted walnuts (see page 223)

6 tablespoons fresh basil chiffonade

To make the cabbage, place the shredded red cabbage in a large mixing bowl and toss with the umeboshi vinegar. Cover with plastic wrap, and place 2 or 3 plates on top. Let marinate at room temperature for at least 2 hours or refrigerated for 8 hours before using. (Store refrigerated, in an airtight container, for up to 2 weeks.)

Heat the olive oil in a large sauté pan over medium-high heat. Add the onion and garlic, and sauté for 3 minutes, or until the garlic just starts to brown. Drain the cabbage of excess vinegar. Stir the caraway seeds into the onion mixture, followed by the cabbage. Toss in the pan for 3 to 5 minutes, until heated through. Remove from the heat, and add the balsamic vinegar and black pepper.

To serve, line each serving plate with a bed of the spinach chiffonade. Top with 1 cup of the cabbage mixture, and then 2 tablespoons of the walnuts, and 1 tablespoon of the basil chiffonade.

NUTRITIONAL INFORMATION

PER SERVING: 260 calories (75% from fat), 8 g protein, 19 g carbohydrate, 19 g fat, 0 mg cholesterol, 1125 mg sodium, 4.6 g fiber

Avocado, Sea Vegetable, *and* Plum *with* Creamy Wasabi Dressing *and* Spicy Candied Peanuts

SERVES 6

Inspired by avocado sushi with its creamy texture and spicy "twang" of wasabi, this salad will be sure to please anyone who loves sushi. At the restaurant, we use fresh ogo seaweed from Hawaii. For this recipe, I have offered instructions for the more commonly available dried sea palm, which is available in most health food markets. Also try this with arame, hijiki, or a prepared sea vegetable salad found in many Japanese markets. E.T.

SPICY CANDIED PEANUTS

1 1/2 cups raw peanuts
1 1/2 teaspoons tamari
1 tablespoon unrefined sugar
1/2 teaspoon ground Szechuan peppercorns
1/4 teaspoon cayenne pepper

CREAMY WASABI DRESSING

2 teaspoons wasabi powder, mixed with enough water
    to form a smooth paste
1/2 teaspoon Dijon mustard
1 teaspoon light miso
1 teaspoon Florida Crystals (see page 224)
1 scallion, green part only, coarsely chopped
1/4 cup rice vinegar
2 tablespoons water
1/2 cup canola oil
1 tablespoon dark sesame oil
Salt

6 heads limestone or small butter lettuce, washed and
    cored
3 avocados, peeled, pitted, and each sliced into
    12 segments
3 red-fleshed plums, each sliced into 12 segments
1 ounce dried sea palm, reconstituted (see page 223)
2 scallions, white and green parts, thinly sliced on the
    diagonal, for garnish

To make the peanuts, preheat the oven to 350°F. Toss all of the ingredients together in a bowl. Place on a baking pan, and bake for 15 minutes, or until golden brown and fragrant, moving the nuts with a steel spatula every 5 minutes. Let cool to room temperature. (Store in an airtight container for up to 4 days.)

To make the dressing, combine the wasabi, mustard, miso, sugar, scallion, vinegar, and water in a blender. Blend until thoroughly combined. With the blender running, slowly add the canola and sesame oils, and blend until thick and creamy. Add salt to taste. (Store refrigerated for up to 1 week.)

To serve, place 1 head of lettuce in the center of each plate. Around each head of lettuce, place 6 avocado slices, followed by 6 of the plum slices between the avocados. Sprinkle 1/4 cup of the peanuts over the salad. Place one-sixth of the sea palm on top of each head of lettuce. Drizzle 2 tablespoons of the dressing over the entire plate, and sprinkle with sliced scallions.

NUTRITIONAL INFORMATION

PER SERVING: 530 calories (74% from fat), 14 g protein, 24.5 g carbohydrate, 35 g fat, 0 mg cholesterol, 197 mg sodium, 7.6 g fiber

PER 2 TABLESPOONS DRESSING: 142 calories (95% from fat), 0.2 g protein, 1.4 g carbohydrate, 15 g fat, 0 mg cholesterol, 49 mg sodium, 0.1 g fiber

PER 1/4 CUP PEANUTS: 216 calories (69% from fat), 9.6 g protein, 8.1 g carbohydrate, 18 g fat, 0 mg cholesterol, 90 mg sodium, 3.2 g fiber

Nori Salad Roll *with* Spicy, Sweet, *and* Sour Kumquat-Lime Dressing

SERVES 6

This nori roll contains no rice, but rather crunchy crisp bean sprouts and Napa cabbage, watercress, mango, and grapefruit, as well as aromatic fresh mint and cilantro. The dressing is our spin on a traditional Thai dipping sauce, minus the fish sauce but not shy on chile. The whole thing is oil free. Embellish on the filling as you see fit. Serve with our Asian-Style Smoked Tofu (page 150) for a more substantial entrée salad. E.T.

Spicy, Sweet, and Sour Kumquat-Lime Dressing

6 tablespoons unrefined sugar or fructose

1 cup water

$^1/_2$ teaspoon crushed red pepper flakes, plus more as needed

6 kumquats, thinly sliced

1 teaspoon peeled and minced or grated fresh ginger

Juice of 6 limes ($^1/_2$ cup)

$^1/_2$ teaspoon salt

$^1/_4$ teaspoon guar gum

Nori Rolls

6 sheets toasted nori (yakinori)

$1^1/_2$ cups shredded Chinese cabbage

$1^1/_2$ cups loosely packed watercress

$1^1/_2$ cups bean sprouts

1 cup plus 2 tablespoons shredded peeled carrot

1 mango, peeled and thinly sliced

1 red grapefruit, peeled and supremed (see page 222)

$^2/_3$ cup chopped toasted peanuts (see page 222)

$^1/_3$ cup mint chiffonade

$^1/_3$ cup cilantro leaves

18 watercress or mint sprigs, for garnish

To make the dressing, place a saucepan over medium heat and add the sugar and water. Cook for 2 minutes, or until the sugar is dissolved. Remove from the heat. Add the pepper flakes, kumquat, ginger, lime juice, salt, and guar gum. Whisk thoroughly to dissolve the guar gum. Let cool to room temperature, or chill, before serving. (Store refrigerated for up to 1 week.)

To make the rolls, lay a nori sheet flat on a plate. Spread $^1/_4$ cup each of the cabbage, the watercress, and the bean sprouts over the nori. Follow with 3 tablespoons of the carrot, one-sixth of the mango and the grapefruit, 2 teaspoons of the peanuts, and one-sixth of the mint chiffonade and cilantro leaves. Drizzle 1 tablespoon of the dressing over the salad ingredients, dampen the edge of the sheet, and then roll tightly to seal. Repeat with the remaining 5 rolls.

To serve, slice each roll into thirds, and place the thirds vertically in the center of each plate. Spoon about 3 tablespoons of the dressing around the plate. Sprinkle 1 tablespoon of the peanuts around the plate. Place a sprig of the watercress or mint in the center of each roll.

NUTRITIONAL INFORMATION

PER SERVING: 361 calories (44% from fat), 12.2 g protein, 42 g carbohydrate, 18 g fat, 0 mg cholesterol, 223 mg sodium, 9.4 g fiber

PER 2 TABLESPOONS DRESSING: 51 (0.3% from fat), 0.4 g protein, 13.9 g carbohydrate, 0 g fat, 0 mg cholesterol, 136 mg sodium, 1.5 g fiber

SOUTHWEST SALAD TIMBALE *with* NOPAL CACTUS

SERVES 6

Feel free to embellish on the ingredients for this color-ful and festive salad. Try using fresh corn and peppers in the summer or a tropical fruit such as mango in place of the grapefruit. If you can't find fresh nopal cactus, use a quality jarred marinated cactus, avail-able in Hispanic markets. To press this salad together, we use a ring mold made of acrylic tubing 2¹/2 inches in diameter and 4 inches long, but common stainless-steel molds of different sizes and shapes work well, too.
E.T.

MARINATED NOPAL CACTUS

Juice of 2 lemons
Juice of 1 orange
¹/4 cup extra virgin olive oil
1 clove garlic, minced
¹/2 teaspoon dried Mexican oregano
1 teaspoon salt
¹/4 teaspoon freshly ground black pepper
2 nopal cactus pads, charred and burred (see page 222),
     sliced into ¹/2-inch-thick strips

STRAWBERRY-CHIPOTLE BALSAMIC

1¹/2 cups balsamic vinegar
³/4 cup fresh apple juice
8 strawberries, halved
3 dried chipotle chiles
Salt and freshly ground black pepper

2 cups small-diced peeled jicama
¹/4 cup small-diced red onion
1 teaspoon minced seeded jalapeño chile
2 tablespoons coarsely chopped cilantro
Salt as needed
Juice of 1¹/2 limes
2 avocados, peeled, pitted, and cut into small dice
2 jarred roasted pimientos, cut into small dice
2 pink grapefruits, peeled and supremed (see page 222)
³/4 cup cilantro oil (page 215), for garnish
¹/2 cup pumpkin seeds, toasted (see page 222; optional)
Cilantro leaves, for garnish

To marinate the cactus, in a mixing bowl, whisk together the lemon juice, orange juice, olive oil, gar-lic, oregano, salt, and pepper. Place the cactus strips in the marinade, and marinate for 2 hours at room tem-perature. (Store refrigerated in the marinade for up to 1 week.) Cut the cactus strips into small dice.

To make the balsamic, combine the balsamic vinegar, apple juice, strawberries, and chipotle chiles in a small saucepan. Bring to a boil. Decrease the heat to low and simmer for 15 minutes, until the chipotles are soft. Let cool to room temperature, and then purée in a blender. Strain into a bowl. Add salt and pepper to taste. (Store refrigerated for up to 2 weeks.)

To make the timbales, toss the jicama, onion, jalapeño, cilantro, two-thirds of the lime juice, and salt to taste together in a mixing bowl. In a separate bowl, mix the avocado with the remaining lime juice. Sprinkle with ¹/4 teaspoon salt.

Place 6 ring molds on a flat surface. To each, add one-sixth of the jicama mixture, one-sixth of the marinated cactus, one-sixth of the roasted pimiento, one-sixth of the avocado, and one-sixth of the grapefruit. With the bottom of a glass the same size as the inside of the mold, or with some other flat surface, press the ingre-dients down toward the plate for about 30 seconds to set up the timbale.

To serve, drizzle 2 tablespoons of the balsamic and 2 tablespoons of the cilantro oil over each plate. Using a spatula, move 1 timbale to the center of the plate. Carefully remove the mold while gently pressing down on the ingredients inside. Sprinkle the plate with pumpkin seeds, and top with cilantro leaves.

NUTRITIONAL INFORMATION

PER SERVING: 284 calories (68% from fat), 4 g protein, 28 g carbohydrate, 17.9 g fat, 0 mg cholesterol, 719 mg sodium, 8.7 g fiber

PER 2 TABLESPOONS DRESSING: 36 (4.7% from fat), 0.3 g protein, 9.2 g carbohydrate, 0.2 g fat, 0 mg choles-terol, 316 mg sodium, 1.1 g fiber

GRILLED RADICCHIO DE TREVISO *with* PINK GRAPEFRUIT, PINK PEPPERCORNS, *and* GARLIC-TARRAGON RANCH DRESSING

SERVES 4

Our version of a ranch dressing is simply addictive. Serve it as a dip with crudités or to dress other grilled vegetables at your next barbecue. Seek out the pink peppercorns in specialty and gourmet food stores—they are key to the dressing's unique flavor. Radicchio de Treviso is an elongated head versus the round bulb of the more common radicchio. Look for radicchio de Treviso in the fall and winter. E.T.

GARLIC-TARRAGON RANCH DRESSING

1/4 cup cashews
1 teaspoon Dijon mustard
2 cloves garlic, minced
1 teaspoon nutritional yeast (see page 224)
2 tablespoons water, plus more as needed
Juice of 1 lemon
1/2 teaspoon grated lemon zest
3 tablespoons champagne vinegar
1 teaspoon pink peppercorns
1/3 teaspoon dried thyme
1 scallion, white and green parts, minced
3 tablespoons minced fresh tarragon
1 tablespoon minced fresh dill
2 teaspoons light miso
1/2 cup extra virgin olive oil
Salt and freshly ground black pepper

GRILLED RADICCHIO DE TREVISO

1 clove garlic, minced
2 teaspoons balsamic vinegar
2 teaspoons extra virgin olive oil
1/4 teaspoon salt
1/4 teaspoon freshly ground black pepper
2 heads radicchio de Treviso, halved lengthwise

2 pink or ruby grapefruits, peeled and supremed (see page 222)
2 teaspoons pink peppercorns, for garnish
4 teaspoons minced fresh chives, for garnish

To make the dressing, combine the cashews, mustard, garlic, yeast, 2 tablespoons of the water, the lemon juice and zest, vinegar, peppercorns, thyme, scallions, tarragon, dill, and miso in a blender. Blend until smooth. With the blender running on low, add the oil. If the dressing is too thick, add another tablespoon of water. Season with salt and pepper to taste. (Store refrigerated for up to 1 week.)

To grill the radicchio, preheat the grill or broiler. In a bowl, combine the garlic, vinegar, oil, salt, and pepper. Add the radicchio halves, and coat with the marinade. Grill or broil for 1 minute per side, or until slightly charred and wilted.

To serve, coat the bottom of each plate with about 2 tablespoons of the dressing. Place the radicchio cut side up in the center of the plate. Drizzle with more dressing. Arrange the grapefruit segments around and on the radicchio. Sprinkle with the pink peppercorns and the minced chives.

NUTRITIONAL INFORMATION

PER SERVING: 204 calories (65% from fat), 1.8 g protein, 7.9 g carbohydrate, 18.6 g fat, 0 mg cholesterol, 150 mg sodium, 1.4 g fiber

PER 2 TABLESPOONS DRESSING: 173 calories (89% from fat), 1.4 g protein, 3.3 g carbohydrate, 17 g fat, 0 mg cholesterol, 71 mg sodium, 0.6 g fiber

ROASTED TOMATO PANZANELLA SALAD *with* BRAISED GARLIC *and* ZINFANDEL VINAIGRETTE

SERVES 6

For our spin on a quintessential summer salad, we roast tomatoes to intensify their flavor, combine them with some soft braised garlic cloves, purple basil, and toasted bread, and pack the whole thing into a mold to create a vertical presentation. The Zinfandel dressing is very easy: take some quality Zin and cook it down to almost a syrup. Then combine it with some balsamic vinegar and the oil reserved from the braised garlic. Serve this salad with a glass of good Zinfandel as we did at our first Ravenswood Winery Dinner. Don't even think about this salad until you can get your hands on the best-quality organic vine-ripened red tomatoes you can find—the more varieties the better! E.T.

ZINFANDEL VINAIGRETTE

2 cups Zinfandel
1/2 cup balsamic vinegar
1/4 teaspoon salt, plus more as needed
1/4 cup olive oil, or oil reserved from Millennium Oil-Braised Garlic (page 212)
Freshly ground black pepper

PANZANELLA

6 tomatoes, cut into 1-inch dice (4 cups)
1/2 loaf crusty French or Italian-style bread, cut into 1/2-inch dice (3 cups)
1/2 cup Millennium Oil-Braised Garlic (page 212)
1/2 cup purple basil chiffonade
2 tablespoons chopped parsley
Salt and freshly ground black pepper
1 1/2 cups baby arugula or assorted baby salad greens

To make the vinaigrette, place a saucepan over low heat, and add the Zinfandel and vinegar. Cook for 20 minutes, or until reduced to about 1/2 cup. Pour the reduction into a small mixing bowl, and then place the mixing bowl on top of another larger bowl filled with ice. Let cool for 30 minutes, or until close to a refrigerated temperature. The reduction should be very dark and slightly thick. Add the salt, and slowly whisk in the oil. Add salt and pepper to taste.

To make the panzanella, preheat the broiler. Spread the tomatoes on a baking sheet and place under the broiler. Broil for 10 minutes, or until slightly charred all over, turning the tomatoes after 5 minutes. They will be soft and have released a lot of moisture. Remove from the broiler and let cool to room temperature. Drain the tomatoes of the accumulated liquid, reserving 1/2 cup for the dressing. (The tomatoes can be stored refrigerated overnight.)

Place a small saucepan over low heat, and add the tomato liquid. Reduce by one-half, about 15 minutes. Strain through a strainer to remove any seeds. Let cool until slightly syrupy; it should yield about 1/4 cup.

Preheat the oven to 350°F. Place the bread on a baking sheet and bake for 15 to 20 minutes, turning every 5 minutes until the bread is crisp and dry. Let cool to room temperature before using. (Store in an airtight container for up to 1 week.)

Toss the tomatoes, toasted bread, braised garlic, 1/4 cup of the purple basil, parsley, and 1/4 cup of the Zinfandel vinaigrette together in a bowl. Add salt and pepper to taste. In another bowl, toss the baby arugula with 1/4 cup of the Zinfandel vinaigrette.

To serve, place 1/2 cup of the dressed arugula in the center of each plate. Pack a 1-cup ring mold tightly with the tomato mixture. Place over the arugula and remove the mold. Top with one-sixth of the remaining basil chiffonade. Drizzle one-sixth of the remaining vinaigrette and one-sixth of the tomato reduction around the plate.

NUTRITIONAL INFORMATION

PER SERVING: 243 calories (48% from fat), 3.9 g protein, 24 g carbohydrate, 10 g fat, 0 mg cholesterol, 200 mg sodium, 3.7 g fiber
PER 2 TABLESPOONS VINAIGRETTE: 102 calories (91% from fat), 0 g protein, 1.4 g carbohydrate, 6 g fat, 0 mg cholesterol, 61 mg sodium, 0 g fiber

White Nectarine *and* Canary Melon Salad *with* Gewürztraminer, Pistachio, *and* Kaffir Lime Leaf Vinaigrette

SERVES 6

This simple and elegant summer fruit salad juxtaposes the exotic floral flavors of Kaffir lime leaf and Thai basil, with the subtle sting of white pepper. Use any orange-fleshed melons and any variety of nectarine. We use verjus (sour grape juice) as the acid for this dressing, although a citrus juice, such as lime, will work just fine. E.T.

GEWÜRZTRAMINER VINAIGRETTE

1^1/2 cups Gewürztraminer

^{1}/3 cup verjus, or juice of 2 limes

1 teaspoon grated lime zest

^{1}/2 cup pistachios, toasted (see page 222) and coarsely ground

1 teaspoon peeled and minced fresh ginger

^{1}/4 teaspoon salt

^{1}/4 teaspoon ground white pepper

2 Kaffir lime leaves, very thin chiffonade

3 heads limestone or butter lettuce, cored and cleaned

^{1}/3 canary melon, flesh cut into ^{1}/2-inch dice

1 white nectarine, diced

1 canary melon, cut into 18 thin slices

2 white nectarines, cut into 18 thin slices total

^{1}/4 cup coarsely chopped pistachios, for garnish

^{1}/4 cup Thai basil chiffonade, for garnish

1^1/2 teaspoons ground white pepper, for garnish

6 teaspoons pistachio oil, for garnish

To make the vinaigrette dressing, heat the wine in a small saucepan over medium and reduce to ^{2}/3 cup, about 20 minutes. Let cool in a bowl immersed in an ice-water bath until room temperature. Whisk in the verjus, lime zest, pistachios, ginger, salt, white pepper, and lime leaves. (Store refrigerated for up to 1 week.)

To make the salad, toss the lettuce, diced melon, and diced nectarine with ^{1}/2 cup of the dressing in a mixing bowl.

To serve, mound one-sixth of the lettuce mixture in the center of each plate. Fan 3 slices of the melon and 3 slices of the nectarine around the plate. Drizzle about 1 tablespoon of the dressing around the melon and nectarine. Sprinkle the pistachios, basil, and white pepper around the salad. Drizzle 1 teaspoon of the pistachio oil around the salad.

NUTRITIONAL INFORMATION

PER SERVING: 325 calories (22% from fat), 4.6 g protein, 24 g carbohydrate, 12 g fat, 0 mg cholesterol, 101 mg sodium, 3.7 g fiber

PER 2 TABLESPOONS DRESSING: 90 calories (56% from fat), 0.8 g protein, 2.5 g carbohydrate, 1.9 g fat, 0 mg cholesterol, 30 mg sodium, 0.5 g fiber

HEIRLOOM TOMATO STACK *with* BITTER GREENS, AVOCADO, BASIL, *and* CURRIED HAZELNUT MOJO DRESSING

SERVES 6

For this Caribbean slant on the summer classic of tomatoes and basil, we layer avocado slices, basil, and bitter greens between slices of a whole tomato and serve over a curried hazelnut dressing. Use as many varieties of basil as you can find: try purple ruffled basil, Thai basil, lemon basil, and Mexican Albaca basil. E.T.

HAZELNUT MOJO DRESSING

2 tablespoons extra virgin olive oil
4 cloves garlic, minced
Juice of 2 oranges
Juice of 1 lemon
Juice of 1 lime
1 teaspoon grated orange zest
1/2 teaspoon grated lime zest
1 tablespoon balsamic vinegar
1 teaspoon peeled and minced fresh ginger
1 tablespoon chipotle paste (page 214)
1 1/2 teaspoons mild curry powder, toasted
   (see page 223)
1 1/2 teaspoons agave nectar (see page 224)
1/3 cup whole hazelnuts, toasted (see page 222)
Water, as needed
1/4 cup coarsely ground toasted hazelnuts
   (see page 222)
Salt

2 cups loosely packed assorted basil leaves
2 cups loosely packed baby bitter greens, such as
   arugula, mizuna, and watercress
6 heirloom tomatoes, cored
3 ripe but firm Haas avocados, peeled, pitted, and cut
   into 36 slices total
6 tablespoons toasted hazelnuts, coarsely chopped,
   for garnish
2 tablespoons purple basil leaves, chiffonade, for
   garnish

To make the dressing, heat the olive oil in a small sauté pan over medium heat. Add the garlic, and sauté for 5 to 7 minutes, until lightly browned, stirring often to prevent scorching. Transfer the sautéed garlic and oil to a bowl, and let cool to room temperature. In a blender, combine the sautéed garlic, the orange, lemon, and lime juices, orange and lime zests, balsamic vinegar, ginger, chipotle paste, curry powder, agave, and whole hazelnuts. Blend to a smooth purée, adding enough water to thin the dressing to the consistency of heavy cream. Transfer to a bowl, fold in the ground hazelnuts, and add salt to taste. (Store refrigerated for up to 4 days.)

To make the stack, toss the basil leaves and bitter greens with 1/4 cup of the dressing in a mixing bowl. Slice 1/4 inch off the bottom of each tomato to create a flat surface, and then slice each tomato into 4 equal slices. On the bottom slice of each tomato, layer 2 slices of avocado and a small amount of the basil and greens. Repeat two more times, rebuilding the tomatoes with the greens and avocado between the slices, and ending with the tomato tops.

To serve, drizzle 2 tablespoons of the dressing on each plate. Place a tomato stack in the center of the plate. Sprinkle the whole plate with 1 tablespoon of the toasted hazelnuts and 1 teaspoon of the purple basil chiffonade.

NUTRITIONAL INFORMATION

PER SERVING: 317 calories (69% from fat), 6 g protein, 20.5 g carbohydrate, 26 g fat, 0 mg cholesterol, 238 mg sodium, 5.8 g fiber

PER 2 TABLESPOONS DRESSING: 58 calories (71% from fat), 0.8 g protein, 3.3 g carbohydrate, 4.8 g fat, 0 mg cholesterol, 120 mg sodium, 1 g fiber

ASIAN GUACAMOLE SALAD *with* CRISP RICE NOODLES *and* MIZUNA GREENS

SERVES 6

This guacamole variation gets an Asian twist with ginger, toasted sesame seeds, and Szechuan peppercorns. We serve it with crisp puffed rice noodles, mizuna greens (reminiscent of western arugula), and citrus fruit, such as blood orange and kumquat. We serve this salad with the same kumquat-lime dressing that we use for the nori salad roll (page 53). E.T.

ASIAN GUACAMOLE

2 scallions, green part only, minced
1 clove garlic, minced
$1/2$ jalapeño chile, seeded and minced
1 teaspoon peeled and minced fresh ginger
1 cup $1/4$-inch-diced jicama
$1/2$ cup $1/4$-inch-diced cucumber
1 avocado, peeled, pitted, and cut into $1/4$-inch dice
Juice of 1 lime
2 teaspoons sesame seeds, toasted (see page 223)
1 teaspoon ground Szechuan peppercorns, toasted (see page 223)
$1/2$ teaspoon salt

CRISP RICE NOODLES

2 cups canola oil, for deep-frying
$1/4$ (16-ounce) package dried rice stick noodles, broken into 3-inch pieces

3 cups loosely packed mizuna or arugula
2 blood oranges, peeled and supremed (see page 222)
$3/4$ cup Spicy, Sweet, and Sour Kumquat-Lime Dressing (page 53)
$1/4$ cup toasted sesame oil, for garnish
1 tablespoon black sesame seeds, toasted (see page 223), for garnish

To make the guacamole, combine all of the ingredients in a mixing bowl. (Store refrigerated, in an airtight container, with plastic wrap over the guacamole to minimize browning, for up to 1 day.)

To make the noodles, heat the oil in a 1-quart saucepan over high heat until very hot (about 350°F). Test by dropping a small piece of noodle in the oil; it should puff up and become opaque white instantly. When the oil is the right temperature, drop a handful of noodles in the saucepan. When they puff up, transfer with a slotted spoon to a paper towel–lined plate, and repeat until all of the noodles are fried.

To make the salad, toss the mizuna greens and blood oranges with $1/4$ cup of the kumquat-lime dressing in a bowl, reserving the remaining dressing for the garnish.

To serve, in the center of each plate, mound about $1/2$ cup of the dressed mizuna and blood orange segments. Top with one-sixth of the puffed rice noodles, followed by a $1/3$-cup scoop of Asian guacamole. Top with a few strands of rice noodles. Drizzle 1 tablespoon of the remaining dressing around the plate, and 2 teaspoons of the sesame oil over the salad. Sprinkle with black sesame seeds.

NUTRITIONAL INFORMATION

PER SERVING: 302 calories (57% from fat), 2.5 g protein, 43.3 g carbohydrate, 15 g fat, 0 mg cholesterol, 250 mg sodium, 5.3 g fiber

Spanish Marble Potato Salad *with* Grilled Frisée, *and* Creamy Sherry Vinaigrette

SERVES 4

This is a luxurious spin on a typical potato salad, perfect for spring, when new potatoes and fresh English peas come into season. We use thirty-year-old sherry vinegar, which has an exceptionally warm, woody quality. Look for it (as well as for caperberries and green peppercorns) in specialty food stores, but feel free to substitute any quality sherry vinegar. E.T.

CREAMY SHERRY VINAIGRETTE

1/4 cup cashews
2 teaspoons Dijon mustard
2 tablespoons Millennium Oil-Braised Garlic or Oil-Free Braised Garlic (page 212)
2 teaspoons nutritional yeast (see page 224)
2 tablespoons water
1/4 cup sherry vinegar
2 teaspoons green peppercorns
1 teaspoon Spanish paprika
1/4 teaspoon salt, plus more as needed
1/2 cup extra virgin olive oil

GRILLED FRISÉE

2 teaspoons balsamic vinegar
2 teaspoons extra virgin olive oil
1 clove garlic, minced
1/4 teaspoon salt
Pinch of freshly ground black pepper
1 large head frisée

POTATO SALAD

1 pound marble-sized new red potatoes or new potatoes, halved
1 cup fresh shelled English peas
1 Granny Smith apple, cut into 1/3-inch dice and tossed with freshly squeezed lemon juice to prevent discoloring
1 celery stalk, cut into 1/3-inch dice
1 scallion, white and green parts, minced
12 radicchio de Treviso leaves or Belgian endive spears

1 teaspoon green peppercorns packed in brine, drained, for garnish

12 caperberries, for garnish
12 chervil sprigs, for garnish

To make the vinaigrette, combine the cashews, mustard, garlic, yeast, water, vinegar, peppercorns, paprika, and 1/4 teaspoon of the salt in a blender. Blend until smooth. With the blender running, slowly add the oil and blend until the dressing is thick and emulsified. Add salt to taste. (Store refrigerated for up to 1 week.)

To make the frisée, preheat the grill. In a bowl, combine the vinegar, oil, garlic, salt, and pepper. Add the frisée head side down to the marinade, and toss to coat. Grill head side down for 2 minutes, or until wilted. Turn over, and grill for 1 minute more. (Alternatively, heat a large sauté pan over high. When the pan is hot, add the frisée head side down and sauté for 1 minute, until wilted. Sauté core side down for 1 minute.) Let cool. Remove the core and slice into 4 pieces.

To make the potato salad, bring 2 quarts salted water to a boil. Add the potatoes and boil for 5 to 7 minutes, until al dente. Drain and let cool. Blanch the peas for 1 minute, or until just al dente (see page 223). Drain and let cool in a cold water bath. Toss the potatoes, peas, apple, celery, and scallions with all but 1/4 cup of the vinaigrette.

To serve, place 1 piece of the frisée at one end of each plate. Mound one-quarter of the potato salad on the plate, and place the radicchio spears on the plate with the ends touching the potato salad and spears facing the edge of the plate. Top each salad with 1/4 teaspoon of the peppercorns, 3 caperberries, and 3 chervil sprigs. Drizzle 2 teaspoons of the vinaigrette over the radicchio spears.

NUTRITIONAL INFORMATION

PER SERVING: 298 calories (26% from fat), 7 g protein, 33 g carbohydrate, 18 g fat, 0 mg cholesterol, 961 mg sodium, 5.3 g fiber

PER 2 TABLESPOONS VINAIGRETTE: 150 calories (90% from fat), 1.2 g protein, 2.5 g carbohydrate, 15 g fat, 0 mg cholesterol, 77 mg sodium, 0.4 g fiber

GRILLED WHITE ASPARAGUS *with* BABY LOLA ROSA LETTUCE *and* VANILLA-LAVENDER AÏOLI

SERVES 4

The grill in our restaurant is located near the salad station. The warm, smoky grill flavors counterbalance the acid of vinaigrettes and also temper bitter greens such as frisée and radicchio de Treviso, as well as white asparagus, an effect that gives this salad its complex flavor.

Grown underground, white asparagus is a little more fibrous than its green counterpart—hence the peeling and longer cooking time. It can be found in spring at specialty food markets. Although white asparagus is well worth the extra cost and prep time, its green cousin also works just fine for this salad.

The subtle flavors of vanilla and lavender, together with hazelnuts, perfectly complement the subtly nutty-flavored asparagus. Serve with a glass of Viognier or another dry and intense white wine and some crusty bread to mop up the extra dressing. E.T.

VANILLA-LAVENDER AÏOLI

2 teaspoons extra virgin olive oil
2 cloves garlic, minced
Juice of 1 lemon
1 teaspoon nutritional yeast (see page 224)
1/2 vanilla bean, seeds scraped and reserved
1/2 teaspoon pure vanilla extract
1/2 teaspoon unrefined sugar or agave nectar
  (see page 224)
1/2 teaspoon salt, plus more as needed
2 teaspoons green peppercorns in brine, drained
1/4 teaspoon freshly ground black pepper, plus more
  as needed
2 teaspoons Dijon mustard
1/3 cup olive oil
1/3 cup canola oil
1/2 teaspoon dried lavender, plus more as needed

SUN-DRIED TOMATO VINAIGRETTE

1/2 cup sun-dried tomatoes, softened in warm water
  for 15 minutes, drained, and cut into 1/4-inch dice
2 tablespoons tomato paste
1 tablespoon balsamic vinegar

2 tablespoons water
2 tablespoons hazelnut oil
1/2 teaspoon green peppercorns in brine, drained
Salt

GRILLED WHITE ASPARAGUS

20 white asparagus spears
Juice of 1 lemon
1 tablespoon extra virgin olive oil
1/4 teaspoon salt

4 heads Baby Lola Rosa lettuce or red butter lettuce,
  cored and washed
1/4 cup coarsely ground hazelnuts, toasted (see page
  222), for garnish
12 caperberries, for garnish
4 strawberries, sliced into fans, for garnish

To make the aïoli, place a sauté pan over medium heat and add the extra virgin olive oil. Add the garlic and sauté for 5 to 7 minutes, until lightly browned. Transfer the garlic to a small bowl and refrigerate for 30 minutes, or until cool.

Place the garlic, lemon juice, yeast, vanilla bean, vanilla extract, sugar, 1/2 teaspoon of the salt, the peppercorns, 1/4 teaspoon of the black pepper, and the mustard in a blender. Blend until smooth. With the blender running, slowly add the olive oil and canola oil, followed by 1/2 teaspoon of the lavender. Add salt, pepper, and lavender to taste. (Store refrigerated for up to 1 week.)

To make the vinaigrette, whisk all of the ingredients together in a mixing bowl. (Store refrigerated for up to 1 week.)

To make the grilled asparagus, snap off the last inch of the stem and discard. Peel the asparagus, starting at the base of the stem and stopping about 1 inch from the top of the spear. Bring 4 quarts of water to a boil in a large saucepan or pot. Blanch the white asparagus for 7 minutes, or until the asparagus is slightly soft (see page 223). Drain and let cool in a cold water bath.

Preheat the grill or broiler. Mix together the lemon, olive oil, and salt in a bowl large enough to fit the white asparagus. Add the asparagus, and toss to coat. Grill the asparagus, turning often, for 2 minutes, or until there are grill marks on all sides. (Alternatively, preheat the broiler. Broil, turning often, for 3 minutes, or until there is a little blackening all over.) Remove from the heat source, and let cool slightly.

To serve, place a head of lettuce at the edge of each plate. Fan 5 asparagus spears out from the lettuce across the plate. Drizzle 2 tablespoons of the vanilla-lavender aïoli over the lettuce and asparagus. Drizzle 2 tablespoons of the vinaigrette over the asparagus.

Sprinkle 1 tablespoon of the hazelnuts over the salad. Place 3 caperberries on the salad. Fan 1 of the strawberries across the top of the lettuce.

NUTRITIONAL INFORMATION

PER SERVING: 381 calories (74% from fat), 5.9 g protein, 13.6 g carbohydrate, 35 g fat, 0 mg cholesterol, 322 mg sodium, 4.7 g fiber

PER 2 TABLESPOONS AÏOLI: 234 calories (96% from fat), 0.4 g protein, 1.5 g carbohydrate, 25 g fat, 0 mg cholesterol, 179 mg sodium, 0.1 g fiber

PER 2 TABLESPOONS VINAIGRETTE: 56 calories (69% from fat), 0.9 g protein, 3.7 g carbohydrate, 4.7 g fat, 0 mg cholesterol, 138 mg sodium, 0.8 g fiber

INDIAN SUMMER GRILLED FIG *and* RADICCHIO *on a* ROSEMARY SKEWER *with* CHERRY TOMATO SALAD

SERVES 4

This salad typifies early fall produce in the San Francisco Bay Area: heirloom tomatoes are at their peak, sun-ripened figs make a brief appearance, and chicory crops are just starting to be harvested. The rosemary branch perfumes the radicchio and figs as it grills. You can also prepare this salad with rehydrated dried figs, which have an intense flavor and chewy texture. The fig balsamic keeps indefinitely and makes a great marinade. E.T.

FIG BALSAMIC VINEGAR

8 to 10 black Mission figs, halved
2 cups balsamic vinegar
1 cup Marsala wine
Peeled zest of $1/2$ orange
Juice of 1 orange
$1/2$ teaspoon ground cardamom
1 teaspoon pure vanilla extract
1 dried chile de árbol (optional)
$1/2$ teaspoon allspice berries (optional)
$1/4$ teaspoon whole cloves (optional)

FIG SKEWERS

1 clove garlic, minced
3 tablespoons walnut oil (optional), plus more as needed
1 teaspoon minced fresh rosemary
Salt and freshly ground black pepper
1 large head radicchio, cut into 8 wedges
12 firm black Mission figs or 12 dried figs soaked for
    1 hour in warm water and then drained
4 rosemary stalks, leaves stripped

2 tablespoons extra virgin olive oil
2 cloves garlic, minced
1 (12-ounce) basket assorted cherry tomatoes,
    stemmed and halved
4 to 6 radishes, thinly sliced
2 tablespoons minced fresh herbs (such as tarragon,
    oregano, and basil)
Salt and freshly ground black pepper
$1/4$ cup lightly crushed toasted walnuts (page 223),
    for garnish

To make the fig balsamic, combine all of the ingredients in a 2-quart nonreactive saucepan over medium heat and bring to a boil. Decrease the heat to low, and simmer for 20 to 30 minutes, until reduced by one-third. Strain though a fine sieve. Let cool to room temperature. (Store refrigerated for up to 2 months.)

To make the skewers, preheat the grill or broiler. In a large bowl, combine the garlic, 3 tablespoons fig balsamic, walnut oil, rosemary, salt, and pepper. With a wood or metal skewer, make a hole through each radicchio wedge, near the stem. Toss the radicchio wedges and figs in the marinade to coat.

Using a rosemary stalk, skewer a fig, then a radicchio wedge, and repeat until the skewer contains 3 figs and 2 radicchio wedges. Repeat with the remaining 3 skewers. Grill or broil for $1 1/2$ minutes per side, or until the radicchio is slightly charred.

To make the salad, place a sauté pan over medium heat and add the olive oil. Add the garlic, and sauté for 2 to 3 minutes, until the garlic just turns golden. Remove from the heat and transfer to a mixing bowl. Add the cherry tomatoes, radishes, fresh herbs, 2 tablespoons of the fig balsamic, and salt and pepper to taste.

To serve, place one-quarter of the cherry tomato salad in the center of each plate. Place a fig skewer over it. Sprinkle with 1 tablespoon of the toasted walnuts, and drizzle with more fig balsamic and walnut oil, if desired.

NUTRITIONAL INFORMATION

PER SERVING: 365 calories (56% from fat), 4.2 g protein, 41 g carbohydrate, 22 g fat, 0 mg cholesterol, 15 mg sodium, 12.4 g fiber
PER 2 TABLESPOONS FIG BALSAMIC: 32 calories (3% from fat), 0.2 g protein, 6 g carbohydrate, 0.1 g fat, 0 mg cholesterol, 1 mg sodium, 1.3 g fiber

BITTER GREENS *with* FENNEL *and* BEETS, ASIAN PEAR, *and* POMEGRANATE VINAIGRETTE *with* WHITE TRUFFLE OIL

SERVES 6

This simple fall salad is elegant. The earthy notes of the truffle oil contrast with the sweet and sour of the pomegranate and add a touch of decadence. The pomegranate vinaigrette makes a lot more than you'll need for this salad; fortunately, it keeps indefinitely refrigerated and makes a great gift for your culinary-inclined friends. E.T.

POMEGRANATE VINAIGRETTE

2 cups fresh pomegranate juice (see page 224)

2 cups balsamic vinegar

Grated zest of $1/2$ orange

Juice of 1 orange

1 quarter-sized slice peeled fresh ginger

$1/2$ teaspoon ground cardamom

1 teaspoon pure vanilla extract

$1/2$ teaspoon allspice berries (optional)

$1/4$ teaspoon whole cloves (optional)

4 cups assorted bitter greens (such as arugula, cress, endive, frisée, and radicchio)

$1/4$ cup hazelnut oil

$1/2$ teaspoon white truffle oil, plus more as needed

Salt and freshly ground black pepper

2 fennel root bulbs, very thinly sliced

2 small to medium Chioggia beets, very thinly sliced

2 small to medium yellow beets, very thinly sliced

$1/2$ red onion, very thinly sliced

1 firm Asian pear, halved, cored, and sliced into thin crescents

6 tablespoons loosely packed tarragon leaves, for garnish

6 tablespoons chopped peeled hazelnuts, toasted (see page 222), for garnish

$1/2$ cup pomegranate seeds, for garnish

To make the vinaigrette, combine all of the ingredients in a nonreactive 2-quart saucepan over high heat. Bring to a boil, and decrease to a simmer. Simmer for 20 to 30 minutes, until reduced by one-half. Strain though a fine-mesh strainer. Let cool to room temperature before using. (Store refrigerated indefinitely.)

To make the salad, toss the greens with 2 tablespoons of the vinaigrette, 2 tablespoons of the hazelnut oil, the truffle oil, and salt and pepper to taste together in a bowl.

To serve, divide the greens among 6 plates. In the same bowl, toss the fennel, Chioggia and yellow beets, red onion, and Asian pear with 2 tablespoons vinaigrette, and the remaining hazelnut oil. Add salt and pepper to taste. Top each plate of greens with one-sixth of this mixture. Drizzle additional truffle oil around each plate. Garnish with tarragon, chopped hazelnuts, and pomegranate seeds.

NUTRITIONAL INFORMATION

PER SERVING: 164 calories (52% from fat), 2.7 g protein, 18 g carbohydrate, 10.1 g fat, 0 mg cholesterol, 47 mg sodium, 2.6 g fiber

PER 2 TABLESPOONS DRESSING: 24 calories (2% from fat), 0.2 g protein, 7 g carbohydrate, 0.1 g fat, 0 mg cholesterol, 4 mg sodium, 0 g fiber

SOUPS

For me, soups are always one of the most satisfying parts of a meal. A good soup can, in fact, be a meal in itself. Here we present a great selection of soups uniquely Millennium. These soups cross all boundaries: African yam with teff croutons; Asian roasted kabocha squash with star anise and a sesame cream; a slightly whimsical yet mushroom-intense porcini cappuccino with truffle foam; a soul-warming cactus gumbo. None is textbook authentic, yet each either suggests an ethnic style or is an authentically seasoned vegan adaptation of a classic. We end the chapter with some simple summer-cooling chilled soups, such as tomato-watermelon soup with a lime and chile ice.

Saffron–Sea Palm and Fennel Soup with Oyster Mushrooms,
Crostini, and Rouille ᔥ 78

Chanterelle Mushroom Chana Dal ᔥ 81

Corn and Smoked Oyster Mushroom Chowder ᔥ 82

Mother's Artichoke-Tomato Bisque ᔥ 83

Chilled Tomato and Watermelon Soup with Lime Ice ᔥ 84

Chilled White Peach Soup with Black Pepper and
Rose-Lavender Cream ᔥ 85

Chilled Avocado, Tomatillo, and Cucumber Soup with
Saffron-Lime Ice ᔥ 87

Chilled Potato Vichyssoise with Black Truffle Sorbet ᔥ 88

Chilled Yellow Doll Watermelon Soup with Cardamom Cream ᔥ 89

Japanese Yam *and* Cauliflower Purée *with* Spicy Szechuan Vinaigrette *and* Pickled Spring Garlic

SERVES 6

Japanese yams (technically, sweet potatoes) have a wonderful chestnutlike flavor and silky texture when puréed. This soup is rich but mild in spice, with a kick from its drizzle of spicy red Szechuan vinaigrette and some pungency from its miso-pickled spring garlic.

The garlic recipe comes from line chef Elisha Trotter, who lived in Japan "for the pickles." Spring garlic is a green that resembles a scallion but has a distinct garlic taste; look for it in Asian markets. Try this recipe with other vegetables. The pickling time will vary depending on the vegetable. Cucumber slices will need only 30 minutes to absorb the miso flavor. Mature garlic cloves need 2 days in the marinade. E.T.

MISO-PICKLED SPRING GARLIC

4 spring garlic stalks, ends removed, cut into 1-inch pieces
1/2 cup barley miso or a lighter miso
1 tablespoon Dijon mustard
3 tablespoons water

SZECHUAN VINAIGRETTE

2 tablespoons tomato paste
2 teaspoons peeled and grated fresh ginger
1/2 teaspoon ground Szechuan peppercorns, toasted (see page 223)
1/4 teaspoon ground white pepper
1 teaspoon unrefined sugar
Juice of 1 lemon
2 teaspoons tamari
1 tablespoon water
1 1/2 tablespoons toasted sesame oil

PURÉE

2 lemongrass stalks, white parts only
2 teaspoons canola oil
2 yellow onions, cut into thin crescents
1 tablespoon peeled and minced fresh ginger
1/3 teaspoon ground nutmeg
1 cup dry sherry
2 Japanese yams, peeled and cut into 1-inch dice (2 cups)

2 cups cauliflower florets
6 cups vegetable stock (page 205) or Asian vegetable stock (page 206)
1/4 cup shiro or white miso
Salt

To make the pickled garlic, place the spring garlic in a small bowl or a plastic storage container. In a separate bowl, whisk together the miso, mustard, and water. Pour the marinade over the garlic, coating evenly. Cover the container, and let pickle for at least 4 hours at room temperature or overnight in the refrigerator.

To make the vinaigrette, combine all of the ingredients in a mixing bowl and whisk until incorporated.

To make the purée, lightly crush the lemongrass stalks with the back of a knife and wrap them in cheesecloth. Place a soup pot over medium heat and add the canola oil. Add the onions and sauté for 5 to 7 minutes, until translucent. Add the ginger and nutmeg, and sauté for 1 minute more. Add the sherry and stir to scrape up the browned bits from the bottom of the pot. Add the yams, cauliflower, lemongrass, and stock, and simmer for 30 minutes, or until the yams and cauliflower are very soft. Remove the lemongrass wrapped in cheesecloth. Using a handheld immersion blender, purée the soup with the miso. Add salt to taste.

To serve, mince the pickled garlic. Ladle the purée into 6 soup bowls. Drizzle each serving with 1 tablespoon of the Szechuan vinaigrette and place some pickled garlic on top.

NUTRITIONAL INFORMATION

PER CUP PURÉE: 175 calories (18% from fat), 3.9 g protein, 21 g carbohydrate, 2 g fat, 0 mg cholesterol, 441 mg sodium, 3.2 g fiber

PER SERVING GARLIC: 54 calories (24% from fat), 3.1 g protein, 7.8 g carbohydrate, 1.5 g fat, 0 mg cholesterol, 870 mg sodium, 1.3 g fiber

PER TABLESPOON VINAIGRETTE: 30 calories (72% from fat), 0.4 g protein, 1.9 g carbohydrate, 2.6 g fat, 0 mg cholesterol, 116 mg sodium, 0.3 g fiber

MEDITERRANEAN FIVE-LENTIL *and* CHARD SOUP *with* WALNUT GREMOLATA

SERVES 6

This soup is full of texture, with walnuts, citrus, and herbs rounding out and sharpening its flavors. It's best to cook the lentils separately to keep their different textures intact. Feel free to use only one or two kinds of lentils or another bean altogether. E.T.

GREMOLATA

1/2 cup walnuts, toasted (see page 223) and coarsely ground
Grated zest of 1 lemon
Juice of 1 lemon
2 tablespoons minced parsley
2 tablespoons minced dill
1/4 teaspoon salt

FIVE-LENTIL SOUP

2 teaspoons extra virgin olive oil, or 1/4 cup white wine or vegetable stock (page 205) for oil free
1 red onion, cut into small dice
6 cloves garlic, minced
1 tablespoon peeled and minced fresh ginger
2 teaspoons cumin seeds, toasted (see page 223) and ground
1 teaspoon caraway seeds, toasted (see page 223) and ground
1 teaspoon dill seeds, ground
1 teaspoon dried thyme
1/2 teaspoon ground allspice
4 bay leaves
1/4 cup dry sherry
2 teaspoons Sucanat (see page 224)
2 teaspoons balsamic vinegar
2 cups chopped canned tomatoes
1/4 cup dried red lentils, cooked (see page 220)
1/4 cup dried Drench lentils, cooked (see page 220)
1/4 cup dried green lentils, cooked (see page 220)
1/4 cup dried black beluga lentils, cooked (see page 220)
1/4 cup yellow split peas, cooked
6 cups vegetable stock (page 205)
2 cups chopped red chard
1/4 cup light miso
Salt and freshly ground black pepper

To make the gremolata, combine all of the ingredients in a bowl. Serve, or store refrigerated, covered, overnight.

To make the soup, heat the olive oil in a soup pot over medium heat. Add the onions, garlic, and ginger and sauté for 10 minutes, or until lightly browned. Add the cumin, caraway, dill, thyme, allspice, and bay leaves. Sauté, stirring constantly, for 2 minutes. Add the sherry, Sucanat, vinegar, tomatoes, red lentils, Drench lentils, green lentils, black beluga lentils, peas, and vegetable stock. Simmer for 30 minutes. Add the chard and simmer for 10 minutes, or until wilted. Whisk in the miso. Remove and discard the bay leaves, and season with salt and pepper to taste.

To serve, ladle the soup into 6 soup bowls. Garnish each portion with 1 tablespoon of the gremolata.

NUTRITIONAL INFORMATION

PER CUP SOUP: 258 calories (12% from fat), 14 g protein, 39 g carbohydrate, 3.3 g fat, 0 mg cholesterol, 623 mg sodium, 14 g fiber

PER TABLESPOON GREMOLATA: 50 calories (72% from fat), 2 g protein, 1.8 g carbohydrate, 4.4 g fat, 0 mg cholesterol, 60 mg sodium, 0.7 g fiber

SAFFRON, SWEET POTATO, FENNEL, *and* ROASTED GARLIC BISQUE *with* MEYER LEMON CREAM

SERVES 6

This is a favorite soup in the winter. It is especially popular around Valentine's Day, because of the aphrodisiac qualities of the saffron, garlic, and pine nuts.
E.T.

MEYER LEMON CREAM

1/2 cup raw cashews
2 teaspoons light miso
Juice of 4 Meyer lemons (1/2 cup)
1 cup water

BISQUE

12 to 16 large cloves garlic
2 teaspoons extra virgin olive oil, or vegetable stock (page 205) for oil free
1 yellow onion, cut into small dice
1/2 teaspoon dried thyme
1/2 teaspoon ground fennel seeds
1 teaspoon ground cumin
1 teaspoon chipotle paste (page 214)
1/3 teaspoon saffron threads, soaking in 1/4 cup vegetable stock (page 205)
1/2 cup dry sherry
1 sweet potato, peeled and cut into 1/2-inch dice (2 cups)
2 fennel bulbs, cut into 1/2-inch dice (1 1/2 cups)
1/4 cup arborio rice
1 tablespoon tomato paste
2 quarts vegetable stock (page 205)
2 teaspoons balsamic vinegar
1 1/2 teaspoons salt
Freshly ground black pepper
2 tablespoons Pernod (optional)
2 tablespoons pine nuts, toasted (see page 222), for garnish

To make the cream, place the cashews, miso, lemon juice, and 1/4 cup of the water in a blender. Blend to make a thick, coarse purée. With the machine running, slowly add the remaining water. The blended mixture should have the consistency of heavy cream. (Store refrigerated, in an airtight container, for up to 4 days.)

To make the bisque, place the garlic cloves in a dry sauté pan over high heat. Dry-toast for 5 to 7 minutes, until half of each clove is charred. Remove from the heat.

In a soup pot, heat the oil over medium heat. Add the onion and sauté for 7 minutes, or until translucent. Add the thyme, fennel seeds, cumin, chipotle chile paste, and charred garlic. Sauté for another 2 minutes. Add the saffron and its soaking liquid. Add the sherry and stir to scrape up the browned bits from the bottom of the pot. Add the sweet potato, fennel, rice, tomato paste, and stock. Decrease the heat to medium-low. Cover and simmer for 40 minutes, or until the fennel is soft. Purée all of the soup in a blender for a velvety cream, or leave up to half of it unpuréed for a chunky consistency. Add the balsamic, salt, and pepper to taste, and add the Pernod.

To serve, ladle into 6 soup bowls. Garnish each bowl with 1 tablespoon of the lemon cream and sprinkle with 1 teaspoon of toasted pine nuts.

NUTRITIONAL INFORMATION

PER CUP BISQUE: 230 calories (18% from fat), 4.3 g protein, 33 g carbohydrate, 3.7 g fat, 0 mg cholesterol, 531 mg sodium, 5 g fiber

PER TABLESPOON CREAM: 13 calories (61% from fat), 0.4 g protein, 1 g carbohydrate, 1 g fat, 0 mg cholesterol, 14 mg sodium, 0.2 g fiber

ASIAN MATSUTAKE TONIC *with* SPAGHETTI SQUASH *and* AROMATICS

SERVES 6

This exotic hot and sour soup is from our Millennium New Year's Eve Dinner, and it is an invigorating winter tonic. The restorative aromatics of ginger, galangal, and ginseng root enhance this shiitake and matsutake mushroom broth, and the spaghetti squash adds even more texture and color. Fresh matsutake mushrooms are not easy to find and are quite expensive, but a few go a long way. Look for them October through January in specialty food and Japanese markets, but freely substitute fresh shiitake or maitake mushroom if they are not available. Sea palm is a dried seaweed with a crunchy texture; we prefer Mendocino Sea Vegetable Company brand. E.T.

SPAGHETTI SQUASH AND AROMATICS

1/3 spaghetti squash, steamed, cooled, and flesh removed in strands with a fork
1 (4-ounce) package enoki mushrooms, mushrooms broken apart
2 tablespoons Thai basil chiffonade
2 tablespoons tightly packed cilantro leaves
1 teaspoon toasted sesame oil (optional)
1 tablespoon sesame seeds, toasted (see page 223)

MATSUTAKE TONIC

1 tablespoon sesame oil, or dry sherry for oil free
2 leeks, white part only, cleaned and cut into 1/4-inch-thick julienne
4 cloves garlic, minced
1 carrot, peeled and sliced into 1/4-inch matchsticks
1 beet, peeled and sliced into 1/4-inch matchsticks
2 tablespoons thin slices peeled fresh ginger
1/2 serrano or Thai chile, very thinly sliced
1/2 cup thinly sliced fresh shiitake mushrooms
1/2 cup sliced fresh matsutake mushrooms (1 to 2 small to medium mushrooms)
1/4 cup Shaoxing Chinese rice wine or sake or dry sherry
6 cups Asian vegetable stock (page 206)
1 tablespoon dried sea palm, or soaked and shredded wakame seaweed

1 tablespoon dried wood ear mushroom
1 tablespoon seedless tamarind paste, thinned in 1/4 cup vegetable stock (page 205)
1 lemongrass stalk
1 1/2-inch piece fresh galangal root
1 small ginseng root
1/2 cup thinly sliced lotus root
1/4 cup shiro miso
2 teaspoons Sucanat (see page 224)
Juice of 1 lime
Tamari
White pepper

To make the squash and aromatics, combine all of the ingredients in a mixing bowl.

To make the tonic, place a 4-quart saucepan over medium heat, and add the oil. Add the leeks, garlic, carrots, and beets, and cook for 10 minutes, or until just softened. Add the ginger, chile, shiitake and matsutake mushrooms, and sauté for 2 minutes, or until the mushrooms are soft. Add the Shaoxing wine and stir to scrape up the browned bits from the bottom of the pot. Add the stock, followed by the sea vegetable, wood ear, and tamarind paste.

Break the lemongrass stalk into 2-inch pieces and crack with the back of a knife. Tie together the lemongrass, galangal, and ginseng in cheesecloth. Add to the tonic. Decrease the heat to low and simmer for 20 minutes. Add the lotus root and simmer for 10 minutes, or until cooked through. Add the miso, Sucanat, and lime juice. Season with tamari and white pepper to taste. Remove the cheesecloth and discard.

To serve, the tonic ladle into 6 soup bowls. Top with 2 to 3 tablespoons of the squash and aromatics.

NUTRITIONAL INFORMATION

PER CUP TONIC: 167 calories (19% from fat), 4 g protein, 26 g carbohydrate, 3.4 g fat, 0 mg cholesterol, 467 mg sodium, 4.5 g fiber

PER SERVING SQUASH AND AROMATICS: 29 calories (49% from fat), 0.8 g protein, 3.2 g carbohydrate, 1.7 g fat, 0 mg cholesterol, 6 mg sodium, 0.4 g fiber

AFRICAN YAM SOUP *with* GROUND NUTS *and* TEFF CROUTONS

SERVES 6

This hearty, rich, sweet potato–based soup has the aromatics of clove, cardamom, and cinnamon and is enhanced with peanut butter. At the restaurant, we serve this soup with chopped peanuts, lime, and croutons made from the traditional West African grain teff, which is used in Ethiopian injera bread. It is available in most health food stores. E.T.

AFRICAN YAM SOUP

2 teaspoons extra virgin olive oil, or $1/4$ cup vegetable stock (page 205) for oil free

2 red onions, chopped

4 cloves garlic, minced

2 teaspoons peeled and minced fresh ginger

$1/3$ teaspoon ground clove

$1/2$ teaspoon ground cardamom

$1/2$ teaspoon ground allspice

1 teaspoon ground cinnamon

1 teaspoon ground cumin

2 teaspoons ground mild chile powder

$1/4$ teaspoon cayenne pepper

1 cup freshly squeezed orange juice

$1/2$ teaspoon grated orange zest

3 yams or sweet potatoes, peeled and cut into 1-inch dice (4 cups)

1 (16-ounce) can diced tomatoes (2 cups)

6 cups vegetable stock (page 205)

$1/2$ cup creamy peanut butter (optional; omit for lower fat)

$1/4$ cup light miso

Salt and freshly ground black pepper

Cayenne pepper

TEFF CROUTONS (OPTIONAL)

2 cups water

$1/2$ teaspoon salt

$1/2$ cup dried teff

1 teaspoon canola oil

6 lime wedges, for garnish

6 teaspoons coarsley chopped peanuts, toasted (see page 222), for garnish

6 teaspoons chopped cilantro leaves, for garnish

To make the soup, heat the olive oil in a 4-quart pot over medium heat. Add the onions and garlic, and sauté, stirring often, for 10 minutes, or until the onions are lightly caramelized. Add the ginger, cloves, cardamom, allspice, cinnamon, cumin, chile powder, and cayenne pepper, and sauté for 1 minute. Add the orange juice and zest and stir to scrape up the browned bits from the bottom of the pot. Add the yams, tomatoes, and stock, and simmer for 40 minutes, or until the yams are very soft. Add the peanut butter and the miso and purée the soup in batches in a blender or with a handheld immersion blender until smooth. Add salt, pepper, and cayenne pepper to taste.

To make the croutons, preheat the oven to 400°F. Line a baking pan with parchment paper. Bring the water to a boil in a 1-quart saucepan. Add the salt, and whisk in the teff. Decrease the heat to low and continue to whisk the teff for 10 minutes, or until it pulls away from the side of the pan and is thick. Transfer from the heat onto the baking pan. Spread and smooth the teff out until uniformly $1/2$ inch thick, and let cool to room temperature. Slice into $1/2$-inch croutons. Bake, turning often, for 15 minutes, or until crisp. Let cool.

To serve, ladle into 6 soup bowls. Garnish each bowl with 1 lime wedge on the side, and 1 teaspoon of the chopped peanuts, 1 teaspoon of the chopped cilantro, and 4 or 5 teff croutons on top.

NUTRITIONAL INFORMATION

PER CUP SOUP: 401 calories (34% from fat), 11 g protein, 55 g carbohydrate, 15 g fat, 0 mg cholesterol, 707 mg sodium, 9.3 g fiber

PER SERVING CROUTONS: 60 calories (15% from fat), 2 g protein, 11 g carbohydrate, 1.1 g fat, 0 mg cholesterol, 162 mg sodium, 2 g fiber

CARAMELIZED THREE-ONION *and* PORCINI CAPPUCCINO *with* TRUFFLED SOY FOAM

SERVES 6

This fun and decadent cappuccino makes a great start to a meal. Feel free to substitute dried morels or shiitakes for the porcini. The intense onion-mushroom soup is served in a latte bowl and topped with truffle oil–enhanced soy milk foam. E.T.

PORCINI CAPPUCCINO

2 ounces dried porcini mushrooms

2 cups vegetable stock (page 205)

2 teaspoons extra virgin olive oil, or red wine
    for oil free

2 leeks, white part only, cut into thin rounds

12 shallots, thinly sliced

3 red onions, thinly sliced

1/2 teaspoon salt

2 teaspoons Sucanat (see page 224)

1 cup sliced cremini mushrooms

1 cup sliced fresh shiitake mushrooms

1/4 teaspoon ground caraway seeds

2 bay leaves

2 teaspoons fresh rosemary, minced

1 shot strong espresso coffee

2 cups Cabernet, Zinfandel, or other good-quality
    red wine

4 cups roasted vegetable dark stock (page 207)
    or mushroom stock (page 206)

1/4 cup dark miso

Salt and freshly ground black pepper

SOY FOAM

1/2 cup whole soy milk

1 1/2 teaspoons white truffle oil

Ground nutmeg, for garnish

In a small saucepan, heat the porcini mushrooms with the vegetable stock over low heat until hot but not boiling. Remove from the heat, and let the mushrooms reconstitute for 30 minutes. Remove the mushrooms and check for grit. Strain and reserve the stock. Mince the mushrooms.

In a 4-quart saucepan, heat the olive oil over medium heat. Add the leeks, shallots, and red onions, and sauté for 5 minutes, or until just soft. Add the salt and Sucanat. Continue to sauté, stirring often, for 15 minutes, or until the onion mixture is dark caramel in color. Add the cremini, shiitake, and porcini mushrooms, followed by the caraway seeds, bay leaves, and rosemary. Sauté for 2 minutes. Add the espresso and stir to scrape up the browned bits from the bottom of the pot. Add the red wine and dark vegetable stock. Decrease the heat to medium-low, and simmer for 1 hour, or until reduced by one-third. Transfer 2 cups of the liquid to a bowl. Whisk the miso into the 2 cups, and then return the liquid to the soup. Remove and discard the bay leaves, and season with salt and pepper to taste.

To make the soy foam, place the soy milk and truffle oil in a 2-cup mug or pitcher. With the steamer attachment of an espresso machine, steam until foaming.

To serve, ladle the soup into 6 latte bowls. Cover with soy foam, and sprinkle with ground nutmeg.

NUTRITIONAL INFORMATION

PER CUP CAPPUCCINO: 281 calories (10% from fat), 6.9 g protein, 45 g carbohydrate, 2.8 g fat, 0 mg cholesterol, 642 mg sodium, 6.5 g fiber

PER SERVING FOAM: 16 calories (78% from fat), 0.6 g protein, 0.4 g carbohydrate, 1.5 g fat, 0 mg cholesterol, 2 mg sodium, 0.3 g fiber

CARROT BROTH *with* FRESH CRANBERRY BEANS, SORREL, *and* TARRAGON OIL

SERVES 6

This flavorful broth is light and has a stunning orange glow. Part of the secret to this soup is to add the carrot juice right before you serve it. We've prepared it in the early fall, when fresh cranberry beans are available. It is also good in the spring with fresh English peas or fava beans. E.T.

3 celery stalks
4 leeks, white part only, cleaned and diced
4 carrots, peeled and diced
6 dried shiitake mushrooms
2 cups Chardonnay
3 lemon thyme sprigs
5 bay leaves
1 sage sprig
1 2-inch rosemary sprig
1/3 teaspoon saffron threads
1 dried chipotle chile, seeded
1 teaspoon salt
11 cups water
2 cups shelled fresh cranberry beans
2 cups fresh carrot juice
1/4 teaspoon white pepper
Salt
8 leaves fresh sorrel, chiffonade, for garnish
2 scallions, green part only, cut into 1-inch-long chiffonade, for garnish
4 tablespoons tarragon oil (page 215)

To make the broth, dice 2 of the celery stalks and cut the remaining stalk in half. In a 4-quart saucepan, place the leeks, diced celery, carrots, shiitake mushrooms, and Chardonnay over medium heat. Simmer for 7 minutes, or until the wine evaporates and the leeks soften. Add 2 sprigs of the lemon thyme, 3 of the bay leaves, the sage, rosemary, saffron, chile, salt, and 8 cups of the water. Simmer for 1 hour, or until reduced to 6 cups. Strain the broth through a fine-mesh strainer into another saucepan.

Place the cranberry beans, the celery halves, the 2 remaining bay leaves, the 1 remaining sprig thyme, and the 3 remaining cups water in a saucepan over medium heat. Simmer for 20 minutes, or until the beans are cooked through but still firm to the touch. Drain the beans. Add to the carrot broth. Heat to serving temperature. Add the carrot juice and white pepper, and season with salt to taste.

To serve, ladle the soup into 6 soup bowls. Place a mound of sorrel chiffonade and scallions in the center of each bowl. Drizzle 2 teaspoons of the tarragon oil around the soup.

NUTRITIONAL INFORMATION

PER CUP BROTH: 284 calories (3% from fat), 9.5 g protein, 50 g carbohydrate, 1 g fat, 0 mg cholesterol, 492 mg sodium, 12 g fiber

Asian Roasted Kabocha Squash *with* Star Anise Soup *and* Sesame–Szechuan Peppercorn Cream

SERVES 6

Roasting the kabocha for this filling winter soup intensifies the subtle nutty flavor of the squash. The star anise adds licorice notes to the soup, and the sesame–Szechuan peppercorn cream adds both nutty depth and palate-invigorating pungency. E.T.

SESAME–SZECHUAN PEPPERCORN CREAM

1/4 cup sesame seeds, toasted (see page 223)

2 ounces silken tofu

1 teaspoon light miso

1/2 teaspoon ground toasted Szechuan peppercorns (page 223)

1/2 cup water

KABOCHA SOUP

1/2 teaspoon toasted sesame oil

1 kabocha squash, halved

1 teaspoon canola oil (optional)

2 yellow onions, cut in half crosswise and thinly sliced into crescents

1/4 cup dry sherry

1/2 teaspoon Sucanat (see page 224)

2 tablespoons peeled and minced fresh ginger

1/2 teaspoon ground allspice

1 teaspoon ground star anise

6 cups vegetable stock (page 205)

1/4 cup light miso

Salt and white pepper

2 scallions, green part only, thinly sliced on the diagonal, for garnish

6 whole star anise, for garnish

To make the cream, combine all of the ingredients in a blender, and blend until smooth. (Store refrigerated for up to 2 days.)

To make the soup, preheat the oven to 400°F. Brush the sesame oil over a baking pan. Place the squash cut side down on the pan. Cover with aluminum foil and bake for 30 to 40 minutes, until the flesh is very soft. Remove from the oven and let cool to room temperature. Remove the seeds and discard. Remove the flesh and reserve.

In a large saucepan, heat the canola oil over medium heat. Add the onions, sherry, and Sucanat. Cook, stirring often, for 15 minutes, or until amber and caramelized. Add the ginger, allspice, and star anise. Sauté for 2 minutes. Add the reserved squash flesh and the vegetable stock. Bring to a boil. Decrease the heat and simmer for 15 minutes, or until heated through. Transfer to a blender, add the miso, and blend until smooth. Return to the pan. Add salt and white pepper to taste.

To serve, ladle the soup into 6 soup bowls. Top each serving with 1 tablespoon of the sesame cream, some scallions, and 1 whole star anise.

NUTRITIONAL INFORMATION

PER CUP SOUP: 142 calories (15% from fat), 3.4 g protein, 23 g carbohydrate, 2.2 g fat, 0 mg cholesterol, 425 mg sodium, 4.3 g fiber

PER TABLESPOON CREAM: 23 calories (62% from fat), 1 g protein, 1 g carbohydrate, 2 g fat, 0 mg cholesterol, 22 mg sodium, 0.3 g fiber

CACTUS GUMBO

SERVES 6

I got the inspiration for this soup while working with nopal cactus pads (nopales) *to make a grilled antipasto plate. As I cut the leaves I noticed a gummy viscosity similar to that of okra. I thought a-ha! Cactus gumbo! It blends Southwestern flavors with Cajun style.* B.E.

TORTILLA STRIPS

2 corn tortillas
1 teaspoon canola oil
Pinch of salt

CACTUS GUMBO

1 teaspoon olive oil, or sherry for oil free
1 yellow onion, cut into $1/4$-inch dice
1 carrot, peeled and cut into $1/4$-inch dice
2 celery stalks, cut into $1/4$-inch dice
2 cloves garlic, minced
2 teaspoons salt
1 bay leaf
1 teaspoon Mexican oregano
$1/2$ tablespoon chile powder, plus more as needed, or 1 dried ancho chile, toasted (see page 222) and ground
$1/4$ teaspoon cayenne pepper
1 large nopal cactus leaf, charred and burred (see page 222), sliced into $1/2$-inch-thick strips
2 tomatoes, peeled, seeded, and diced
Kernels from 1 ear corn
3 cups vegetable stock (page 205)
2 tablespoons corn masa flour

1 avocado, peeled, pitted, and sliced, for garnish
6 sprigs cilantro, for garnish

To make the tortilla strips, preheat the oven to 350°F. Cut the tortillas into long, thin strips. Place them in a bowl and add the oil and salt. Toss, stirring with your fingertips to create curly strands. Bake, agitating frequently to bake evenly, for 10 minutes, or until dry and crisp.

To make the gumbo, place a soup pot over medium heat and add the olive oil. Add the onions, carrots, celery, garlic, salt, bay leaf, oregano, chile powder, and cayenne pepper. Cook for 5 minutes, or until soft. Add the cactus strips, tomatoes, corn, and vegetable stock. Bring to a simmer and cook for 3 minutes, or until just heated through. In a separate pan, toast the masa flour for 3 minutes, or until aromatic and slightly darker. Whisk into the gumbo. Continue to simmer for 5 minutes, or until the flavors have begun to combine.

To serve, ladle the gumbo into 6 soup bowls. Garnish with tortilla strips, sliced avocado, and 1 cilantro sprig.

NUTRITIONAL INFORMATION

PER CUP GUMBO: 106 calories (13% from fat), 3.2 g protein, 20.4 g carbohydrate, 1.7 g fat, 0 mg cholesterol, 672 mg sodium, 4.2 g fiber

PER SERVING TORTILLA STRIPS: 34 calories (27% from fat), 0.7 g protein, 5.8 g carbohydrate, 1.1 g fat, 0 mg cholesterol, 59 mg sodium, 0.7 g fiber

SAFFRON–SEA PALM *and* FENNEL SOUP *with* OYSTER MUSHROOMS, CROSTINI, *and* ROUILLE

SERVES 8

Sea palm is a type of seaweed harvested fresh all along the coastline of the Pacific Northwest. It has long, fettucine-like strands, and this recipe places its pleasant crunch and delicious briny flavor into a classic Mediterranean context. Saffron, fennel, and orange zest classically season bouillabaisse. For the rouille, use all cold ingredients and chill the blender to improve emulsification. To reduce the fat, you can replace the bread and olive oil with 1 package of silken tofu, blended until smooth. The leftover rouille makes a fun addition to sandwiches or salads. B.E.

SAFFRON STOCK

2 leeks, white and green parts, coarsely chopped
2 carrots, peeled and chopped
1 fennel bulb
2 celery stalks, chopped
1/2 orange, peel on
1/2 lemon, peel on
3 small dried porcini mushrooms
8 cups water
1 generous pinch of saffron threads
1/4 cup warm vegetable stock (page 205) or water
1 teaspoon whole coriander
1 teaspoon whole fennel seed
1 bay leaf
2 teaspoons nutritional yeast (see page 224)

ROUILLE

4 cloves garlic
1 cup loosely packed crustless bread
1 dried chipotle pepper, soaked in hot water and stemmed (seeds removed if reduced heat is desired)
1 1/2 teaspoons sweet paprika, toasted (see page 223)
1/2 teaspoon salt
Juice of 1 lemon
2 teaspoons Dijon mustard
1/2 cup olive oil
1/2 cup canola oil
1/2 cup cold water

CROSTINI

1/2 loaf bread, cut into thin slices
1 tablespoon olive oil
1/8 teaspoon salt

SEA PALM SOUP

2 teaspoons olive oil
1 large white onion, halved crosswise and cut into thin crescents
1 fennel bulb, cored, julienne
6 ounces oyster mushrooms
3 cloves garlic, minced
3 teaspoons salt
1 large tomato, peeled, seeded, and diced
Juice of 2 oranges
Grated zest of 2 oranges
1/2 ounce dried sea palm, reconstituted (see page 223)
2 teaspoons capers
1/4 cup pitted green olives, sliced

Fresh oregano, for garnish
1 orange, peeled and supremed (see page 222), for garnish
1 fennel frond, for garnish

To make the stock, place a large stockpot over medium-high heat. Add the leeks, carrots, fennel, celery, orange, lemon, porcini, and water, and bring close to a boil. Decrease the heat to low, and simmer for 45 minutes, or until reduced by one-third.

Meanwhile, steep the saffron threads in the vegetable stock for at least 20 minutes.

Add the coriander, fennel, bay leaf, and nutritional yeast to the soup. Simmer for 15 minutes more, or until the broth is flavorful. Strain the broth through a fine-mesh strainer, and immediately add the saffron threads.

To make the rouille, place 3 cloves of garlic in a dry sauté pan over high heat. Dry-toast for 5 to 7 minutes, until half of each clove is charred.

(continued)

SAFFRON SEA–PALM AND FENNEL SOUP, *continued*

Soak the bread in warm water until soft. Drain well. Put the bread, the toasted garlic, the remaining clove raw garlic, the chipotle, paprika, salt, lemon juice, and mustard in a blender. Blend on low. With the blender running, add the olive and canola oils and then the cold water in a slow, steady stream. Blend until emulsified. (Store refrigerated for up to 1 week.)

To make the crostini, preheat the oven to 350°F. In a bowl, toss the bread with the olive oil and salt. Place the bread slices flat on a baking sheet. Bake for 12 minutes, watching closely to prevent burning, until toasted. Let cool.

To make the soup, heat the olive oil in a soup pot over medium heat. Add the onions, fennel, mushrooms, garlic, and salt. Sauté for 7 minutes, or until the mushrooms are soft. Add the tomatoes, orange juice and zest, sea palm, capers, olives, and saffron stock, and bring to a boil. Decrease the heat and simmer for 20 minutes, letting the flavors mingle.

To serve, ladle the soup into 8 soup bowls. Garnish each bowl with a slice of crostini, 2 tablespoons rouille, oregano leaves, 2 orange supremes, and a tiny sprig of fennel frond on the side.

NUTRITIONAL INFORMATION

PER CUP SOUP: 96 calories (11% from fat), 3.7 g protein, 19 g carbohydrate, 1.4 g fat, 0 mg cholesterol, 1057 mg sodium, 4 g fiber

PER 2 TABLESPOONS ROUILLE: 134 calories (90% from fat), 0.5 g protein, 2.8 g carbohydrate, 13 g fat, 0 mg cholesterol, 91 mg sodium, 0.3 g fiber

CHANTERELLE MUSHROOM CHANA DAL

SERVES 4 TO 6

Chana dal *is the Indian name for baby split garbanzo beans, which you can find in most Indian markets. The word* dal *refers to both the legume and the preparation, which in India is a common bean purée. The chanterelles are a magical and tasty addition. Pappadam is a thin wafer made lentil flour. You can find it in Indian markets. B.E.*

2 teaspoons sesame oil

2 teaspoons canola oil

1 large yellow onion, diced

1 (1-inch) piece fresh ginger, peeled and minced

2 cloves garlic, minced

1 serrano chile, seeded and minced, plus more as needed

1 teaspoon salt

1 1/2 tablespoons mild curry powder

2 cups chanterelle mushrooms, torn into bite-sized pieces

2 cups dry chana dal beans

5 cups vegetable stock (page 205)

6 pappadams, for garnish

1/2 cup cucumber raita (page 214), for garnish

To make the dal, place a large soup pot over medium heat and add the sesame and canola oils. Add the onions, ginger, garlic, serrano, and salt. Sauté, stirring often, for 3 to 5 minutes, until the onions are soft. Add the curry powder and cook for 1 minute. Add the chanterelles, and cook for 5 minutes, or until soft. Add the chana dal and stock and bring to a boil. Decrease the heat, and simmer for 45 minutes, or until the beans are soft.

To serve, ladle the dal into 6 soup bowls. Garnish each bowl with a pappadam and 2 tablespoons raita.

NUTRITIONAL INFORMATION

PER 1/2 CUP DAL: 184 calories (21% from fat), 8 g protein, 27 g carbohydrate, 4 g fat, 0 mg cholesterol, 199 mg sodium, 7.7 g fiber

CORN *and* SMOKED OYSTER MUSHROOM CHOWDER

SERVES 6

This soup evokes memories of creamy clam chowder but is something new altogether. The dulse seaweed flakes add a briny quality, and the hearty smoked mushrooms are a treat you will find yourself craving again and again. Serve with crackers or crostini to sop up every last bit of this tasty chowder. B.E.

12 to 14 oyster mushrooms
1 teaspoon canola oil, or dry sherry for oil free
4 cups vegetable stock (page 205)
2 white onions, cut into $1/4$-inch dice
1 clove garlic, minced
Pinch of ground nutmeg
1 teaspoon fresh thyme
1 bay leaf
Salt and freshly ground black pepper
Kernels from 2 ears corn
2 russet potatoes, peeled and cut into $1/2$-inch dice
1 red bell pepper, roasted (see page 222), peeled, seeded, and finely diced
Dulse flakes, for garnish
6 thyme sprigs, for garnish

To smoke the mushrooms, in a bowl, toss the oyster mushrooms with the oil. Smoke for 20 minutes (see page 219).

To make the chowder, in a soup pot, heat 2 tablespoons of the stock over medium heat. Add the onions, garlic, nutmeg, thyme, and bay leaf, and salt and pepper to taste. Cover and braise, stirring often, for 10 minutes, or the onions are soft. Add the corn, potatoes, and the remaining vegetable stock. Bring to a boil. Decrease the heat to medium-low. Simmer for 10 minutes, or until the potatoes are fork-tender.

Remove and discard the bay leaf. Using a blender, pulse-blend the soup until creamy but not puréed.

Tear the mushrooms into smaller bite-sized pieces. Stir the mushrooms and bell pepper into the soup. Simmer for 5 minutes, letting the flavors mingle. Season with salt and pepper to taste.

To serve, ladle the chowder into 6 soup bowls. Garnish each serving with a pinch of dulse flakes and a sprig of thyme.

NUTRITIONAL INFORMATION

PER CUP CHOWDER: 220 calories (7.8% from fat), 8 g protein, 43 g carbohydrate, 1.9 g fat, 0 mg cholesterol, 42 mg sodium, 6.1 g fiber

MOTHER'S ARTICHOKE-TOMATO BISQUE

SERVES 6

A popular soup I used to prepare at Mother's Café & Garden in Austin, Texas, inspired me to create this recipe. The café has been making vegetarians (and a bunch of other people) happy since the seventies, with home-style and hearty comfort food. Its version of this soup was so popular that the regular customers would threaten to revolt if it wasn't served every Tuesday. My version is different, but I definitely owe credit to Mother's—thanks, guys!

One key to this recipe is to slice the artichokes paper-thin using a sharp knife or with the slicing blade of a food processor. Any bits that are not paper-thin will take longer to cook and will probably be bitter in the finished soup. B.E.

CHILE-TOASTED ALMONDS

3 tablespoons almonds
$1/2$ teaspoon freshly squeezed lemon juice
$1/8$ teaspoon salt
Pinch of cayenne pepper
$1/2$ teaspoon sweet paprika

ARTICHOKE-TOMATO BISQUE

3 cups vegetable stock (page 205)
1 yellow onion, diced
1 carrot, peeled and diced
2 cloves garlic, minced
$1/4$ pound baby artichokes (4 to 5 artichokes), hearts only, prepared (see page 222) and sliced paper-thin
1 teaspoon dried oregano
2 teaspoons salt
$1/2$ teaspoon freshly ground black pepper
Pinch of crushed red pepper flakes
1 teaspoon nutritional yeast (see page 224)
4 large ripe tomatoes, peeled (see page 223), seeded, and chopped
1 cup cooked brown basmati rice

To make the almonds, toss all of the ingredients together in a sauté pan over medium heat. Toast for 5 minutes, or until aromatic (see page 222).

To make the bisque, place a soup pot over medium heat and add $1/4$ cup of the stock. Add the onions, carrots, garlic, artichokes, oregano, salt, black pepper, red pepper, and yeast. Cover and cook for 5 minutes, or until the artichokes are limp. Add the tomatoes, rice, and the remaining $2^3/4$ cups stock. Bring to a simmer, and cook, stirring regularly, for 20 minutes, or until the soup begins to thicken just slightly and the rice begins to dissolve. Add salt and black pepper to taste.

To serve, ladle the bisque into 6 soup bowls and garnish with almonds.

NUTRITIONAL INFORMATION

PER CUP BISQUE: 103 calories (6% from fat), 3.4 g protein, 21 g carbohydrate, 0.8 g fat, 0 mg cholesterol, 662 mg sodium, 3.6 g fiber
PER SERVING ALMONDS: 26 calories (74% from fat), 0.9 g protein, 0.9 g carbohydrate, 2.3 g fat, 0 mg cholesterol, 2 mg sodium, 0.3 g fiber

CHILLED TOMATO *and* WATERMELON SOUP *with* LIME ICE

SERVES 6

The key to this soup (and to cooking in general) is in selecting good ingredients. The tomatoes should be small (larger tomatoes tend to be watery), dense, and rich in color: they should smell like tomatoes. The watermelon should be heavy for its size, yellowed on one side (to show it ripened on the vine), and with the stem broken, not cut; a ripe melon falls off the vine. Serve this refreshing soup in bowls, or serve in glasses as an agua fresca. B.E.

LIME ICE

1 cup freshly squeezed lime juice
2 tablespoons agave nectar (see page 224)

TOMATO AND WATERMELON SOUP

6 red tomatoes, peeled and seeded
4 cups seeded watermelon flesh
Salt and freshly ground black pepper

Cilantro sprigs, for garnish

To make the ice, whisk together the lime juice and agave nectar. Freeze for 2 hours, stirring every 20 minutes.

To make the soup, blend the tomatoes with the watermelon flesh. Add salt and pepper to taste. Strain, and refrigerate for 1 hour, or until well chilled.

To serve, ladle the soup into 6 soup bowls or glasses. Garnish with lime ice shavings and sprigs of fresh cilantro. Serve immediately.

NUTRITIONAL INFORMATION

PER SERVING SOUP: 63 (11.5% from fat), 2 g protein, 14 g carbohydrate, 1 g fat, 0 mg cholesterol, 15 mg sodium, 2 g fiber

PER SERVING ICE: 27 calories (1% from fat), 0.2 g protein, 8.7 g carbohydrate, 0 g fat, 0 mg cholesterol, 0 mg sodium, 0.2 g fiber

CHILLED WHITE PEACH SOUP *with* BLACK PEPPER *and* ROSE-LAVENDER CREAM

SERVES 6

This sweet chilled soup starts off a summer meal simply, refreshingly, and elegantly. E.T.

ROSE AND LAVENDER CREAM

1/4 cup cashews
1 teaspoon light miso
1/2 teaspoon dried lavender
2 teaspoons rose water
1/4 teaspoon ground nutmeg
1/2 cup water

WHITE PEACH SOUP

11 cups water
4 large ripe white peaches
Juice of 1 orange
Juice of 1/2 lemon
1 teaspoon fresh ginger juice (see page 222)
1/4 teaspoon salt
Coarsely ground black pepper

To make the cream, combine the cashews, miso, lavender, rose water, nutmeg, and 1/4 cup of the water in a blender. Blend to a coarse purée. With the blender running, slowly add the remaining water. Blend until smooth.

To make the soup, bring 8 cups of the water to a boil. Cut an X pattern just through the skin at the top of the peaches. Decrease the heat to a simmer, and blanch the peaches for 30 seconds (see page 223). Transfer to ice water to cool. Drain. Peel, halve, and pit the peaches.

Transfer to a blender and add the orange and lemon juices, ginger juice, the remaining 3 cups of water, and the salt. Blend until smooth. Refrigerate for 3 hours, or until well chilled.

To serve, ladle the soup into 6 soup bowls. Top each serving with 2 teaspoons of the rose-lavender cream, and sprinkle with pepper to taste.

NUTRITIONAL INFORMATION

PER SERVING SOUP: 41 calories (2% from fat), 0.7 g protein, 10 g carbohydrate, 0.1 g fat, 0 mg cholesterol, 82 mg sodium, 1.7 g fiber

PER TABLESPOON CREAM: 12 calories (68% from fat), 0.4 g protein, 0.7 g carbohydrate, 1 g fat, 0 mg cholesterol, 14 mg sodium, 0.1 g fiber

CHILLED AVOCADO, TOMATILLO, *and* CUCUMBER SOUP *with* SAFFRON-LIME ICE

SERVES 6

This creamy, smooth, luxurious chilled green soup is easy to make and hard not to like. Anyone who likes avocados will love it. The ice is also easy: put it in a shallow pan, freeze it, and scrape it up with a fork.
E.T.

SAFFRON-LIME ICE

Juice of 2 limes
1/4 teaspoon saffron threads, soaked in 1/4 cup
   warm water for 20 minutes
1 teaspoon unrefined sugar
1 teaspoon Hungarian paprika or Spanish paprika,
   toasted (see page 223)
1/2 cup water
1/3 teaspoon salt

AVOCADO, TOMATILLO, AND CUCUMBER SOUP

1/2 yellow onion, cut into 1/2-inch dice
4 cloves garlic, peeled
1 jalapeño chile
3 ripe avocados, peeled and pitted
8 tomatillos, peeled
1 English cucumber, halved lengthwise and seeded
1/2 cup loosely packed cilantro leaves
1 teaspoon dried oregano, toasted (see page 223)
1/4 teaspoon ground nutmeg
1/4 teaspoon freshly ground black pepper
Juice of 1 lime
2 teaspoons light miso
3 cups water
Salt
Cayenne pepper (optional)
1/3 cup slivered almonds, toasted (see page 222),
   and very coarsely crushed, for garnish

To make the ice, mix all of the ingredients together in a bowl, and pour into a 2-inch-deep pan. Freeze for 3 to 4 hours, until frozen solid.

To make the soup, heat a large nonstick sauté pan over high heat. Add the onions, garlic, and jalapeño. Dry-toast, stirring frequently, for 7 to 10 minutes, until half of the onions, garlic, and jalapeño are charred. Remove from the pan and let cool to room temperature. Peel and seed the jalapeño.

Place the avocado in a mixing bowl with the cooled onion, garlic, and jalapeño. Add the tomatillos, cucumber, cilantro, oregano, nutmeg, black pepper, lime juice, miso, and water. In a blender, or using a handheld immersion blender, blend the ingredients in batches until smooth. Add salt and cayenne pepper to taste. Refrigerate for 2 hours, or until well chilled.

To serve, ladle the soup into 6 martini glasses. Sprinkle toasted almonds over the top of each. Scrape the saffron ice crystals off the pan with a fork, and place 2 teaspoons on each serving of soup. Serve immediately.

NUTRITIONAL INFORMATION

PER SERVING SOUP: 203 calories (64% from fat), 4.7 g protein, 15 g carbohydrate, 15 g fat, 0 mg cholesterol, 84 mg sodium, 3.5 g fiber

PER SERVING ICE: 3 calories (5% from fat), 0 g protein, 0.7 g carbohydrate, 0.1 g fat, 0 mg cholesterol, 40 mg sodium, 0.1 g fiber

CHILLED POTATO VICHYSSOISE
with BLACK TRUFFLE SORBET

SERVES 6

Here is our take on the classic potato vichyssoise. It's great with just a sprinkle of fresh dill and chopped chive, and even better with our Black Truffle Sorbet. If you do not have a sorbet machine, use the sorbet recipe for a Black Truffle Cream. E.T.

BLACK TRUFFLE SORBET

1/4 cup unsalted cashews

1 teaspoon white miso

Juice of 1/2 lemon

1 teaspoon nutritional yeast (see page 224)

1/4 teaspoon ground nutmeg

1/2 teaspoon salt

1 1/2 teaspoons white or black truffle oil

1/2 cup water, plus more as needed

1 tablespoon minced fresh black truffle or jarred truffle shavings

CHILLED POTATO VICHYSSOISE

2 teaspoons olive oil, or 1/4 cup vegetable stock (page 205) for oil free

4 leeks, white part only, cleaned and cut into 1/2-inch dice

1/2 teaspoon dried thyme

2 bay leaves

1/4 cup dry sherry

3 large waxy potatoes (such as Yukon Gold, White Rose, or red skinned), peeled and cut into 1-inch dice

4 cups vegetable stock (page 205)

1 tablespoon white miso

2 cups soy milk

2 tablespoons fresh tarragon leaves or dill

Salt and white pepper

2 tablespoons chopped chives, for garnish

6 thin lemon rounds, for garnish

To make the sorbet, combine the cashews, miso, lemon juice, yeast, nutmeg, salt, truffle oil, and 1/4 cup of the water in a blender. Blend until coarsely puréed. Add the remaining 1/4 cup water, plus more if needed, and continue to blend until smooth and the consistency of cream. Add the minced truffle. Freeze in a sorbet machine according to the manufacturer's instructions. (Store frozen for up to 1 week.) Defrost slightly before serving.

To make the vichyssoise, place a 2-quart pot over medium heat, and add the olive oil. Add the leeks, and sauté for 5 to 7 minutes, until wilted and translucent. Add the thyme and bay leaves. Add the sherry and stir to scrape up the browned bits from the bottom of the pan. Add the potatoes and stock. Cover and simmer for 20 minutes, or until the potatoes are soft and crush easily with the back of a spoon. Let cool for 20 minutes.

Remove and discard the bay leaves. Add the miso, soy milk, and tarragon, and transfer to a blender. Blend in batches until smooth. Refrigerate for 30 to 45 minutes, until cool (50° to 55°F), but not as cold as the refrigerator (38° to 45°F). Just before serving, add salt and white pepper to taste.

To serve, ladle the vichyssoise into 6 soup bowls. Garnish each bowl with 2 tablespoons of the sorbet, 1 teaspoon chopped chives, and a lemon round. Serve immediately.

NUTRITIONAL INFORMATION

PER SERVING VICHYSSOISE: 158 calories (21% from fat), 4.9 g protein, 23 g carbohydrate, 3 g fat, 0 mg cholesterol, 129 mg sodium, 3.4 g fiber

PER 2 TABLESPOONS SORBET: 53 calories (69% from fat), 1.3 g protein, 2.8 g carbohydrate, 4.2 g fat, 0 mg cholesterol, 194 mg sodium, 0.4 g fiber

CHILLED YELLOW DOLL WATERMELON SOUP
with CARDAMOM CREAM

SERVES 6

Here's another chilled soup that makes a perfect start to a meal in the August heat. It is refreshing and invigorates the palate. ℰ.𝒯.

CARDAMOM CREAM

$1/4$ cup unsalted cashews
1 teaspoon white miso
$1/2$ teaspoon ground cardamom
$1/4$ teaspoon salt
$1/2$ cup water

YELLOW DOLL WATERMELON SOUP

4 cups yellow watermelon flesh, seeded
1 tablespoon peeled and minced ginger
2 cups water
Juice of 1 lime
1 teaspoon unrefined sugar
$1/4$ teaspoon cayenne pepper
Salt

2 tablespoons loosely packed small peppermint leaves, for garnish

To make the cream, place all of the ingredients in a blender and blend until smooth. Refrigerate for 4 hours, or until well chilled.

To make the soup, place the melon, ginger, water, lime juice, sugar, and cayenne pepper in a blender and blend until smooth. Add salt to taste. Refrigerate for 4 hours, or until well chilled.

To serve, ladle the soup into 6 soup bowls and garnish each serving with 2 teaspoons of cardamom cream. Scatter peppermint leaves over the top.

NUTRITIONAL INFORMATION

PER SERVING SOUP: 39 calories (10% from fat), 0.8 g protein, 9 carbohydrate, 0.5 g fat, 0 mg cholesterol, 5 g sodium, 0.6 fiber

PER 2 TEASPOONS CREAM: 16 calories (67% from fat), 0.5 g protein, 1 g carbohydrate, 1.4 g fat, 0 mg cholesterol, 57 mg sodium, 0.2 g fiber

MILLENNIUM
exotic vegetarian cuisine

PASTAS

In this chapter, we offer recipes using our hand-made fresh pasta, which you can find in the basics chapter (page 208). The recipe is really quite easy: use semolina flour, water, and salt. After that, flavor the pasta however you like. We prefer to stick with one element that will remain distinct when combined with a sauce. A pasta machine helps, but a rolling pin and a knife can also be used to produce great results—rustic, thick, chewy ribbons in want of thick, rich, intense sauce. Check out Bruce's Buckwheat Pappardelle for just such a dish—or some of the other simple yet exotic pasta sauce recipes and serving suggestions that can be whipped up in no time.

Penne Noodles with Peanut-Coconut Sauce, Smoked Tofu,
and Broccoli ⚘ 108

Buckwheat Pappardelle with Wasabi-Miso Sauce and
Sea Vegetable Salad ⚘ 109

Roasted Beet Lasagnette with Tahini Crème, Tofu Ricotta,
and Gremolata ⚘ 110

Swiss Chard Cannelloni with Smoked Cherries
and Parsnip Cream ⚘ 112

Samosa Ravioli with Beet-Tamarind Chutney ⚘ 114

BROAD NOODLES *with* SOUTHEAST ASIAN PEANUT PESTO *and* FIVE-SPICE BAKED TOFU

SERVES 4

This pesto gets an Asian spin from the aromatic Kaffir lime leaf, ginger, and Thai chiles. Serve with any broad noodle, such as fettuccine, pappardelle, or Chinese chow fun. Thin out the pesto and use it for a dipping sauce for pot stickers, satés, or vegetable crudités. E.T.

FIVE-SPICE TOFU

3 tablespoons tamari

3 tablespoons mirin

1 tablespoon toasted sesame oil

1 teaspoon unrefined sugar

1 1/2 teaspoons five-spice powder

1/2 teaspoon Szechwan peppercorns, toasted
  (see page 223) and ground

1 pound firm tofu, cut into 1/2-inch-thick by
  2-inch-long strips

PEANUT PESTO

1/2 cup fresh peanuts, roasted

1/2 bunch cilantro leaves

1/2 bunch mint leaves

2 fresh Kaffir lime leaves

4 cloves garlic

1 serrano or Thai chile, seeded

1 tablespoon peeled and minced fresh ginger

2 teaspoons sesame oil

1 teaspoon salt

1 teaspoon grated lime zest

1 tablespoon white miso

Juice of 2 limes

BROAD NOODLES

1 teaspoon canola oil

1/2 red onion, thinly sliced

2 cloves garlic, minced

1 head Chinese broccoli, sliced into bite-sized pieces

1 red bell pepper, sliced into thin strips

1/4 pound mung bean sprouts

3/4 pound fettucine, cooked al dente (see page 208)

1/2 cup peanuts, toasted (see page 222), for garnish

To make the tofu, preheat the oven to 400°F. In a mixing bowl, combine the tamari, mirin, sesame oil, sugar, five-spice powder, and peppercorns to make the marinade. Place the tofu strips in the marinade and toss to coat. Place the tofu on a baking pan and bake for 20 to 30 minutes, until light brown. Turn the tofu and cook for 10 minutes. Baste with more marinade and cook for 10 minutes, or until the tofu has a caramel glaze. Set aside.

To make the pesto, put all of the ingredients in a food processor fitted with the metal blade. Blend, adding water as needed, to achieve a smooth, thin paste. (Store refrigerated, in an airtight container, for up to 2 days.)

To make the noodles, heat the canola oil in a wok or large nonstick sauté pan over high heat. Add the onions and garlic and sauté for 30 seconds, or until just browned. Add the broccoli and bell pepper and sauté for 1 minute, or until lightly wilted. Add the tofu and bean sprouts, followed by the pesto and the pasta, and cook for 3 minutes, or until heated through. Add a small amount of water to thin out the sauce if needed, and toss well. Add salt to taste.

To serve, divide the noodles among 4 pasta bowls, and top with toasted peanuts.

NUTRITIONAL INFORMATION

PER SERVING: 603 calories (49% from fat), 28 g protein, 71 g carbohydrate, 21 g fat, 0 mg cholesterol, 1600 mg sodium, 12.3 g fiber

PER 1/3 CUP PESTO: 154 calories (64% from fat), 6 g protein, 8.6 g carbohydrate, 11 g fat, 0 mg cholesterol, 636 mg sodium, 2.9 g fiber

PER SERVING TOFU: 145 calories (55% from fat), 10 g protein, 5 g carbohydrate, 8 g fat, 0 mg cholesterol, 763 mg sodium, 2 g fiber

YELLOW FINN POTATO GNOCCHI *with* BEET-MERLOT REDUCTION, ROASTED BEETS, *and* WALNUTS

SERVES 6

Here's a dish from a dinner we put on with Frog's Leap Winery. We paired this dish with one of their extraordinary Merlots, and it was quite a success.
E.T.

YELLOW FINN POTATO GNOCCHI

6 large yellow Finn potatoes
1 russet potato
2/3 cup unbleached flour, plus more as needed
1 teaspoon salt

ROASTED BEETS

4 small red beets, peeled and quartered
4 small Chiogga beets, peeled and quartered
2 teaspoons canola oil
1/3 cup vegetable stock (page 205)
1/4 teaspoon ground allspice
1/4 teaspoon ground clove
1/2 teaspoon salt

BEET-MERLOT REDUCTION

1 teaspoon extra virgin olive oil
6 shallots, halved
1 red beet, peeled and quartered
1 thyme sprig
1/2 rosemary sprig
1/3 teaspoon salt, plus more as needed
2 tablespoons dried porcini mushrooms
2 cups roasted vegetable dark stock (page 207) or mushroom stock (page 206)
2 cups Merlot
1/4 cup dried cherries
1 teaspoon balsamic vinegar
2 teaspoons cornstarch, dissolved in 2 tablespoons water
Freshly ground black pepper

2 tablespoons extra virgin olive oil
2 cloves garlic, minced
2 tablespoons chopped fresh parsley
6 tablespoons chopped walnuts, toasted (see page 223), for garnish

6 teaspoons tarragon oil (page 215), for garnish
1 tablespoon drained green peppercorns in brine, for garnish

To prepare the gnocchi, preheat the oven to 400°F. Prick the skin of the yellow Finn and russet potatoes with a fork. Bake for 40 minutes, or until tender when pierced with a knife. Let cool to room temperature.

Scrape the flesh of the potatoes into a bowl, and mash. Add the flour and salt to the potatoes. Knead for about 2 minutes to form a soft dough. If the dough is sticky, add more flour.

Cut off one-quarter of the dough and roll it with your hands into a 1-inch-thick rope. Use the remaining dough to make 3 more ropes. Cut each rope into 1/2-inch-long segments, and pinch in the sides of each piece of the dough so that it looks like a bow tie. Place the finished gnocchi on a floured pan. Repeat with the remaining dough. Freeze the gnocchi for at least 1 hour.

To roast the beets, preheat the oven to 400°F. Toss all of the ingredients together in a bowl, and place on a roasting pan. Bake for 25 minutes, or until the beets are just tender. Remove from the heat.

To make the reduction, heat the olive oil in a saucepan over medium heat. Add the shallots and sauté for 10 minutes, or until lightly caramelized. Add the beet, thyme, rosemary, salt, and porcini and sauté for 1 minute. Add the stock and wine. Simmer over low heat for 20 minutes, or until reduced by one-half. Strain the mixture into another saucepan, add the dried cherries, and simmer for 15 minutes, or until reduced by one-third. Add the vinegar, and whisk in the cornstarch slurry. Add salt and pepper to taste. The sauce should be just thick enough to coat the back of a spoon.

To cook the gnocchi, bring at least 1 gallon of salted water to a boil. Add half of the gnocchi to the boiling water. Cook for 5 to 6 minutes, until the gnocchi

(continued)

YELLOW FINN POTATO GNOCCHI, *continued*

float to the surface. Using a slotted spoon, transfer the gnocchi to a plate. Toss with a little extra virgin olive oil to prevent sticking. Repeat with remaining half of the gnocchi.

Place a large skillet over medium-high heat. Add the oil and the garlic and sauté for 30 seconds. Add the gnocchi and sauté, shaking the pan often to prevent the gnocchi from sticking, for 2 minutes, or until the gnocchi start to brown. Remove from the heat, add the parsley, and toss together.

To serve, divide the gnocchi among 4 large dinner plates. Spoon $1/4$ cup of reduction around the gnocchi on each plate, and place 6 to 8 segments of roasted beet around the plate. Sprinkle the gnocchi with 1 tablespoon of the chopped walnuts, drizzle with 1 teaspoon of the tarragon oil, and sprinkle with $1/2$ teaspoon of the peppercorns.

NUTRITIONAL INFORMATION

PER SERVING: 425 calories (31% from fat), 9.9 g protein, 71 g carbohydrate, 9.6 g fat, 0 mg cholesterol, 605 mg sodium, 6.8 g fiber

PER $1/4$ CUP REDUCTION: 93 calories (12% from fat), 1.8 g protein, 15.4 g carbohydrate, 1 g fat, 0 mg cholesterol, 90 mg sodium, 0.7 g fiber

PER SERVING BEETS: 31 calories (45% from fat), 0.6 g protein, 3.7 g carbohydrate, 1.6 g fat, 0 mg cholesterol, 187 mg sodium, 1.1 g fiber

FUSILLE *with* WINTER VEGETABLES *and*
SOUTHWESTERN ROASTED CARROT PURÉE

SERVES 6

This hearty, satisfying pasta dish can be made with little or no oil. Roasting the onion and carrots with the cumin and chile intensifies their flavors and gives the purée a subtle, smoky quality. Use precooked cubes of any hearty winter root vegetable or squash. Smoked tempeh or tofu would be a nice complement to this pasta. E.T.

ROASTED CARROT PURÉE

1 yellow onion, cut into 1/2-inch dice
2 carrots, peeled and cut into 1/2-inch dice
1 celery stalk, diced
1 teaspoon extra virgin olive oil, or sherry or vegetable stock (page 205) for oil free
2 teaspoons cumin seeds
1/2 teaspoon fresh Mexican oregano
1/3 teaspoon salt
1 dried ancho chile, seeded
2 cups vegetable stock (page 205), or 1 cup vegetable stock and 1 cup carrot juice, plus more as needed
Salt and freshly ground black pepper

FUSILLE WITH VEGETABLES

1 teaspoon extra virgin olive oil, or 1/4 cup vegetable stock (page 205) for oil free
2 fennel bulbs, thinly sliced
4 cloves garlic, minced
1 cup sliced portobello mushrooms
3 cups winter squash or root vegetable, cut into 1/2-inch dice and cooked al dente
1 cup tightly packed spinach leaves
3/4 pound fusille, cooked al dente (see page 208)
Salt and freshly ground black pepper

Cilantro leaves, for garnish
6 lime wedges, for garnish

To make the purée, preheat the oven to 400°F. In a bowl, toss the onion, carrots, and celery together with the olive oil, cumin, oregano, and salt. Place in a shallow baking dish deep enough for only one layer of vegetables. Bake for 20 minutes, stirring the vegetables after 10 minutes, or until lightly browned.

Add the ancho chile and 1 cup of the vegetable stock. Return the pan to the oven and bake for 20 minutes, or until the carrots are soft. Let cool to room temperature.

Transfer to a blender and blend (in batches if needed) with the remaining 1 cup vegetable stock, adding more stock if needed to achieve a smooth purée. Add salt and pepper to taste.

To make the noodles and vegetables, heat the olive oil in a large sauté pan over high heat. Add the fennel and garlic and sauté for 1 minute, or until it just starts to brown. Add the mushrooms and the squash and sauté for 2 to 3 minutes, until the mushrooms are just soft. Add the spinach leaves and the carrot purée and cook for 2 to 3 minutes, until heated through. Toss in the pasta, and season with salt and pepper to taste.

To serve, divide the pasta among 6 pasta bowls. Garnish each serving with cilantro leaves and a lime wedge.

NUTRITIONAL INFORMATION

PER SERVING: 331 calories (10% from fat), 11.3 g protein, 66 g carbohydrate, 3 g fat, 0 mg cholesterol, 357 mg sodium, 9.9 g fiber

PER 1/2 CUP PURÉE: 67 calories (16% from fat), 1.6 g protein, 13 g carbohydrate, 1.2 g fat, 0 mg cholesterol, 144 mg sodium, 3.7 g fiber

CHANTERELLE *and* STINGING NETTLE RAVIOLI *with* SORREL PURÉE, SAFFRON AÏOLI, *and* CANDY CAP MUSHROOM–BALSAMIC REDUCTION

SERVES 6

This recipe comes from our Exotic Mushroom Dinner. Besides showcasing wild chanterelles, it shows off another one of our favorite mushrooms: candy caps (Lactarius fragilis). These small, tawny-capped mushrooms, found from California north through the Pacific Northwest, have a wonderful, rich, caramel- or maple syrup–like flavor. They're worth seeking out, but if you can't find them, substitute dried porcini.

The recipe also features foraged greens from Bolinas, California. Stinging nettles are served over mixed greens, including wild arugula and watercress, also from Bolinas. Substitute fresh spinach for stinging nettles and domesticated varieties of arugula and watercress for the wild varieties, if necessary. If you happen to live in an area with wild greens, go out and forage them. E.T.

SORREL PURÉE

2 cups loosely packed sorrel leaves
2 tablespoons extra virgin olive oil
Vegetable stock (page 205) or water, as needed
Salt and freshly ground black pepper

CANDY CAP–BALSAMIC REDUCTION

4 cups vegetable stock (page 205)
2 tablespoons dried candied cap mushrooms
1 cup balsamic vinegar
$^1/_2$ teaspoon salt

RAVIOLI

$^1/_2$ pound stinging nettles
1 tablespoon extra virgin olive oil
8 to 10 shallots, cut into small dice
$^3/_4$ pound chanterelles, cut into $^1/_2$-inch dice
$^1/_4$ teaspoon salt
$^1/_2$ teaspoon dried thyme
2 tablespoons dry sherry
$^1/_2$ teaspoon ground nutmeg
8 ounces firm tofu, crumbled

1 teaspoon salt
$^1/_4$ teaspoon freshly ground black pepper
1 recipe fresh pasta sheets (page 208), cut into
   36 (3-inch-diameter) circles

3 cups assorted bitter greens (such as arugula, watercress, and radicchio)
$^1/_2$ cup saffron tofu aïoli (page 213)
Fresh chives or tarragon, chopped, for garnish

To make the purée, bring 2 quarts of water to a boil. Blanch the sorrel leaves for 10 seconds (see page 223). Shock in ice water, drain, and squeeze dry.

In a blender, purée the sorrel with the olive oil until smooth. You may need to add a bit of stock or water to thin out. Add salt and pepper to taste.

To make the reduction, place a saucepan over low heat and add the stock and dried candied cap mushrooms. Simmer for 15 minutes. Remove from the heat and let steep for 30 minutes. Strain the liquid into another saucepan. Add the vinegar and salt and simmer over low heat for 15 minutes, or until the mixture reduces to a syrupy consistency of about $^1/_2$ cup. Let cool to room temperature.

To make the ravioli, bring 1 gallon of water to a boil. Blanch the nettles for 1 minute (see page 223), being careful not to touch them with your bare hands. Shock in ice water, drain, and let cool. Squeeze the nettles dry, and coarsely chop the greens.

Place a large skillet over medium heat and add the oil. Add the shallots, chanterelles, and salt. Sauté, stirring often, for 8 to 10 minutes, until the mushrooms are dry and the shallots are lightly caramelized. Stir in the thyme. Add the sherry and stir to scrape up the browned bits from the bottom of the skillet. Add the nutmeg and nettles. Sauté, stirring often, for 3 to 5 minutes, until the liquid from the nettles evaporates. Remove from the heat. Stir in the tofu, salt and pepper. Let cool to room temperature.

Place 2 to 3 heaping tablespoons of the filling in the center of a pasta round. Brush the edges of the pasta round with water, and place a second sheet over the filling. Crimp the edges with a fork. Repeat with the remaining pasta rounds and filling to make 18 ravioli.

In a pot, bring 1 gallon of salted water to a boil, and add the ravioli. Cook for 5 to 7 minutes, until the ravioli float to the surface. Drain in a colander.

Dress the greens with 2 tablespoons of the balsamic reduction and 2 tablespoons of the sorrel purée.

To serve, place ¹/₂ cup of the bitter greens in the center of each plate. Place 3 ravioli on top of the greens.

Drizzle about 2 tablespoons of the aïoli over the ravioli. Place 2 tablespoons of the sorrel purée and 1 tablespoon of the balsamic reduction around the plate. Garnish with chopped chives.

NUTRITIONAL INFORMATION

PER SERVING: 409 calories (15% from fat), 19.8 g protein, 61 g carbohydrate, 10.5 g fat, 0 mg cholesterol, 848 mg sodium, 14.2 g fiber

PER 2 TABLESPOONS PURÉE: 31 calories (96% from fat), 0.1 g protein, 0.2 g carbohydrate, 3 g fat, 0 mg cholesterol, 1 mg sodium, 0 g fiber

PER TABLESPOON REDUCTION: 16 (0.8% from fat), 0.1 g protein, 2.8 g carbohydrate, 0.1 g fat, 0 mg cholesterol, 118 mg sodium, 0.1 g fiber

Pasta Ribbons *in* Shiitake–Butternut Squash Broth *with* Asian Greens, Mushrooms, *and* Chile Oil

SERVES 6

Our friend Bernard in Santa Rosa makes us wide buckwheat black sesame seed pappardelle ribbons for this dish. Feel free to substitute fresh rice chow fun noodles or hearty whole-wheat pasta. The broth is an Asian mushroom stock with puréed butternut squash added to give it a bit of viscosity. Try this pasta dish with our five-spice tofu (page 93), baked marinated tempeh (page 211), or smoked baked tofu (see page 211). Garnish with rau ram, *known as Vietnamese mint or Vietnamese coriander, which has a minty, peppery taste. E.T.*

BROTH

1 teaspoon canola oil
1 teaspoon toasted sesame oil
1 bulb garlic, cloves removed, peeled and coarsely chopped
1 red onion, coarsely chopped
2 tablespoons peeled and sliced fresh ginger
1 tablespoon fermented black beans
2 lemongrass stalks, coarsely chopped
1/2 teaspoon Szechuan peppercorns
Grated zest of 1/2 orange
1 dried chile de árbol or Thai red chile
4 star anise

2 ounces dried shiitake mushrooms
Fresh mushroom stems (optional)
8 cups water
2 tablespoons dark barley miso
2 cups diced butternut squash
Salt

PASTA WITH GREENS AND MUSHROOMS

1/2 teaspoon salt, plus more as needed
4 teaspoons canola oil
1 pound fresh pappardelle noodles
1 cup 1/2-inch dice butternut squash
4 cloves garlic, minced
1 bunch scallions, green part only, coarsely chopped
1 tablespoon peeled and minced fresh ginger
1/2 pound fresh Asian mushrooms (such as shiitake, oyster, and honshimeji)
4 heads (2- to 3-inch) baby bok choy, sliced in quarters
8 ounces firm tofu, diced (1 cup)
1 to 1 1/2 pounds fresh buckwheat noodles, cooked al dente (see page 208)
Tamari

1/4 cup Millennium Seven-Secret Chile Oil (page 12), for garnish
1 cup mung bean sprouts, for garnish
1/2 bunch cilantro leaves, for garnish
1/2 bunch *rau ram* or Thai basil, for garnish

To make the broth, place a 4-quart saucepan over medium heat and add the canola and sesame oils. Add the garlic and onions and sauté for 4 to 5 minutes, until soft and lightly browned. Add the ginger, fermented black beans, lemongrass, peppercorns, orange zest, dried chiles, and star anise. Sauté, stirring, for 1 minute. Add the shiitakes, mushroom stems, and water. Bring to a boil. Decrease the heat to medium-low. Simmer for 45 minutes, or until reduced by one-third.

Blanch the squash for 2 to 3 minutes, until al dente (see page 223). Shock in ice water and drain. Transfer to a blender and blend until puréed.

Remove the broth from the heat and strain into another saucepan. Whisk in the miso. Add the squash purée. Add salt to taste.

To make the pasta, bring a large pot of water to a boil. Add the salt and 1 teaspoon of the canola oil. Add the pasta and cook for 2 minutes, or until al dente. Drain and refresh under cold running water. Drain and toss with 1 teaspoon of the canola oil.

Blanch the squash for 2 to 3 minutes, until al dente (see page 223). Shock in ice water and drain.

Heat the remaining 2 teaspoons canola oil in a large, deep skillet or wok over high heat. Add the garlic, scallion greens, and ginger, and sauté for 1 minute, or until light brown. Add the mushrooms and baby bok choy and sauté for 2 minutes, or until just wilted. Add the butternut squash and tofu, followed by the broth. Bring it to a boil. Add the cooked noodles, and cook for 2 to 3 minutes, until heated through. Add salt and tamari to taste.

To serve, divide the pasta evenly among 6 deep bowls. Garnish each portion with 2 teaspoons of the chile oil, and even amounts of the bean sprouts, cilantro leaves, and *rau ram.*

NUTRITIONAL INFORMATION

PER SERVING: 417 calories (24% from fat), 14.8 g protein, 79.8 g carbohydrate, 7.1 g fat, 0 mg cholesterol, 560 mg sodium, 8.8 g fiber

PER CUP BROTH: 39 calories (40% from fat), 1.3 g protein, 5.2 g carbohydrate, 2 g fat, 0 mg cholesterol, 211 mg sodium, 0.9 g fiber

Lemon–Pine Nut Ravioli *over* Baby Artichoke–Golden Tomato Ragoût

SERVES 4

At the end of summer and early fall, local baby artichokes come into season, and heirloom tomatoes are at their peak. We stew the artichokes with sweet Golden Jubilee tomatoes and fresh rosemary and serve them beneath this lemon–pine nut ravioli, courtesy of Paul Rose, our in-house pasta guru. For the basil aïoli, use Genovese basil, which has a potent flavor that makes it also a favorite for pesto. E.T.

BASIL AÏOLI

1/2 cup small-diced quality white bread, crusts removed
1/2 bunch basil leaves
2 cloves garlic, minced
1 teaspoon Dijon mustard
Juice of 1 lemon
1/2 teaspoon grated lemon zest
1/2 cup extra virgin olive oil
1/2 teaspoon salt

BABY ARTICHOKE–GOLDEN TOMATO RAGOÛT

1 lemon, halved
3 bay leaves
1/2 teaspoon salt
12 baby artichokes, prepared (see page 222) and halved
2 tablespoons extra virgin olive oil
2 leeks, white part only, chopped into small dice
12 to 16 cloves garlic, peeled
2 teaspoons fresh rosemary, minced
1 pound yellow tomatoes (Golden Jubilee or gold plum), seeded and diced
1/2 cup Sauvignon Blanc or other white wine
1/4 teaspoon crushed red pepper flakes
Salt and freshly ground black pepper

RAVIOLI

1 cup pine nuts, toasted (see page 222) and finely chopped
Grated zest of 2 lemons

Juice of 2 lemons
1/2 bunch basil, minced
4 ounces firm tofu, pressed to squeeze out moisture, and crumbled
1 teaspoon umeboshi vinegar
1 teaspoon nutritional yeast (see page 224)
1/4 teaspoon white pepper
Salt
1 recipe fresh pasta sheets (page 208), cut into 32 (2-inch) squares
Water for brushing

To make the aïoli, place the bread in a mixing bowl. Add enough warm water to slightly cover the bread. Soak for 15 minutes. Remove the bread and squeeze out the excess moisture. Place the bread in a blender or, if using an immersion blender, in a mixing bowl. Add the basil, garlic, mustard, lemon juice, zest, and 1/4 cup of the oil. Blend the mixture until very thick. Slowly add the remaining 1/4 cup oil. Blend until you have a thick aïoli. Add salt and adjust the seasonings to taste. (Store refrigerated, in an airtight container, for up to 1 week.)

To make the ragoût, bring 1 gallon of water to a boil. Add the lemon to the water. Add 1 of the bay leaves and the salt. Add the artichokes to the boiling water, and boil for 10 to 15 minutes, until soft. Drain and let cool.

Place a large, deep skillet or sauté pan over medium heat and add the olive oil. Add the leeks and garlic. Sauté for 8 to 10 minutes, until lightly caramelized. Add the rosemary, the remaining 2 bay leaves, the tomatoes, and the cooked baby artichokes. Add the white wine and pepper flakes. Decrease the heat to medium-low and simmer for 15 to 20 minutes, until the ragoût thickens. Remove from the heat. Remove and discard the bay leaves, and add salt and pepper to taste.

To make the ravioli filling, combine all of the ingredients in a mixing bowl. Mash with the back of a fork until thoroughly incorporated. Add salt to taste.

To make the ravioli, for each ravioli, place 1 to 2 teaspoons of the filling in the center of a pasta sheet. Brush the edges with water. Place another sheet on top, and crimp the edges with a fork. Repeat with the remaining pasta rounds to make 16 ravioli. Refrigerate for 2 hours, or freeze for 1 hour.

In a pot, bring 1 gallon of water to a boil. Boil the ravioli, in batches if necessary, for 2 to 3 minutes, until they float to the surface. If you like your ravioli with a crispy shell, at this point place them in large skillet with 2 teaspoons canola oil, and sauté over medium-high heat for 1 1/2 minutes per side, or until slightly browned.

To serve, place equal portions of the ragoût in the center of a deep pasta bowl or soup bowl. Place 4 ravioli over the ragoût, and drizzle 2 tablespoons of the basil aïoli over the top.

NUTRITIONAL INFORMATION

PER SERVING: 491 calories (41% from fat), 33 g protein, 58 g carbohydrate, 23 g fat, 0 mg cholesterol, 600 mg sodium, 7.8 g fiber

PER 1/2 CUP RAGOÛT: 104 calories (43% from fat), 2.9 g protein, 11.6 g carbohydrate, 4.9 g fat, 0 mg cholesterol, 219 mg sodium, 4 g fiber

PER 2 TABLESPOONS AÏOLI: 100 calories (81% from fat), 0.8 g protein, 4 g carbohydrate, 9.4 g fat, 0 mg cholesterol, 124 mg sodium, 0.4 g fiber

ASPARAGUS-RHUBARB CANNELLONI *with* TURMERIC-ORANGE SAUCE *and* HERB AÏOLI

SERVES 6

In this spring dish, rhubarb, a rare treat, gets a savory application. You'll find that its piquant presence perfectly counters the asparagus—so much so, in fact, that you may find yourself slipping it into other savory dishes. I say, don't be shy—let your rhubarb shine!

To prevent the green herbs from turning brown, chill all aïoli ingredients and a blender for 30 minutes before beginning. The aïoli can be made up to 1 day ahead of time. If you want to substitute whole-wheat bread for the sourdough, push the finished aïoli through a fine-mesh strainer to remove any chunks. This recipe yields 2 cups of aïoli, which is more than is needed for this dish. Serve the remainder with the bread, or reserve it for sandwiches. B.E.

HERB AÏOLI

$^1/_2$ cup loosely packed crustless bits of sourdough bread
$^1/_2$ cup olive oil
5 cloves garlic, minced
2 teaspoons Dijon mustard
$^1/_4$ cup loosely packed assorted fresh herbs (such as fennel frond, basil, rosemary, oregano, and sage)
$^1/_2$ cup canola oil
$^1/_2$ cup water
2 ice cubes (optional)
$^1/_2$ teaspoon salt

TURMERIC-ORANGE SAUCE

1 teaspoon olive oil
1 yellow onion, diced
1 (1-inch) piece fresh turmeric, peeled and minced, or $^1/_2$ teaspoon dried ground tumeric
2 star anise
1 teaspoon salt, plus more as needed
$^1/_4$ teaspoon freshly ground black pepper, plus more as needed
2 cups California Chardonnay or other dry white wine
3 cups fresh orange juice
Shredded zest of 1 orange
2 tablespoons all-purpose flour, dissolved in 3 tablespoons water

ASPARAGUS-RHUBARB CANNELLONI

1 tablespoon olive oil
1 tablespoon balsamic vinegar
1 tablespoon tamari
1 tablespoon Sucanat (see page 224)
$^1/_2$ teaspoon coarsely ground black pepper
1 (16-ounce) block tempeh
$^1/_2$ yellow onion, diced
$^1/_2$ cup Zinfandel or other red wine
1 cup vegetable stock (page 205)
36 asparagus spears, hard, fibrous ends removed
2 rhubarb stalks, cut into long, thin strips (12 total)
12 (4 by 6-inch) cooked fresh pasta sheets (page 208)

To make the aïoli, soak the bread in warm water for 10 minutes. Drain. Place a pot over medium heat and add a dash of the olive oil. Add three-quarters of the garlic and cook for 3 to 5 minutes, until brown and caramelized. Let cool.

Fill a chilled blender with the soaked bread, mustard, herbs, cooked and raw garlic, and the remaining olive oil. Blend on low until creamy. While the blender is running, add the canola oil and water in a slow, steady stream. Add the ice cubes only if the aïoli starts to break. Add salt to taste. (Store refrigerated for up to 3 days.)

To make the sauce, place a saucepan over medium-high heat and add the olive oil. Add the onion, turmeric, anise, salt, and pepper. Sauté for 1 to 2 minutes, until the onion is transparent. Add the wine, and bring to a boil. Decrease the heat to a simmer, and cook for 15 minutes, or until reduced by one-half. Add the orange juice and zest, and return to a boil. Whisk in the dissolved flour. Decrease the heat to low, and continue to whisk for 1 minute, or until the flour has cooked. Add salt and pepper to taste.

To make the cannelloni, preheat the oven to 400°F. In a mixing bowl, mix $^1/_2$ tablespoon of the olive oil with the vinegar, tamari, Sucanat, and black pepper. Add the tempeh and marinate for at least 20 minutes.

(continued)

ASPARAGUS-RHUBARB CANNELLONI, *continued*

Smoke the tempeh well (see page 219), for at least 30 minutes, reserving the marinade. Crumble the tempeh. In a cast-iron or heavy-bottomed skillet, heat the remaining oil over medium-high heat. Add the onion and sauté for 1 to 2 minutes, until the onion starts to soften. Add the tempeh, the reserved marinade, the red wine, and stock. Cook, stirring often, for 20 minutes, or until the liquid is well absorbed and the tempeh has the consistency of ground beef. Let cool.

Blanch the asparagus in boiling, salted water for 1 minute (see page 223). Shock in ice water and drain. Place 3 asparagus spears, 1 strip of rhubarb, and 1 heaping tablespoon of tempeh in each pasta sheet. Roll into plump cigar shapes. Put the cannelloni in a baking pan, cover with sauce, and bake for 15 minutes, or until warmed through.

To serve, place 2 cannelloni on each plate, and garnish with 2 tablespoons of the aïoli.

NUTRITIONAL INFORMATION

PER SERVING: 565 calories (43% from fat), 19.5 g protein, 57 g carbohydrate, 24 g fat, 0 mg cholesterol, 577 mg sodium, 7 g fiber

PER ½ CUP SAUCE: 110 calories (12% from fat), 1.3 g protein, 15 g carbohydrate, 1 g fat, 0 mg cholesterol, 239 mg sodium, 1.1 g fiber

PER 2 TABLESPOONS AÏOLI: 137 calories (89% from fat), 0.6 g protein, 3.2 g carbohydrate, 13 g fat, 0 mg cholesterol, 98 mg sodium, 0.2 g fiber

BLACK PEPPER LINGUINE *with* DULSE *and* HONSHIMEJI MUSHROOMS

SERVES 6

Honshimejis are a cultivated mushroom also known by the trade names of clamshell and beech. They have a pronounced seafood flavor and a crunchy texture. If you have trouble finding them, you can substitute the more common oyster mushroom. B.E.

1¹/₂ tablespoons olive oil (optional), or 1 tablespoon
    vegetable stock (page 205) for oil free
6 shallots, thinly sliced
12 ounces honshimeji mushrooms
3 cloves garlic, minced
3 teaspoons salt
1¹/₂ cups dry white wine
1¹/₂ cups vegetable stock (page 205)
¹/₄ cup cashew butter
3 teaspoons nutritional yeast (see page 224)
1 pound black pepper linguine (add 1 teaspoon
    freshly ground black pepper to the fresh pasta recipe
    on page 208), cooked (see page 208)
2 tablespoons dulse flakes, for garnish
2 tablespoons minced fresh Italian parsley, for garnish

To make the linguine, place a large skillet over medium-high heat, and add the olive oil. Add the shallots, mushrooms, garlic, and salt. Sauté for 3 minutes, or until the mushrooms are cooked. Add the white wine and vegetable stock. Bring to a boil and cook for 7 to 10 minutes, until reduced by one-half. Whisk in the cashew butter and yeast. Simmer for 1 to 2 minutes, until thick and creamy.

Toss the pasta with the sauce in the skillet. Add seasonings to taste.

To serve, divide the linguine among 6 plates, and garnish with 1 teaspoon dulse flakes and 1 teaspoon parsley.

NUTRITIONAL INFORMATION
PER SERVING: 390 calories (25% from fat), 15 g protein, 50 g carbohydrate, 9 g fat, 0 mg cholesterol, 1190 mg sodium, 3.2 g fiber

PENNE NOODLES *with* PEANUT-COCONUT SAUCE, SMOKED TOFU, *and* BROCCOLI

SERVES 4

This pasta is quick, easy, and fun to make, and it's guaranteed to please fans of Thai cooking. To adjust the spice, increase the number of chiles (we recommend extra hot!). B.E.

PEANUT-COCONUT SAUCE

1/4 cup peanut butter
3/4 cup coconut milk, or 3/4 cup rice milk plus
 1/4 teaspoon coconut extract
Juice of 3 limes
Grated zest of 3 limes
2 tablespoons coarsely chopped cilantro
2 tablespoons coarsely chopped fresh spearmint
2 teaspoons peeled and minced fresh ginger
2 cloves garlic, minced
1 jalapeño chile, plus more as needed, seeded and
 minced
1 teaspoon cumin seeds, toasted (see page 223)
1/4 teaspoon coriander, toasted (see page 223)
1/3 cup tamari

PENNE NOODLES

1 teaspoon toasted sesame oil
5 to 7 scallions, white and green parts, sliced on the
 long diagonal
2 cups broccoli florets, cut into small pieces or
 blanched (see page 223)
2 carrots, peeled and cut diagonally into matchsticks
8 ounces smoked baked tofu (see page 211), cut into
 1/2-inch dice
1 cup Chinese cabbage, shredded
1 pound penne pasta, cooked (see page 208)

1/2 cup loosely packed fresh Thai basil, for garnish
1 tablespoon sesame seeds, for garnish

To make the sauce, blend all of the ingredients in a blender until smooth.

To make the noodles, place a wok or large skillet over high heat. When extremely hot, add the sesame oil. Add the scallions, and stir-fry for 30 seconds, or until browned. Add the broccoli, carrots, and tofu, and continue to cook for 5 minutes, or until just soft. Add the cabbage, penne, and the peanut sauce. Toss to coat, stirring constantly, until heated through.

To serve, divide the pasta among 4 pasta bowls, and garnish with Thai basil and sesame seeds.

NUTRITIONAL INFORMATION

PER SERVING: 535 calories (40% from fat), 22 g protein, 62 g carbohydrate, 24 g fat, 0 mg cholesterol, 1620 mg sodium, 8.6 g fiber
PER 1/4 CUP SAUCE: 149 calories (70% from fat), 5 g protein, 6 g carbohydrate, 12 g fat, 0 mg cholesterol, 951 mg sodium, 1 g fiber

BUCKWHEAT PAPPARDELLE *with* WASABI-MISO SAUCE *and* SEA VEGETABLE SALAD

SERVES 6

This quick pasta is a playful Asian take on horseradish cream sauce. If buckwheat pappardelle is unavailable, try substituting one-third (²/₃ cup) buckwheat flour for semolina in the fresh pasta recipe (page 208), or use buckwheat soba or udon (available at most Asian groceries and health food stores). B.E.

WASABI-MISO SAUCE

2 tablespoons wasabi paste or grated fresh wasabi root

1 tablespoon peeled and grated fresh ginger

2 cloves garlic, minced

4 teaspoons granulated sugar

3 teaspoons rice vinegar

2 tablespoons light miso

1 teaspoon salt

2 teaspoons sesame oil (optional)

1 cup vegetable stock (page 205) or water

6 ounces silken tofu

SEA VEGETABLE SALAD

¹/₂ cup sea vegetable (such as sea palm, wakame, or arame), reconstituted (see page 223)

¹/₄ cup sprouts (such as mung bean, radish, onion, or sunflower)

¹/₂ carrot, peeled and shredded

1 tablespoon tamari

2 teaspoons rice vinegar

BUCKWHEAT PAPPARDELLE

2 teaspoons sesame oil, or 1 tablespoon vegetable stock (page 205) for oil free

1 leek, white and green parts, cut into thin diagonal slices

1 (8 to 10-inch-long) burdock root, halved lengthwise and cut into thin diagonal slices

1 large sweet red pepper, seeded, julienne

1 cup shiitake mushrooms, stemmed and sliced

1 pound buckwheat pappardelle, cooked (see page 208)

1 tablespoon sesame seeds, toasted (see page 223), for garnish

To make the wasabi-miso sauce, blend the ingredients in a blender until smooth.

To make the salad, in a bowl, mix together and toss all of the ingredients.

To make the pappardelle, heat a wok or sauté pan over high heat until very hot, and add the oil. Add the leeks, burdock, red pepper, and shiitakes. Stir-fry for 3 to 5 minutes, until crisp-tender. Add the pappardelle and wasabi sauce and toss to coat.

To serve, divide the pasta among 6 pasta bowls. Garnish with sesame seeds and equal parts sea vegetable salad.

NUTRITIONAL INFORMATION

PER SERVING: 366 calories (19% from fat), 15.1 g protein, 65 g carbohydrate, 8.2 g fat, 0 mg cholesterol, 880 mg sodium, 5.5 g fiber

PER ¹/₂ CUP SAUCE: 75 calories (46% from fat), 5.3 g protein, 8 g carbohydrate, 5 g fat, 0 mg cholesterol, 464 mg sodium, 0.1 g fiber

PER ¹/₄ CUP SALAD: 7.5 calories (3.2% from fat), 0.6 g protein, 1.5 g carbohydrate, 0.1 g fat, 0 mg cholesterol, 171 mg sodium, 0.4 g fiber

ROASTED BEET LASAGNETTE *with* TAHINI CRÈME, TOFU RICOTTA, *and* GREMOLATA

SERVES 6

My mother used to prepare an American classic, Harvard beets, as one of many vegetable sides to accompany the Sunday roast. Consequently, I grew up loving and looking forward to this sweet, succulent root vegetable. I was surprised later to find that not everyone shares my fond appreciation. Beets add rich depth of flavor, beautiful color, and a firm, agreeable texture to any meal. B.E.

TOFU RICOTTA

8 ounces firm tofu
2 tablespoons tahini
1 teaspoon umeboshi vinegar
1 teaspoon nutritional yeast (see page 224)
1 teaspoon light miso

LEMON, DILL, AND PINE NUT GREMOLATA

$1/4$ cup pine nuts, toasted (see page 222) and coarsely chopped
Grated zest of 2 lemons
$1/4$ cup fresh dill, stemmed and coarsely chopped

ROASTED BEET LASAGNETTE FILLING

$1^1/2$ bunches baby red beets (12 to 14 small beets), quartered, greens removed and reserved
2 spring onions, whites only, cut in half lengthwise and thinly sliced
1 teaspoon balsamic vinegar
1 teaspoon Sucanat (see page 224)
1 teaspoon tamari
$1/4$ teaspoon dill seeds
$1/4$ teaspoon ground allspice
1 teaspoon salt
$1/4$ teaspoon freshly ground black pepper
$1/2$ teaspoon olive oil

TAHINI CRÈME WITH PEAS AND MORELS

$3/4$ cup tahini
Juice of 2 lemons
1 small white onion, cut into $1/4$-inch dice

3 cloves garlic, minced
$1/4$ teaspoon cumin seeds, toasted (see page 223) and ground
$1/4$ teaspoon coriander seeds, toasted (see page 223) and ground
$1/8$ teaspoon fenugreek seeds, ground
1 teaspoon salt
$1^1/2$ cups vegetable stock (page 205)
$1/4$ cup fresh English peas
1 teaspoon olive oil
1 cup morel mushrooms, cleaned and sliced into rounds

18 (3 by 3-inch) cooked fresh pasta sheets (page 208)

To make the ricotta, combine all of the ingredients in a bowl. Mix well using clean hands until thoroughly combined. Blend half of the mixture in a food processor fitted with the metal blade. Return the mixture to the bowl, and fold in. Cover and refrigerate for 1 hour to overnight.

To make the gremolata, combine all of the ingredients. Set aside for up to 2 hours.

To make the lasagnette filling, preheat the oven to 400°F. Add all of the ingredients to a mixing bowl and stir to combine. Spread the mixture evenly on a small baking sheet or in a baking dish. Cover with aluminum foil and roast for 30 to 45 minutes, uncovering for the last 10 minutes, until the beets are fork-tender.

To make the crème, place the tahini, lemon juice, half of the onion, half of the garlic, the cumin, coriander, fenugreek, salt, and stock in a blender. Blend until smooth.

Blanch the peas for 30 to 40 seconds (see page 223). Shock in ice water, drain, and let cool.

Place a saucepan over medium-high heat and add the olive oil. Add the remaining onion and garlic and sauté for 1 to 2 minutes, until soft. Add the peas and morels and sauté for 2 minutes, or until the morels are well cooked. (Undercooked morels may cause digestive distress.) Stir in the tahini crème and cook until just warmed through (do not boil or the sauce will curdle and may lose its creamy color).

To serve, spoon equal parts of the crème onto 6 plates or pasta bowls. On each plate, layer 1 sheet pasta, 2 tablespoons warm tofu ricotta, and 1/4 cup (or one-twelfth) of the roasted beets. Repeat this process for the second layer, working quickly to prevent cooling. Top with a pasta sheet and the gremolata. (If necessary, reheat the lasagnettes briefly in the oven before adding the gremolata.) Serve immediately.

NUTRITIONAL INFORMATION

PER LASAGNETTE: 478 calories (60% from fat), 18 g protein, 52 g carbohydrate, 23 g fat, 0 mg cholesterol, 1029 mg sodium, 7.3 g fiber

PER 2 TABLESPOONS TOFU RICOTTA: 46 calories (60% from fat), 3.2 g protein, 1.7 g carbohydrate, 3.3 g fat, 0 mg cholesterol, 160 mg sodium, 0.6 g fiber

PER 1/2 CUP CRÈME: 204 calories (67% from fat), 6.3 g protein, 11 g carbohydrate, 16 g fat, 0 mg cholesterol, 318 mg sodium, 2.2 g fiber

PER 1 TABLESPOON GREMOLATA: 35 calories (74% from fat), 1.6 g protein, 1.1 g carbohydrate, 3 g fat, 0 mg cholesterol, 0 mg sodium, 0.4 g fiber

Swiss Chard Cannelloni *with* Smoked Cherries *and* Parsnip Cream

SERVES 6

Chard is related to the beet and is sometimes referred to as beet spinach. It is larger and more leathery than spinach, however, and comes in a beautiful array of colors. In California, organically grown chard is available almost year-round. We love to show it off in late fall and winter, when other colorful vegetables have started to wane. The smoked cherries in this dish make it an excellent match for a jammy California red Zinfandel or a French Carignan. The caramelized garlic can be made up to 2 days ahead of time and kept in the refrigerator, but serve at room temperature or slightly warm. B.E.

CARAMELIZED GARLIC

1 teaspoon olive oil
20 whole cloves garlic, peeled
1 teaspoon tamari
Grated zest of 1 orange
2 cups roasted vegetable dark stock (page 207), or 2 cups vegetable stock (page 205) plus 1 teaspoon molasses

PARSNIP CREAM

1/4 cup cashews
2 cups vegetable stock (page 205), or 1 cup water plus 1 cup vegetable stock
1 teaspoon olive oil, or dry sherry for oil free
3 shallots
2 parsnips, peeled and diced
1 clove garlic, minced
1/4 teaspoon salt, plus more as needed
1/8 teaspoon white pepper, plus more as needed
1 cup dry white wine
Pinch of grated nutmeg
1 teaspoon nutritional yeast (see page 224)
2 tablespoons dry sherry

BREADCRUMBS

2 slices crusty whole-wheat bread
1/2 teaspoon olive oil (optional)
1 teaspoon pine nuts, toasted (see page 222; optional)

Pinch of grated nutmeg
1/2 teaspoon dried thyme

SWISS CHARD CANNELLONI

1/2 cup dried cherries
1 teaspoon olive oil
1 large sweet onion, cut into 1/4-inch-thick wedges
2 cloves garlic, minced
2 teaspoons salt
1/4 teaspoon freshly ground black pepper
1/4 teaspoon coriander, toasted (see page 223) and ground
1/4 teaspoon fennel seeds, toasted (see page 223) and ground
1/2 teaspoon dried oregano
8 cups loosely packed Swiss chard, stemmed and cut into 1-inch-long strips
1/4 cup slivered almonds, toasted (see page 222)
12 (4 by 6-inch) cooked fresh pasta sheets (page 208)

1 tablespoon aromatic herbs (such as thyme, rosemary, and sage), finely minced, for garnish

To make the garlic, preheat the oven to 350°F. Heat a heavy-bottomed oven-proof pan over high heat until very hot. Carefully add the oil and garlic and sear for about 1 minute. Add the tamari, zest, and stock and cover. Bake for 1 hour, or until the garlic is soft and caramelized and the liquid is just syrupy. Remove from the oven, and let cool, reserving the syrup.

To make the cream, in a blender, blend the cashews with 1 cup of the stock until creamy.

Heat the oil in a pot over medium-high heat. Add the shallots, parsnips, garlic, salt, and white pepper. Sauté for 1 to 2 minutes, until soft. Add the white wine and the remaining 1 cup stock, and cook for 15 to 20 minutes, until reduced by half. Whisk in the cashew crème, nutmeg, and yeast. Decrease the heat to a simmer, and simmer for 2 minutes, or until the cashews just begin to thicken the sauce. Add the sherry, and add salt and white pepper to taste. Using a blender or a handheld immersion blender, blend the sauce until smooth. Strain if necessary.

To make the breadcrumbs, toast the bread until dry. Combine with the olive oil, pine nuts, nutmeg, and thyme in a food processor fitted with the metal blade to form a coarse meal.

To make the cannelloni, tie the cherries up in cheesecloth. Reconstitute them in warm water or stock for 15 minutes. Smoke the cherries for 30 minutes (see page 219) while preparing the rest of the filling.

Heat the olive oil in a pan over medium-high heat. Add the onion, garlic, salt, black pepper, coriander, fennel, and oregano. Cook for 2 to 3 minutes, until the onion and garlic are soft but not falling apart. Let cool.

Place a pan over medium heat and add salted water 1/4-inch deep. Add the chard, cover, and steam for 5 to 7 minutes, until soft. Drain well, and add to the cooling onions. Add the toasted almonds and smoked cherries. Combine with the onion and garlic mixture. Let cool.

Preheat oven to 500°F. Lightly oil an ovenproof pan. Place 3 to 4 tablespoons of filling into each pasta sheet, and roll into plump cigar shapes. Place the rolled cannellonis in the ovenproof pan, cover with the parsnip cream, and bake for 10 minutes, or until heated through. Cover the cannelloni with the breadcrumbs, and bake for 5 minutes, or until the crumbs brown.

To serve, place 2 cannelloni on each plate and garnish with caramelized garlic. Drizzle with some of the reserved caramelized garlic syrup and sprinkle with aromatic herbs.

NUTRITIONAL INFORMATION

PER 2 CANNELLONI: 393 calories (25% from fat), 11.7 g protein, 60 g carbohydrate, 8.4 g fat, 0 mg cholesterol, 980 mg sodium, 8 g fiber

PER 1/3 CUP CREAM: 104 calories (35% from fat), 1.7 g protein, 10 g carbohydrate, 3 g fat, 0 mg cholesterol, 75 mg sodium, 2.4 g fiber

PER TABLESPOON BREADCRUMBS: 14 calories (26% from fat), 0.5 g protein, 2.3 g carbohydrate, 0.5 g fat, 0 mg cholesterol, 26 mg sodium, 0.4 g fiber

PER 2 TABLESPOONS GARLIC: 37 calories (22% from fat), 1.2 g protein, 5.6 g carbohydrate, 0.9 g fat, 0 mg cholesterol, 59 mg sodium, 0.4 g fiber

SAMOSA RAVIOLI *with* BEET-TAMARIND CHUTNEY

SERVES 6

This is our version of an Indian samosa pastry turned into a ravioli with fresh fennel pasta. We make basic pasta (page 208) with ground fennel seeds and fennel fronds. The chutney alone is reason enough to try this recipe—it's that addictive! E.T.

BEET-TAMARIND CHUTNEY

3 red beets, peeled and cut into small dice
1/2 red onion, cut into small dice
1 jalapeño chile, seeded and minced
1/2 cup tamarind purée
2 tablespoons agave nectar (see page 224)
1/4 cup champagne vinegar
Salt

SAMOSA RAVIOLI

4 yellow Finn potatoes, cut into 1/4-inch dice
2 tablespoons canola oil
1/2 yellow onion, cut into 1/4-inch dice
2 cloves garlic, minced
1/2 teaspoon mustard seeds
1 teaspoon whole cumin seeds
1/4 teaspoon ground cardamom
1/4 teaspoon ground turmeric
1 cup fresh or frozen peas
1/2 cup dried sour cherries or dried cranberries
2 tablespoons chopped cilantro
Salt and freshly ground black pepper
1 recipe fresh fennel pasta sheets (page 208), cut into 24 (3-inch-diameter) rounds
3/4 cup cucumber raita (page 214)
Cilantro leaves, for garnish

To make the chutney, blanch the beets until cooked through but al dente (see page 223). Remove from the heat and shock in ice water. Drain and reserve. Combine the beets with the onion, jalapeño, tamarind purée, agave, and vinegar. Add salt to taste.

To make the ravioli filling, bring 2 quarts of water to a boil in a 4-quart saucepan. Blanch the yellow Finn potatoes for 4 to 5 minutes, until cooked through but al dente (see page 223). Drain and let cool.

Heat the oil in a large sauté pan over medium heat. Add the onion and garlic, and sauté for 2 minutes, or until just wilted. Add the mustard, cumin, cardamom, and turmeric. Sauté for 2 minutes, or until the mustard seeds start to pop. Add the potatoes, followed by the peas. Sauté, stirring often, for 5 minutes, or until heated through. Add the dried cherries, followed by the cilantro. Remove from the heat. Add salt and pepper to taste.

To make the ravioli, place a round of pasta on a flat surface. Add 2 to 3 tablespoons of the filling. Cover with a second sheet of pasta and crimp the edges with a fork until tightly sealed. Repeat with the remaining pasta rounds to make 12 ravioli.

In a pot, bring 1 gallon of salted water to a boil, and add the ravioli. Cook for 3 minutes, or until the ravioli float to the surface. If you like your ravioli with a crispy shell, at this point place them in a large skillet with 2 teaspoons canola oil over medium-high heat and sauté for 2 minutes per side, or until crisp.

To serve, place 2 ravioli on each of 6 plates. Add a dollop of beet chutney, followed by 2 tablespoons of raita. Garnish with cilantro.

NUTRITIONAL INFORMATION

PER SERVING: 173 calories (13% from fat), 5 g protein, 32 g carbohydrate, 2.7 g fat, 0 mg cholesterol, 64 mg sodium, 3 g fiber

PER 2 TABLESPOONS CHUTNEY: 18 calories (1.7% from fat), 0.3 g protein, 4.8 g carbohydrate, 0.1 g fat, 0 mg cholesterol, 7 mg sodium, 0.5 g fiber

ENTRÉES

All of these entrées are based on cuisine with rustic ethnic origins, dishes like tamales, bean stews, Thai curry, vegetable tagine. What transforms them into haute cuisine is our interpretation: we present a phyllo-wrapped huitlacoche-stuffed tamale; a crisp quinoa cake over a hauntingly smoky Caribbean bean stew; a Thai curry stacked between sesame wafers; a sweet onion stuffed with a cinnamon-spiked mix of roast vegetables. We round out the chapter with a few hearty sandwiches from our Southern Comfort Dinner menu and staff lunches. You'll want to kick back in a recliner with a long neck and watch a Bowl game with one of these babies.

We will separate, contrast, balance, and mirror elements on the plate so they remain distinct, letting the diner recombine them with every forkful, making every bite that much more interesting. We arrange the elements beautifully on the plate with an eye for color and balance. Do you need to go through all of this at home when you prepare these dishes? Maybe not, but I encourage you to try preparing these dishes as we intend so you can understand why we designed them the way we did. I also encourage you to dissect our dissections, to take apart our dishes, simplify them, and make them a part of your culinary repertoire. Capture their essence, and make them your own.

Tamarind and Cardamom–Glazed Tofu Brochette over Zucchini
Cake with Butternut Squash Baduche *ᵍ* 130

Black Quinoa Cake over Smoky Calypso Bean Sauce, Curried
Squash, and Mango-Habanero-Coconut Sauce *ᵍ* 132

Socca Rustica with Chickpea Sangiovese Stew and
Preserved Orange–Olive Relish *ᵍ* 134

Asian Rice Flour Crêpes Filled with Eggplant and
Shiitake Mushrooms over Edamame Sauce *ᵍ* 136

Korean-Style Barbecued Tempeh over Rice Noodle Salad
with Citrus and Kimchee *ᵍ* 138

The Asian Napoleon *ᵍ* 140

Celery Root Ravioli Stuffed with Beets and Matsutake Mushrooms
in a Lobster Mushroom Crème *ᵍ* 142

Root Vegetable Ravioli with Portobello Mushroom Pâté and
Sweet Pepper–Olive Tapenade *ᵍ* 145

Portobello Carpaccio over Carrot and Parsnip Fettuccine with
Raw Pumpkin Seed–Ancho Chile Pesto *ᵍ* 147

Creole Sautéed Mushrooms and Kidney Beans over
Pecan Dirty Rice *ᵍ* 148

Asian-Style Smoked Tofu and Marinated Cabbage Lavash *ᵍ* 150

Oyster Mushroom and Tofu Rémoulade Poorboy *ᵍ* 151

African Teff Cakes with Fava–Wild Mushroom Wat
and Carrot-Chile Chutney *ᵍ* 152

Sloppy Jose *ᵍ* 155

Cajun-Crusted Tempeh with Lemon-Caper-Dill Cream, and Braised
Collard Greens *ᵍ* 156

Fauxlet au Poivre with Syrah Jus, Chicory and Smoked Cherries, and
Roasted Potatoes and Roots *ᵍ* 158

Feijoada with Crispy Yuca Cakes *ᵍ* 160

Smoked Tempeh and Eggplant Muffaletta with Olive and
Cucumber Relish ❧ 161

Huitlacoche-Polenta Roulades with Chocolate Mole
and Carrot-Habanero Sauce ❧ 162

Black Chanterelles en Papillote with Toasted Barley Risotto, Beet-
Cabernet Truffle Foam, and Braised Celery Hearts ❧ 164

Stuffed Poblano Chiles over Forbidden Black Rice Risotto with
Roasted Corn–Avocado Abdi ❧ 167

WHITE BEAN–FILLED PHYLLO PURSE *over* SOFT GARLIC POLENTA *with* PORCINI-ZINFANDEL SAUCE, BROCCOLI RABE, *and* GRILLED PEAR

SERVES 8

This rich and satisfying fall dish with Tuscan roots will make a great centerpiece for any holiday dinner—especially if you want to impress a doubting carnivore. Substitute portobellos in the sauce if the fresh porcini are unavailable, but do not skimp on the porcini stock. The purse filling works well with a variety of mushrooms, so work with whatever is readily available and suits your taste. Take the dish over the top by adding a little truffle oil to the filling. Serve with a contrast of bitter grilled broccoli rabe and sweet grilled pear. E.T.

PORCINI-ZINFANDEL SAUCE

1 tablespoon extra virgin olive oil
12 shallots, cut into small dice
4 cloves garlic, minced
16 ounces porcini mushrooms, diced
1/4 teaspoon salt
1 teaspoon Sucanat (see page 224)
1/2 teaspoon dried thyme
2 teaspoons minced fresh rosemary
2 bay leaves
1 1/2 cups Zinfandel
3 cups mushroom stock (page 206) or roasted vegetable dark stock (page 207)
1 tablespoon tamari
1 tablespoon balsamic vinegar
2 tablespoons all-purpose flour
3 tablespoons vegetable oil
Salt and freshly ground black pepper

SOFT GARLIC POLENTA

4 cups water or vegetable stock (page 205)
1 cup dried polenta
1/4 cup Millennium Oil-Braised Garlic (page 212), or 8 cloves garlic, coarsely chopped and sautéed in 2 tablespoons olive oil until lightly browned
1/4 cup cashew cream (page 212)
1 teaspoon nutritional yeast (see page 224)
2 teaspoons fresh sage chiffonade
1/2 teaspoon salt

PURSE

1 tablespoon extra virgin olive oil
1/2 yellow onion, cut into small dice
2 cloves garlic, minced
1 carrot, peeled and cut into small dice
1 fennel bulb, cut into small dice
1/4 teaspoon dried thyme
1 teaspoon minced fresh sage
16 ounces assorted fresh mushrooms (such as chanterelles, shiitakes, and cremini), thickly sliced
2 tablespoons Marsala, Madeira, or sherry
2 cups cooked white cannellini beans (see page 220)
1/2 cup vegetable stock (page 205) or cooking liquid from the beans
1 cup diced Spicy Fennel Seitan Sausage (page 210), or 1 (8-ounce) package Italian-style vegan sausage, diced (optional)
1/4 teaspoon ground nutmeg
Salt and freshly ground black pepper
White or black truffle oil (optional)
12 (13 by 18-inch) sheets whole-wheat phyllo dough
Vegetable oil, for brushing

GRILLED BROCCOLI RABE

4 tablespoons balsamic vinegar
1 teaspoon chopped garlic
2 teaspoons olive oil
8 small heads broccoli rabe
1/4 teaspoon salt
Freshly ground black pepper

GRILLED PEARS

2 Bosc pears, cut into 4 slices each
2 tablespoons balsamic vinegar
2 tablespoons olive oil

To make the sauce, heat the olive oil in a saucepan over medium heat. Add the shallots and garlic, and cook, stirring often, for 12 to 15 minutes, until lightly caramelized. Add the mushrooms and salt. Cook, stirring often, for 5 to 7 minutes, until the mushrooms

(continued)

WHITE BEAN–FILLED PHYLLO PURSE, *continued*

are dry and browned. Add the Sucanat, and cook for 2 minutes, or until caramelized. Add the thyme, rosemary, and bay leaves. Add the wine and stir to scrape up the caramelized shallots from the bottom of the saucepan. Add the stock, tamari, and balsamic vinegar. Decrease the heat to medium-low and cook for 15 to 20 minutes, until reduced by one-half.

In a small saucepan, whisk together the flour and the vegetable oil to form a roux. Cook over medium-low heat, stirring often, for 15 minutes, or until the roux is dark amber in color. Remove from the heat and let cool to close to room temperature before using.

Slowly whisk the roux into the reduced sauce, using only one-half to two-thirds of the mixture. Simmer for 5 minutes, then check to see if it will coat the back of a spoon. If needed, add the remaining roux and simmer for another 5 minutes. Remove and discard the bay leaves, and add the salt and pepper to taste. Remove from the heat.

To make the polenta, heat the water to a boil in a saucepan. Whisk in the polenta. Decrease the heat to medium-low and cook the polenta, stirring often for 15 to 20 minutes, until it is thick and pulls away from the side of the pan. Remove from the heat and stir in the garlic, followed by the cashew cream. Add the yeast, sage, and salt. Set aside.

To make the purse filling, preheat the oven to 350°F. Heat the oil in a large skillet over medium-high heat. Add the onions, garlic, carrots, and fennel, and sauté for 7 minutes, or until lightly browned. Add the thyme, sage, and mushrooms, and sauté for about 2 minutes. Add the Marsala and stir to scrape up the browned bits from the bottom of the skillet. Add the stock and sausage, and simmer for 10 minutes, or until the mixture is dry. Remove from the heat. Add the nutmeg, and season with salt and pepper to taste. Let cool to room temperature, and then add the truffle oil.

To make the purses, place 2 sheets of phyllo on a dry work surface and brush the top sheet with vegetable oil.

Repeat the procedure two more times, using 6 sheets of phyllo total. Cut the stack of phyllo in half lengthwise and then in half crosswise to yield 4 equal squares. Repeat with the remaining 6 sheets of dough.

Line a baking sheet with parchment paper. Place 1/2 cup of the filling in the center of each phyllo square. Bring up the edges to meet in the center over the filling and squeeze and twist the ends together to form a bundle. Place on the baking sheet. Repeat with the remaining 7 squares, to yield a total of 8 purses. Bake for 25 minutes, or until lightly browned.

To grill the broccoli rabe, preheat the grill. Place all of the ingredients in a bowl and toss together. Grill the rabe for 1 1/2 minutes per side, or until wilted and slightly charred.

To grill the pears, preheat the grill. Place the pears, balsamic, and olive oil in a bowl and toss together. Grill the pears for 2 minutes per side, or until nice grill marks form.

To serve, place 1/4 cup of sauce on the bottom of a plate. Place 1/2 cup of the soft polenta in a mound in the center of the plate. Place a purse on top of the polenta, with some broccoli rabe off to the side. Lean a slice of the grilled pear against the broccoli rabe.

NUTRITIONAL INFORMATION

PER PURSE: 261 calories (24% from fat), 12.8 g protein, 38 g carbohydrate, 6.7 g fat, 0 mg cholesterol, 465 mg sodium, 6 g fiber

PER 1/4 CUP SAUCE: 76 calories (31% from fat), 1.5 g protein, 12 g carbohydrate, 2.5 g fat, 0 mg cholesterol, 111 mg sodium, 1 g fiber

PER 1/2 CUP POLENTA: 118 calories (31% from fat), 2.7 g protein, 17 g carbohydrate, 4 g fat, 0 mg cholesterol, 132 mg sodium, 2.5 g fiber

PER SERVING BROCCOLI RABE: 53 calories (22% from fat), 4.5 g protein, 8.3 g carbohydrate, 1.7 g fat, 0 mg cholesterol, 100 mg sodium, 46 g fiber

PER SERVING PEARS: 51 calories (58% from fat), 0.1 g protein, 5.6 g carbohydrate, 3.5 g fat, 0 mg cholesterol, 0 mg sodium, 0.8 g fiber

Heirloom Tomatoes Stuffed *with* Red Lentil Hummus *and* Basil *with* Sprouted Quinoa–Corn Guacamole

SERVES 6

This raw summer entrée will appeal to anyone who likes fresh tomatoes, basil, hummus, and guacamole. Prepare a couple of days ahead to sprout the quinoa and soak the lentils. If you are short on time, substitute cooked quinoa and cooked lentils or chickpeas. E.T.

GUACAMOLE

Kernels from 1 ear corn
2 scallions, white and green parts, thinly sliced
1/2 English cucumber, seeded and diced
1/2 jalapeño chile, seeded and diced
2 avocados, peeled, pitted, and diced
Juice of 1 lemon
2 tablespoons chopped fresh cilantro leaves
1/2 cup sprouted quinoa (see page 223)
Salt

RAW RED LENTIL HUMMUS

1 cup dried red lentils, soaked (see page 220)
1/3 cup tahini
2 cloves garlic, minced
1 teaspoon ground cumin
1/2 teaspoon ground coriander
1/3 jalapeño chile, seeded
2 teaspoons light miso
1 tablespoon extra virgin olive oil
Salt and freshly ground black pepper

BASIL-CASHEW SOUR CRÈME

1/2 cup unsalted cashews
Juice of 1 lemon
1 cup fresh basil leaves
1/4 teaspoon salt
2/3 cup water, plus more as needed

6 ripe heirloom tomatoes (any variety)
Salt
1/2 head radicchio, finely shredded
1/2 bunch fresh Genovese, purple, or lemon basil leaves
Assorted fresh herbs (such as oregano and thyme)
2 tablespoons sprouted quinoa (see page 223)
6 tablespoons finely diced seeded tomato or watermelon, for garnish

To make the guacamole, combine all of the ingredients in a bowl.

To make the hummus, combine the lentils, tahini, garlic, cumin, coriander, jalapeño, miso, and olive oil in a food processor fitted with the metal blade. Process to a smooth, spreadable consistency, adding water if the mixture seems too thick. Season with salt and pepper to taste. (Store refrigerated for up to 4 days.)

To make the crème, combine the cashews, lemon juice, basil leaves, and salt in a blender with just enough water to cover. Begin blending. When the mixture seizes up, slowly add the remaining water to achieve a pourable consistency.

To serve, slice each tomato into 4 slices of equal width. Season each slice with a pinch of salt.

Drizzle 2 tablespoons of the crème in a spiral pattern over each dinner plate. Place a small mound of the shredded radicchio in the center of the plate. Place 1 tomato slice on top of the radicchio. Spoon about 2 teaspoons of the hummus on the tomato slice. Sprinkle a few basil leaves and some of the herbs over the hummus. Repeat two more times, finishing with the last tomato slice on top.

Place 3 guacamole mounds around the tomato. Sprinkle the rim of the plate with 1 teaspoon of the sprouted quinoa and with chopped tomato.

NUTRITIONAL INFORMATION

PER SERVING: 274 calories (43% from fat), 10.3 g protein, 31 g carbohydrate, 14 g fat, 0 mg cholesterol, 86 mg sodium, 9.2 g fiber

PER 2 TABLESPOONS CRÈME: 24 calories (67% from fat), 0.7 g protein, 1.4 g carbohydrate, 2 g fat, 0 mg cholesterol, 30 mg sodium, 0.4 g fiber

PER SERVING GUACAMOLE: 117 calories (50% from fat), 2.6 g protein, 13 g carbohydrate, 7.1 g fat, 0 mg cholesterol, 7g sodium, 2.1 fiber

Pumpkin Seed–Crusted Portobello Potato Salad *with* Grapefruit Mojo, Jicama-Citrus Salad, *and* Prickly Pear Paint

SERVES 4

Portobello Potato Salad has been on our menu in at least half a dozen variations over the past four years. The gist is that you have a crisp-crunchy pan-fried smoked portobello mushroom atop flavorful roasted potatoes, balanced out with a cool, usually citrus-based salad and some sort of spicy dressing for dipping. This version has a Latin spin with its mojo, pumpkin seed crust, and spicy prickly pear sauce. Look for prickly pear purée in Hispanic markets.

If you decide not to smoke the mushrooms, be sure to at least braise them to cook through. Also feel free to grill or broil the mushrooms without the crust for a lighter and lower fat variation. E.T.

GRAPEFRUIT MOJO

4 cloves garlic, minced
2 teaspoons coarsely ground cumin seeds
1/2 jalapeño or serrano chile
1 teaspoon light miso
1/4 teaspoon salt
2/3 cup freshly squeezed grapefruit juice
Juice of 3 limes

PRICKLY PEAR PAINT

1/3 cup prickly pear purée
1 tablespoon chipotle paste (page 214), or
  2 reconstituted chipotle chiles
1/4 cup water
Salt

JICAMA-CITRUS SALAD

1 grapefruit
2 oranges, mandarins, or tangelos
1 lime
1 jicama, peeled and cut into 1/2-inch dice (11/2 cups)
1 cup cooked black-eyed peas
1/4 cup fresh mint chiffonade
2 tablespoons tightly packed whole cilantro leaves
Salt

ROASTED YUKON GOLD POTATOES

1 pound Yukon Gold, yellow Finn, or German Butterball potatoes, washed and cut into 1/2-inch dice
2 tablespoons extra virgin olive oil
2 cloves garlic, minced
1 teaspoon whole cumin seeds
Salt and freshly ground black pepper

PUMPKIN SEED–CRUSTED PORTOBELLOS

2 cups corn flour
11/2 cups raw pumpkin seeds, coarsely ground
1 dried ancho chile, toasted (see page 222) and
  coarsely ground in a spice mill or coffee grinder
2 teaspoons cumin seeds
1 teaspoon Spanish paprika
1/2 teaspoon dried oregano
1 teaspoon salt
4 portobello mushrooms, smoked (see page 219)
1/4 cup tofu aïoli (page 213), or 1/2 cup soy milk combined with 2 teaspoons Dijon mustard
Vegetable oil

2 cups baby arugula or baby spinach
1/4 cup cilantro oil (page 215), for garnish

To make the mojo, dry-sauté the garlic in a nonstick sauté pan over medium heat, stirring often, for 1 to 2 minutes, until just golden. Add the cumin and chile, and sauté for 1 minute. Remove from the heat and let cool to room temperature. In a blender, combine the garlic-chile mixture with the miso, salt, grapefruit juice, and lime juice. Blend until smooth. (Store refrigerated for up to 1 week.)

To make the paint, combine all of the ingredients in a blender. Purée until thoroughly blended.

To make the salad, with a sharp knife, cut the rinds off the grapefruit, oranges, and lime, exposing the flesh. Be sure to cut away any remaining white pith. Remove the segments of all of the citrus by cutting the flesh away from the membranes. Place the segments in a mixing bowl with all of the accumulated juice. Add the jicama, black-eyed peas, mint, and cilantro. Mix well, and add salt to taste.

To make the potatoes, preheat the oven to 400°F. Place the potatoes in a large bowl with the olive oil, garlic, cumin, salt, and pepper. Toss together. Place the seasoned potatoes on a roasting pan or baking sheet. Roast in the oven for 25 minutes, or until crisp and cooked through. Keep warm until needed.

To make the mushrooms, combine the corn flour, pumpkin seeds, chile, cumin, paprika, oregano, and salt in a mixing bowl.

Place the mushrooms in the dredge. Dip them in the tofu aïoli and then place them back in the dredge.

Add enough vegetable oil to cover the bottom of a large, nonstick skillet and heat over high heat. When the oil is very hot, place the portobellos in the skillet, cap side down. Sauté for 2 minutes per side, or until the crust is golden brown. Transfer to a bowl away from the heat, and keep warm.

To make the wilted greens, drain the oil out of the sauté pan. Place the pan back over high heat. Add the arugula with 1/4 cup of the grapefruit mojo. Toss the greens and dressing together in the pan, or until the greens are coated with dressing and just wilted.

To serve, place 1/2 cup of the jicama salad in the center of each plate. Mound about 1 cup of the potatoes over the jicama salad, and top with one-quarter of the wilted greens.

Thinly slice each portobello mushroom three-quarters of the way through on the diagonal. Place 1 of the sliced portobello mushrooms over the greens on each plate. Drizzle the plate with 3 tablespoons of the grapefruit mojo, 1 teaspoon of the cilantro oil, and 1 to 2 tablespoons of the prickly pear paint.

NUTRITIONAL INFORMATION

PER SERVING DREDGED PORTOBELLOS: 120 calories (69% from fat), 1.4 g protein, 8.2 g carbohydrate, 9.6 g fat, 0 mg cholesterol, 69 mg sodium, 1.6 g fiber

PER SERVING POTATOES: 132 calories (46% from fat), 2 g protein, 16 g carbohydrate, 7 g fat, 0 mg cholesterol, 7 mg sodium, 1.5 g fiber

PER 1/2 CUP JICAMA-CITRUS SALAD: 143 (2.9% from fat), 7 g protein, 28 g carbohydrate, 0.5 g fat, 0 mg cholesterol, 7 mg sodium, 6.2 g fiber

PER 3 TABLESPOONS MOJO: 27 calories (8% from fat), 0.7 g protein, 6 g carbohydrate, 0.3 g fat, 0 mg cholesterol, 129 mg sodium, 0.6 g fiber

PER 2 TABLESPOONS PAINT: 10 calories (9% from fat), 0.2 g protein, 2.3 g carbohydrate, 0.1 g fat, 0 mg cholesterol, 4 mg sodium, 0.8 g fiber

MILLET-BERBER–CRUSTED PORTOBELLO POTATO SALAD
with PEANUT SAUCE *and* PAPAYA-LEMON VINAIGRETTE

SERVES 4

This version of our Portobello Potato Salad takes an East African slant. Although the combination of elements on the plate is hardly authentic, the seasoning of the different components and the use of millet in the crust hold to African culinary roots. Feel free to play around with different components as the salad is based on the seasons. Try this dish with marinated tempeh, tofu, or seitan to replace the mushroom. E.T.

AFRICAN-STYLE PEANUT SAUCE

1 dried ancho chile, toasted (see page 222), seeded, and ground in a spice mill or coffee grinder
1 teaspoon cumin seeds, toasted (see page 223) and ground
1/2 teaspoon caraway seeds, toasted (see page 223) and ground
1 teaspoon coriander seeds, toasted (see page 223) and ground
6 cloves garlic, minced
1 teaspoon Spanish paprika
2 tablespoons tomato paste
1/2 cup smooth peanut butter
2 tablespoons rice vinegar
2 tablespoons tamari
1 cup water, or as needed
1/2 teaspoon salt

PAPAYA-LEMON VINAIGRETTE

1/2 ripe papaya, peeled and seeded
Juice of 3 lemons
1/2 cup water
Pinch of salt

CARAWAY ROASTED YAM AND POTATOES

3 Yukon Gold potatoes, cut into 1/2-inch dice
1 large garnet yam, cut into 1/2-inch dice
1 teaspoon crushed caraway seeds
1 1/2 teaspoons dried spearmint
4 cloves garlic, minced
1/2 teaspoon salt
2 tablespoons extra virgin olive oil

BERBER-MILLET–CRUSTED PORTOBELLOS

1 teaspoon allspice berries
1/2 cinnamon stick
2 tablespoons cumin seeds
2 tablespoons coriander seeds
1 teaspoon fenugreek
1 teaspoon whole cloves
1 teaspoon cardamom seeds
1 teaspoon ground ginger
1/2 teaspoon crushed red pepper flakes
1 teaspoon Spanish paprika
1/2 teaspoon freshly ground black pepper
2 cups millet flour
1 cup whole millet
1 1/2 teaspoons salt
4 portobello mushrooms, smoked (see page 219)
1/4 cup tofu aïoli (page 213), or 1/2 cup soy milk combined with 2 teaspoons Dijon mustard
Vegetable oil

2 cups baby arugula or baby spinach
2 cups Jicama-Citrus Salad (page 122)
2 tablespoons fresh mint, chiffonade, for garnish
1 cup cherry tomatoes (such as Sweet 100s), for garnish

To make the peanut sauce, combine all of the ingredients in a blender, and blend until smooth. The dressing should be a little thicker than heavy cream.

To make the vinaigrette, combine all of the ingredients in a blender, and blend until smooth.

To make the potatoes, preheat the oven to 400°F. Place the potatoes and yam in a mixing bowl. Add the caraway, spearmint, garlic, salt, and olive oil. Toss well. Spread on a baking sheet and bake for 20 to 25 minutes, stirring after the first 10 minutes, until lightly browned and crisp-tender. Keep warm until needed.

To make the mushrooms, grind the allspice, cinnamon, cumin, coriander, fenugreek, clove, cardamom, ginger, pepper flakes, paprika, and pepper in a spice grinder or coffee mill, leaving some of the spices coarsely ground. Combine this spice mix with the flour, millet, and salt in a bowl.

Place the mushrooms in the millet dredge. Dip them in the tofu aïoli and then back in the millet dredge.

Add enough vegetable oil to cover the bottom a large, nonstick skillet and heat over high heat. When the oil is very hot, place the portobellos in the skillet, cap side down. Sauté for 2 minutes per side, or until the crust is golden brown. Transfer to a bowl and keep warm.

To make the wilted greens, drain the oil from the sauté pan and return the pan back to the heat. Add the arugula with $^{1}/_{4}$ cup of the papaya vinaigrette. Toss the greens and dressing together in the pan until the greens are coated with the dressing and just wilted.

To serve, place $^{1}/_{2}$ cup of the jicama salad in the center of each plate. Mound about 1 cup of the potatoes over the jicama salad and top with one-quarter of the wilted greens.

Thinly slice each portobello mushroom three-quarters of the way through on the diagonal. Place 1 of the sliced portobello mushrooms over the greens on each plate. Drizzle the plate with $^{1}/_{4}$ cup of the peanut sauce and 2 tablespoons of the papaya vinaigrette. Sprinkle the mint chiffonade around the plate, and garnish with cherry tomatoes.

NUTRITIONAL INFORMATION

PER SERVING DREDGED PORTOBELLOS: 175 calories (51% from fat), 3.3 g protein, 18 g carbohydrate, 10 g fat, 0 mg cholesterol, 105 mg sodium, 2.6 g fiber

PER CUP POTATOES: 261 calories (24% from fat), 4.5 g protein, 46 g carbohydrate, 7.1 g fat, 0 mg cholesterol, 252 mg sodium, 5.2 g fiber

PER $^{1}/_{4}$ CUP SAUCE: 111 calories (61% from fat), 5 g protein, 7 g carbohydrate, 8 g fat, 0 mg cholesterol, 480 mg sodium, 1.4 g fiber

PER 2 TABLESPOONS VINAIGRETTE: 10 calories (2% from fat), 0.2 g protein, 3.1 g carbohydrate, 0.1 g fat, 0 mg cholesterol, 25 mg sodium, 0.4 g fiber

STUFFED SWEET ONIONS *with* ROASTED VEGETABLES, ISRAELI COUSCOUS SALAD, *and* POMEGRANATE EGGPLANT SAUCE

SERVES 6

This version of our stuffed onion takes on a Middle Eastern tone, with lots of different flavors and textures on the plate. Sumac powder, made from dried dark-red berries, imparts a pungent, slightly bitter fruitiness to the vegetables. Look for it in Middle Eastern grocery stores.

The vegetables are our take on a tagine, a Moroccan stew that is usually cooked in an earthenware pot. Let the seasons dictate what variety of vege-tables and type of sweet onion you use for this dish. E.T.

ROASTED SWEET ONIONS

6 Maui onions or any other type of sweet onion, peeled
1 tablespoon extra virgin olive oil
1/2 teaspoon ground cumin
1 teaspoon ground cinnamon
1/4 teaspoon ground allspice
1 teaspoon salt

POMEGRANATE EGGPLANT SAUCE

1 tablespoon extra virgin olive oil
1/2 red onion, cut into small dice
6 cloves garlic, minced
1/2 teaspoon ground cumin
1/2 teaspoon toasted ground coriander seeds (see page 223)
1/4 teaspoon crushed red pepper flakes
1 Chinese or Japanese eggplant, cut into small dice (11/2 cups)
1/4 teaspoon salt
2 cups fresh pomegranate juice (see page 224)
1/2 cup freshly squeezed orange juice
1 teaspoon cornstarch, dissolved in 2 tablespoons water
1 teaspoon tamari, plus more as needed

ISRAELI COUSCOUS SALAD

1 cup dried Israeli couscous
3 cups water
1/4 teaspoon saffron threads

1 tablespoon extra virgin olive oil (optional)
3 scallions, green part only, thinly sliced
2 plum tomatoes, seeded and diced
1 cup seeded and diced cucumber
1/3 cup diced dried apricots
1/4 cup diced preserved lemons
1/4 cup pistachios or almonds, toasted (see page 222)
1 tablespoon minced fresh parsley
2 tablespoons minced fresh mint
2 tablespoons tahini, thinned with 1/4 cup water
Juice of 1 lemon
Salt and freshly ground black pepper

ROASTED VEGETABLES

1/2 butternut squash, diced (2 cups)
1 red onion, cut into 1/2-inch dice
4 cloves garlic, minced
8 ounces button or cremini mushrooms, diced (1 cup)
11/2 cups cooked fava beans, lima beans, or chickpeas (see page 220)
2 tomatoes, seeded and diced
2 teaspoons extra virgin olive oil
1 teaspoon ground cinnamon
1/2 teaspoon ground cumin
1/4 teaspoon dried thyme
1/2 teaspoon sumac powder, plus more for garnish
Salt and freshly ground black pepper

6 watercress sprigs, for garnish

To make the onions, preheat the oven to 400°F. Cut the bottoms off of each onion, to make a flat surface. Cut off the top 1/4 inch of each onion, and then cut two crisscrossing slits about 1/2 inch deep in the tops. Rub each onion with some of the olive oil and place in a baking dish.

Mix together the cumin, cinnamon, allspice, and salt in a small bowl and sprinkle over the onions. Cover the baking dish with aluminum foil or a lid. Bake for 1 hour 15 minutes, or until the onions are soft when pressed with a fork and still hold their shape. Remove from the oven and let cool to room temperature.

Hollow out the onions, leaving a $1/2$-inch-thick shell.

To make the sauce, heat the olive oil in a deep sauté pan over medium-high heat. Add the onion and garlic and sauté for 3 minutes, or until just soft. Add the cumin, coriander, pepper flakes, eggplant, and salt. Continue to sauté, stirring often, for 5 minutes. Add the pomegranate and orange juice and bring to a boil. Decrease the heat to medium-low and simmer for 5 to 7 minutes, until reduced by one-third. Whisk in the cornstarch mixture and simmer for 2 minutes, or until the sauce is thick enough to coat the back of a spoon. Add tamari to taste. Remove from the heat.

To make the couscous salad, place the Israeli couscous in a 2-quart saucepan over medium-high heat. Toast, stirring often, for 1 minute. Add the water and saffron. Simmer for 7 to 10 minutes. Drain the couscous, and toss with 1 teaspoon of the olive oil. Let cool to room temperature. Combine in a mixing bowl with the scallions, tomatoes, cucumber, apricots, lemons, pistachios, parsley, mint, tahini, lemon juice, and remaining olive oil. Add salt and pepper to taste.

To make the vegetables, preheat the broiler. Preheat the oven to 350°F. Blanch the squash for 2 to 3 minutes, until al dente (see page 223). Shock in ice water and drain.

Combine the onion, garlic, squash, mushrooms, fava beans, and tomatoes in a mixing bowl. Toss with the oil and the cinnamon, cumin, thyme, and sumac powder. Season with salt and pepper to taste.

Place the vegetables on a baking sheet, and then place them under the broiler 2 to 3 inches away from the heat. Broil, stirring often, for 7 to 10 minutes, until the vegetables are lightly browned and the onions are soft.

Let the vegetables cool until cool enough to handle, and then stuff equal amouns of them into the onion shells. Warm the stuffed equal amounts of onions in the oven for 10 minutes, or until hot.

To serve, place about $1/4$ cup of the pomegranate sauce on each dinner plate. Mound $1/2$ cup of the couscous salad in the center of the plate. Place a stuffed onion on top of the couscous. Place a sprig of watercress on top of the onion, and sprinkle the plate with some of the sumac powder.

NUTRITIONAL INFORMATION

PER STUFFED ONION: 206 calories (30% from fat), 10.9 g protein, 34 g carbohydrate, 4.4 g fat, 0 mg cholesterol, 329 mg sodium, 11.1 g fiber

PER $1/2$ CUP VEGETABLES: 150 calories (10% from fat), 8.8 g protein, 26 g carbohydrate, 1.9 g fat, 0 mg cholesterol, 12 mg sodium, 9 g fiber

PER $1/4$ CUP SAUCE: 52 calories (20% from fat), 0.8 g protein, 10 g carbohydrate, 1.3 g fat, 0 mg cholesterol, 73 mg sodium, 0.8 g fiber

PER $1/2$ CUP SALAD: 168 calories (29% from fat), 5 g protein, 25 g carbohydrate, 5 g fat, 0 mg cholesterol, 111 mg sodium, 2.9 g fiber

GRILLED EGGPLANT *with* ROASTED VEGETABLES *and* SHIITAKE MUSHROOMS, TOMATO LAVENDER SAUCE, *and* KAMUT–PINE NUT SALAD

SERVES 4

This dish embodies everything summer here in northern California, if not everywhere you find quality farmers' markets across the United States. Kamut berries (related to the wheat berry) have a wonderful crunchy texture and a nutty quality that suggests the pine nut complement. Remember with the fresh lavender that a little goes a long way. Give the lavender about 15 minutes to release its oils in the sauce before deciding to add more.

Another option is to grill the vegetables when you grill the eggplant instead of roasting them. Then dice the grilled vegetables to layer between the eggplant. This dish is robust enough with its smoky grilled and roasted flavors to complement a nice Rhône-style red wine or your favorite California Zinfandel. E.T.

TOMATO LAVENDER SAUCE

2 teaspoons extra virgin olive oil
2 leeks, white part only, cut into small dice
1/2 cup white wine
4 to 6 gold plum or Golden Jubilee tomatoes, seeded and diced
1 cup vegetable stock (page 205)
1/2 teaspoon salt
1/4 teaspoon white pepper
1 teaspoon minced fresh lavender

ROASTED GARLIC CASHEW CREAM

1/2 cup Millennium Oil-Braised Garlic (page 212)
1 clove garlic, minced
1/3 cup cashews
1/2 teaspoon nutritional yeast (see page 224)
1 1/2 cups water, plus more as needed
1/2 teaspoon salt, plus more as needed
2 teaspoons fresh minced herbs (such as thyme, dill, tarragon, basil, parsley; optional)

KAMUT–PINE NUT SALAD

2/3 cup dried kamut
6 cups water
1/4 teaspoon salt, plus more as needed
1/4 cup pine nuts, toasted (see page 222)
2 scallions, white and light green parts only, minced
1 cup cucumber, seeded and diced
2 tablespoons chopped fresh parsley
2 tablespoons opal or purple basil chiffonade
Juice of 1 lemon
Freshly ground black pepper
1/4 cup roasted garlic cashew cream (page 212)

ROASTED VEGETABLES AND SHIITAKE MUSHROOMS

2 green zucchini, cut into small dice
Kernels from 2 ears corn
4 ounces fresh shiitake mushrooms, stemmed and thinly sliced
1 red bell pepper or fresh pimiento, cut into small dice
1 leek, white part only, cut into small dice
2 cloves garlic, minced
2 teaspoons extra virgin olive oil
1 teaspoon fresh thyme or lemon thyme
Salt and freshly ground black pepper

GRILLED EGGPLANT

2 to 3 globe or Rosa Bianca eggplants, about 3 1/2 to 4 inches in diameter
1 teaspoon salt
1 clove garlic, minced
1 tablespoon Zinfandel or balsamic vinegar
2 tablespoons extra virgin olive oil
1 teaspoon minced rosemary, oregano, or savory
1/2 teaspoon salt

1/4 cup chopped pitted kalamata or Moroccan olives, for garnish
4 purple or opal basil sprigs, for garnish

To make the sauce, heat a deep skillet or saucepan over medium-low heat and add the olive oil. Add the leeks and cook for 15 minutes, or until soft. Add the white wine, tomatoes, and stock. Partially cover and simmer for 20 to 30 minutes, until the tomatoes are very soft. Add the salt and pepper.

Remove from the heat and let cool to close to room temperature. Purée the mixture in batches until the sauce is smooth. Return to the saucepan. Add the lavender and stir to mix.

To make the cream, combine the roasted garlic, minced garlic, cashews, yeast, 3/4 cup of the water, and the salt in a blender. Blend until a smooth, thick paste forms or until the mixture binds up. With the blender still running, slowly add the remaining 3/4 cup water, using more if needed, until the consistency is that of heavy cream. Stir in the herbs. Add salt to taste.

To make the salad, place a saucepan over high heat and add the kamut, water, and salt. Bring to a boil. Decrease the heat and simmer for 45 minutes to 1 hour, until the kamut is cooked thoroughly and is still al dente. Drain and let cool. Place in a mixing bowl with the pine nuts, scallions, cucumber, parsley, basil, lemon juice, pepper, and cashew cream. Add salt and pepper to taste.

To make the vegetables, preheat the broiler or the oven to 450°F. Place the zucchini, corn, mushrooms, pimiento, leeks, and garlic in a mixing bowl. Toss with the olive oil and thyme. Add salt and pepper to taste. Place on a baking sheet. Roast or broil, stirring often, for 7 to 10 minutes, until lightly browned and cooked through. Remove from the heat.

To make the eggplant, preheat the grill or broiler. Slice the eggplants into 8 1/2-inch to 2/3-inch rounds. Pat the sides with salt and cook for 15 minutes.

Place the salted eggplant on a baking sheet or perforated pan. With a paper towel, wipe the salt off and blot any accumulated moisture from the eggplants.

In a mixing bowl, whisk together the garlic, Zinfandel, olive oil, rosemary, and salt. Brush onto the eggplant slices. Grill or broil for 1 1/2 to 2 minutes per side, until the eggplant is cooked yet firm. Keep warm.

To serve, ladle 6 tablespoons of the tomato sauce around the bottom of each plate. In the center of the plate, mound 1/2 cup of the kamut salad, or press 1/2 cup of the salad into a 3-inch ring mold and unmold onto the plate. Place 1 slice of the eggplant on top of the salad. Place about 2/3 cup of the roasted vegetables on top of the eggplant slice, or press into a 3-inch ring mold prior to placing of the eggplant and then unmold onto the eggplant slice. Place another eggplant slice on top of the roasted vegetables. Drizzle 2 tablespoons of the roasted garlic cashew cream around the plate and eggplant. Sprinkle 1 tablespoon of chopped olives around the plate. Top the eggplant stack with a sprig of basil.

NUTRITIONAL INFORMATION

PER SERVING GRILLED EGGPLANT: 240 calories (50% from fat), 6 g protein, 40 g carbohydrate, 10 g fat, 0 mg cholesterol, 390 mg sodium, 9 g fiber

PER 6 TABLESPOONS SAUCE: 33 calories (31% from fat), 0.6 g protein, 4.3 g carbohydrate, 1 g fat, 0 mg cholesterol, 86 mg sodium, 0.8 g fiber

PER 1/2 CUP SALAD: 168 calories (28% from fat), 6.6 g protein, 26 g carbohydrate, 5.8 g fat, 0 mg cholesterol, 135 mg sodium, 5.5 g fiber

PER TABLESPOON CREAM: 36 calories (74% from fat), 0.6 g protein, 1.9 g carbohydrate, 3.2 g fat, 0 mg cholesterol, 41 mg sodium, 0.2 g fiber

PER 2/3 CUP VEGETABLES AND MUSHROOMS: 160 calories (15% from fat), 5.1 g protein, 34 g carbohydrate, 3 g fat, 0 mg cholesterol, 13 mg sodium, 6.5 g fiber

TAMARIND *and* CARDAMOM–GLAZED TOFU BROCHETTE *over* ZUCCHINI CAKE *with* BUTTERNUT SQUASH BADUCHE

SERVES 6

This Middle Eastern–inspired dish is for the early fall when zucchini and tomatoes are at their peak and when butternut squash and quince are just starting to be harvested. You certainly don't need to serve both chutneys in this dish, but I offer both for you to try. Each goes well with our dolmas (page 34), too.

The zucchini cake, bound with chickpea flour, makes a nice side dish to any Middle Eastern or Indian spiced sauté. Or make smaller cakes and serve as an appetizer with one of the chutneys. Baduche is an Armenian yogurt sauce not unlike Indian raita (which, by the way, also tastes great with the zucchini cake).

You will need six 10-inch wood or metal skewers to prepare this dish. The baduche can be made up to 2 hours in advance. E.T.

BUTTERNUT SQUASH BADUCHE

2 tablespoons extra virgin olive oil
2 cloves garlic, minced
1 1/2 cups 1/2-inch-diced butternut squash
Juice of 2 lemons
3/4 cup tahini
1/2 red onion, cut into small dice
2 tomatoes, seeded and diced
1 teaspoon ground coriander seeds, toasted (see page 223)
2 tablespoons chopped fresh parsley
2 tablespoons chopped fresh mint
1/2 teaspoon salt
1/4 teaspoon freshly ground black pepper

QUINCE-GINGER CHUTNEY (OPTIONAL)

2 quince
2 tablespoons peeled and minced fresh ginger
2 teaspoons minced fresh turmeric root, or
1/2 teaspoon dried turmeric
1/3 cup unrefined sugar
1/2 cup rice vinegar
1/2 teaspoon salt

FIG-CHILE CHUTNEY (OPTIONAL)

1/2 teaspoon brown mustard seeds
12 to 16 figs, sliced in quarters
2 scallions, green part only, thinly sliced
1 serrano chile, minced (seeded for less heat, optional)
Juice of 1 lemon
2 tablespoons agave nectar (see page 224)
Salt

TAMARIND-CARDAMOM GLAZE

1 teaspoon Hungarian paprika
1 teaspoon ground cumin
1 teaspoon ground coriander
1 1/2 teaspoons ground cardamom
1/2 cup tamarind purée
1 cup freshly squeezed orange juice
Juice of 1 lemon
2 cloves garlic
1/4 cup diced yellow onion
1 serrano or jalapeño chile, seeded
3 tablespoons unrefined sugar or agave nectar (see page 224)
2 tablespoons sesame seeds, toasted (see page 223)
1 tablespoon light vegetable oil
1/2 teaspoon salt

ZUCCHINI CAKES

1 cup very thinly sliced red onion
2 1/2 cups grated zucchini, excess moisture squeezed out
2 tablespoons chopped fresh cilantro or parsley
1 teaspoon cumin seeds
1/2 teaspoon salt
1/2 cup chickpea flour, plus more as needed
Light vegetable oil

24 ounces extra firm tofu, cut into 18 dice
2 red onions, cut into 9 dice each

To make the baduche, heat the olive oil in a pan over medium heat. Add the garlic and sauté for 3 minutes, or until it just starts to brown. Transfer to a large mixing bowl and let cool to room temperature.

Blanch the squash for 2 to 3 minutes, until al dente (see page 223). Shock in ice water, drain, and let cool.

Whisk the lemon juice and tahini into the garlic mixture. Add the onion, tomatoes, squash, coriander, parsley, mint, salt, and pepper. Toss well with the tahini dressing. Add salt and pepper to taste.

To make the quince chutney, scrub the quince and slice it into small (about 3/8-inch) dice. Store in water to prevent browning. Drain, and combine in a saucepan with the ginger, turmeric, sugar, vinegar, and salt. Bring to a boil. Decrease the heat to medium-low and simmer for 15 minutes, or until the quince are just soft. Let cool to room temperature to thicken before use. (Store refrigerated, in an airtight container, for up to 1 week.)

To make the fig chutney, toast the mustard seeds in a dry skillet over medium heat for 1 minute, or until they just start to pop. Combine in a bowl with the figs, scallions, chile, lemon juice, and agave nectar. Add salt to taste. (Store refrigerated, in an airtight container, for up to 1 week.)

To make the glaze, in a small dry skillet over medium heat, toast the paprika, cumin, coriander, and cardamom for 2 minutes, or until the spices are fragrant and turn a shade darker. Let cool. Place in a blender with the tamarind, orange juice, lemon juice, garlic, onion, chile, sugar, sesame seeds, vegetable oil, and salt. Blend until smooth. Season to taste. (Store refrigerated for up to 4 days.)

To make the cakes, preheat the oven to 200°F. Place the onion, zucchini, cilantro, cumin seeds, and salt in a mixing bowl. With your hands, mix in the chickpea flour until the mixture holds together. Shape the mixture into six 1/2-inch-thick patties. If time allows, refrigerate the cakes for 1 hour before heating.

Place a large skillet over medium-high heat. Add enough oil just to coat. When the oil is very hot, sear the zucchini cakes for 2 minutes per side, or until brown and crisp. Transfer to a plate, and keep warm until ready to serve.

To make the brochettes, preheat the grill or broiler. For each skewer, alternately skewer 3 pieces of tofu and 3 pieces of onion. Place the skewers in a pan and cover with one-half of the glaze. Marinate for 30 minutes. Broil or grill the skewers 4 to 5 minutes per side, until the glaze is caramelized on the tofu.

To serve, place a zucchini cake in the center of each plate. Circle the zucchini with about 2/3 cup of the baduche. Place a skewer over the cake and top with 2 tablespoons of quince or fig chutney. Drizzle the skewer with more glaze.

NUTRITIONAL INFORMATION

PER GLAZED TOFU BROCHETTE: 150 calories (43% from fat), 10 g protein, 16 g carbohydrate, 5.7 g fat, 0 mg cholesterol, 71 mg sodium, 3 g fiber

PER 2/3 CUP BADUCHE: 258 calories (65% from fat), 6.7 g protein, 17 g carbohydrate, 20 g fat, 0 mg cholesterol, 168 mg sodium, 3.3 g fiber

PER 2 TABLESPOONS GLAZE: 35 calories (15% from fat), 0.6 g protein, 8 g carbohydrate, 0.7 g fat, 0 mg cholesterol, 61 mg sodium, 0.4 g fiber

PER ZUCCHINI CAKE: 59 calories (12% from fat), 3 g protein, 11 g carbohydrate, 0.9 g fat, 0 mg cholesterol, 162 mg sodium, 1.7 g fiber

PER 2 TABLESPOONS QUINCE-GINGER CHUTNEY: 28 calories (2% from fat), 0.1 g protein, 7.4 g carbohydrate, 0.1 g fat, 0 mg cholesterol, 60 mg sodium, 0.4 g fiber

PER 2 TABLESPOONS FIG-CHILE CHUTNEY: 28 calories (3% from fat), 0.3 g protein, 7.6 g carbohydrate, 0.1 g fat, 0 mg cholesterol, 1 mg sodium, 1.9 g fiber

Black Quinoa Cake *over* Smoky Calypso Bean Sauce, Curried Squash, *and* Mango-Habanero-Coconut Sauce

SERVES 6

This Caribbean-inspired dish has many layers of flavor. Smoked onions give the bean sauce depth and body. The squash curry is rich and exotic, and the mango sauce is both sweet and fiery. Garnish with some toasted pistachio nuts for added crunch. Feel free to simplify this dish by adding the squash to the bean sauce and eliminating the curry. Sautéed collard greens round out the dish. E.T.

MANGO-HABANERO-COCONUT SAUCE

1 habanero chile (seeded for less heat, optional)
1 very ripe mango, peeled and pitted
$^1/_2$ cup coconut milk
$^1/_4$ teaspoon salt

SMOKY CALYPSO BEAN SAUCE

2 tablespoons extra virgin olive oil
2 red onions, smoked (page 219), halved crosswise, and sliced into thin crescents
4 cloves garlic, minced
1 tablespoon Sucanat (see page 224)
$^1/_2$ teaspoon dried thyme
1 teaspoon ground allspice
$^1/_4$ teaspoon ground cloves
2 cups cooked calypso, kidney, or black beans (see page 220)
3 cups vegetable stock (page 205)
$^1/_2$ teaspoon salt, plus more as needed
Freshly ground black pepper

CURRIED WINTER SQUASH

$^1/_2$ teaspoon ground cumin
$^1/_2$ teaspoon fennel seeds, ground
2 teaspoons mild curry powder
$^1/_4$ teaspoon ground nutmeg
1 tablespoon vegetable oil
1 yellow onion, cut into small dice
2 cloves garlic, minced
1 tablespoon peeled and minced fresh ginger

3 cups winter squash (such as kabocha, kuri, or butternut), cut into $^1/_2$-inch dice
Juice of 1 orange
1 cup water or vegetable stock (page 205)
Salt
Freshly ground black pepper or chile powder

COLLARD GREENS

1 bunch collard greens, stemmed and cut into $^1/_2$-inch strips
2 teaspoons extra virgin olive oil
1 yellow onion, halved crosswise and then sliced into thin crescents
2 teaspoons umeboshi vinegar, or the juice of 1 lemon plus $^1/_2$ teaspoon salt

BLACK QUINOA CAKES

1 tablespoon extra virgin olive oil
$^1/_2$ cup diced yellow onion
$^1/_2$ cup diced celery
$^1/_2$ cup diced peeled carrot
1 teaspoon ground cumin
$^1/_2$ teaspoon dried oregano
Kernels from 1 ear corn (optional)
$^1/_4$ cup pistachio nuts, toasted (see page 222) and coarsely chopped
$1^1/_2$ cups cooked and cooled black quinoa or standard quinoa
Salt and freshly ground black pepper
$^1/_2$ cup dried corn masa, plus more as needed
Water
Vegetable oil

6 tablespoons pistachio nuts, toasted (see page 222) and coarsely chopped, for garnish
$^1/_4$ cup loosely packed cilantro leaves, for garnish

To make the mango sauce, in a blender, combine the habanero, mango, coconut milk, and salt. Blend until smooth.

To make the bean sauce, place a deep skillet over medium-low heat and add the olive oil. Add the onions and garlic and sauté, stirring often, for 10 to 12 minutes, until the onions are lightly caramelized. Add the Sucanat, and sauté for 5 minutes, or until the onions are a deep caramel in color. Add the thyme, allspice, and cloves, followed by the beans and stock. Add the salt, cover, and simmer over low heat for 30 minutes, or until the stock barely covers the beans and has thickened slightly. Season with salt and pepper to taste.

To make the squash, place a sauté pan over medium heat. Toast the cumin, fennel, curry, and nutmeg for 1 minute, or until they just begin to smoke and become one shade darker.

Heat the vegetable oil in a deep skillet over high heat. Add the onions, garlic, and ginger. Sauté for 1 minute, or until lightly browned. Add the toasted spices, and sauté for 30 seconds before adding the squash, orange juice, and water. Decrease the heat to medium-low and simmer for 15 minutes, or until the liquid is absorbed and the squash is cooked through but still al dente. Add salt and pepper to taste.

To make the greens, boil the greens in enough salted water to cover for 10 minutes, or until they are just soft. Drain well.

Meanwhile, heat the olive oil in a large sauté pan over medium-high heat. Add the onions, and cook for 5 to 7 minutes, until soft and just starting to brown. Add the drained collards to the pan, and toss with the onion. Mix in the vinegar.

To make the cakes, preheat the oven to 400°F. Line a baking sheet with parchment paper and brush it with olive oil. Place a skillet over medium heat and add the olive oil. Add the onions, celery, and carrots, and

sauté for 5 minutes, or until just softened. Add the cumin, oregano, and corn, and sauté for 1 minute. Place the mixture in a mixing bowl, and let cool to room temperature. Add the nuts and quinoa, and add salt and pepper to taste. Slowly mix in the corn masa with just enough water for the mixture to hold together. If the mixture is too wet, add more masa.

Shape the mixture by hand or with a 3-inch ring mold into 1-inch-thick round disks. Place the quinoa cakes on the pan. Brush the tops of the cakes with vegetable oil and bake in the oven for 15 to 20 minutes, until the cakes are crisp and light brown on both sides. Keep warm.

To serve, spoon 1/2 cup of the bean sauce on each plate or into a large pasta bowl. Mound a portion of the collard greens in the center of the plate, place 1 quinoa cake over the green, and spoon 1/2 cup of the squash curry on top of the cake. Drizzle with about 2 tablespoons of the mango sauce, and top with chopped pistachios and cilantro leaves.

NUTRITIONAL INFORMATION

PER QUINOA CAKE: 249 calories (19% from fat), 8.4 g protein, 43 g carbohydrate, 5.7 g fat, 0 mg cholesterol, 25 mg sodium, 4.8 g fiber

PER 1/2 CUP BEAN SAUCE: 124 calories (27% from fat), 4.7 g protein, 17 g carbohydrate, 3.8 g fat, 0 mg cholesterol, 121 mg sodium, 3 g fiber

PER 1/2 CUP SQUASH: 80 calories (27% from fat), 1.5 g protein, 13 g carbohydrate, 2.6 g fat, 0 mg cholesterol, 5 mg sodium, 2 g fiber

PER 2 TABLESPOONS MANGO-HABANERO-COCONUT SAUCE: 32 calories (61% from fat), 0.3 g protein, 3.1 g carbohydrate, 2.4 g fat, 0 mg cholesterol, 41 mg sodium, 0.4 g fiber

PER SERVING COLLARD GREENS: 46 calories (30% from fat), 1.4 g protein, 7.4 g carbohydrate, 1.7 g fat, 0 mg cholesterol, 364 mg sodium, 2.9 g fiber

SOCCA RUSTICA *with* CHICKPEA SANGIOVESE STEW *and* PRESERVED ORANGE–OLIVE RELISH

SERVES 6

Socca is a chickpea flat bread or crêpe native to Nice and to all of the Mediterranean rim under a variety of names. Our spin on socca is to stuff black peppercorn-studded chickpea flour crêpes with a hearty braise of chickpeas, sun-dried tomatoes, and dried apricots simmered in Sangiovese or Chianti. We serve it with a pungent relish of preserved oranges, olives, fennel, and pickled garlic cloves, and with grilled broccoli rabe or another bitter green, such as radicchio de Treviso. The relish is best if made a day ahead of time. E.T.

PRESERVED ORANGE–OLIVE RELISH

2 tablespoons extra virgin olive oil
10 to 12 cloves garlic, peeled and halved
1 small fennel bulb, cut into small dice
1/2 teaspoon whole fennel seeds
4 whole dried chiles de árbol, or 1/2 teaspoon crushed red pepper flakes
1 thyme sprig, or 1/2 teaspoon dried thyme
1/2 teaspoon fresh oregano
1 cup Millennium Preserved Oranges or Quick-Preserved Oranges (page 216), diced
1 cup pitted oil-cured black Greek or Italian olives (or other favorite olives)
1/2 cup water or vegetable stock (page 205)
3 tablespoons red wine vinegar

CHICKPEAS BRAISED IN SANGIOVESE

1/4 cup extra virgin olive oil
6 cloves garlic, minced
2 leeks, white part only, cut into small dice
2 carrots, peeled and cut into small dice
1 tablespoon fresh rosemary, coarsely chopped
1 teaspoon whole cumin seeds
1 bay leaf
2 cups Sangiovese or Chianti
4 cups cooked chickpeas
3 cups vegetable stock (page 205)
1 cup coarsely chopped sun-dried tomatoes
1/2 cup coarsely chopped dried apricots
1/2 teaspoon salt, plus more as needed

2 teaspoons cornstarch, dissolved in 3 tablespoons water
Freshly ground black pepper

SOCCA CRÊPES

2 cups chickpea flour
1/2 teaspoon coarsely ground black pepper, plus more as needed
1/2 cup sliced almonds, toasted (see page 222) and crushed
1 teaspoon egg replacer (see page 224)
1/2 teaspoon salt, plus more as needed
1 tablespoon extra virgin olive oil
2/3 cup water, plus more as needed

Grilled Broccoli Rabe (page 118)
6 tablespoons sliced almonds, toasted (see page 222), for garnish

To make the relish, in a small saucepan, heat the olive oil over medium heat. Add the garlic, and sauté for 2 minutes, or until it just starts to brown. Add the fennel bulb, fennel seeds, chiles, thyme, and oregano. Sauté, stirring often, for 1 minute. Add the oranges, olives, water, and vinegar. Simmer for 10 minutes, or until the liquid is reduced by one-half. Remove from the heat and let cool to room temperature. (Store refrigerated indefinitely.)

To make the chickpeas, heat the olive oil in a deep skillet or heavy-bottomed braising pan over medium-high heat. Add the garlic and sauté for 2 minutes, or until it just begins to brown. Add the leeks and carrots, and sauté, stirring often, for 5 minutes, or until the leeks just start to wilt. Add the rosemary, cumin seeds, and bay leaf. Sauté for another minute. Add 1 cup of the wine and stir to scrape up the browned bits from the bottom of the pan. Add the remaining 1 cup wine, the chickpeas, stock, sun-dried tomatoes, apricots, and salt. Simmer on medium-low heat for 20 minutes, or until the liquid is reduced by one-half. Slowly stir in the cornstarch slurry. Add salt and pepper to taste.

To make the crêpes, preheat the oven to 200°F. In a bowl, combine the chickpea flour, pepper, almonds, egg replacer, and salt. In a separate bowl, whisk together the olive oil and water. Slowly whisk the liquid into the dry ingredients, adding more water as needed to achieve a batter as thick as heavy cream. Add salt and pepper to taste.

Place a large nonstick skillet over medium heat. Brush the bottom with a thin coating of vegetable oil. Ladle 1/2 cup of the batter into the center of the skillet. Tilt the skillet to distribute the batter throughout the pan. Cook the crêpe for 2 to 3 minutes, until the edges start to brown and lift up from the pan. Flip the crêpe, and cook for 1 minute.

Transfer the crêpe to a large plate. Cover with a damp kitchen towel and keep warm in a low oven until all of the crêpes are done. Repeat with the remaining batter until you have 6 crêpes total.

To serve, place a warm crêpe in the center of each dinner plate. Fill with about 1 cup of the braised chickpea mixture. Fold the crêpe over and top with 2 tablespoons of the orange relish. Place some of the broccoli rabe next to the crêpe, and sprinkle 1 tablespoon of the almonds on the crêpe.

NUTRITIONAL INFORMATION

PER CUP CHICKPEAS: 273 calories (30% from fat), 9.4 g protein, 38 g carbohydrate, 1.2 g fat, 0 mg cholesterol, 316 mg sodium, 5.5 g fiber

PER 2 TABLESPOONS RELISH: 29 calories (50% from fat), 0.5 g protein, 3.6 g carbohydrate, 1.9 g fat, 0 mg cholesterol, 442 mg sodium, 0.6 g fiber

PER CRÊPE: 218 calories (58% from fat), 7.8 g protein, 20 g carbohydrate, 8 g fat, 0 mg cholesterol, 125 mg sodium, 2 g fiber

ASIAN RICE FLOUR CRÊPES FILLED *with* EGGPLANT *and* SHIITAKE MUSHROOMS *over* EDAMAME SAUCE

SERVES 6

This recipe originated from my favorite Chinese restaurant, China Dynasty, located down the street from where I used to live in San Rafael. China Dynasty prepares a stellar dish with fresh soybeans (edamame) braised with pickled mustard greens and slices of ginger. I used the idea as a sauce for a crêpe filled with a sweet and spicy braise of Chinese eggplant and shiitake mushrooms. The edamame sauce and the sweet and spicy eggplant can stand alone as centerpiece dishes. Look for pickled mustard greens in Asian markets, or substitute a mild kimchee (Korean pickled cabbage). Make the filling immediately before making the crêpes. E.T.

EDAMAME SAUCE

1 teaspoon canola oil
2 teaspoons toasted sesame oil
1 yellow onion, halved crosswise and then sliced into thin crescents
1/4 cup peeled and thinly sliced ginger rounds
1 1/2 cups pickled mustard greens or kimchee, cut into small dice (1 cup)
1 pound fresh or frozen shelled edamame
1 1/2 cups vegetable stock (page 205)
2 teaspoons cornstarch, dissolved in 1/4 cup cold water
Juice of 2 limes
1/2 teaspoon ground white pepper
Salt

ASIAN EGGPLANT AND SHIITAKE FILLING

1 pound Chinese eggplant (about 4 to 5 eggplants), halved lengthwise and cut diagonally into 1-inch-thick slices
2 teaspoons canola oil
1 red onion, halved crosswise and then sliced into thin crescents
6 cloves garlic, minced
1 1/2 teaspoons coarsely chopped fermented black beans
2 teaspoons peeled and minced fresh ginger
1/4 teaspoon crushed red pepper flakes

6 ounces shiitake mushrooms, stemmed and thinly sliced
1 teaspoon tomato paste
2 tablespoons Sucanat (see page 224)
3 tablespoons tamari
1 teaspoon toasted sesame oil

RICE FLOUR CRÊPES

2 cups brown rice flour
1/4 cup cornstarch
2 teaspoons egg replacer (see page 224)
1/2 teaspoon salt
1/2 cup thinly sliced scallions, green part only
2 teaspoons black sesame seeds, toasted (see page 223; optional)
1 teaspoon toasted sesame oil
3/4 cup soy milk, plus more as needed

1/2 bunch Thai basil leaves
6 tablespoons kecap manis (page 215)
6 tablespoons peanuts or cashews, toasted (see page 224), for garnish
6 tablespoons thinly sliced scallions, green part only, for garnish
1 (4-ounce) package enoki mushrooms, for garnish

To make the sauce, heat the canola oil and 1 teaspoon of the sesame oil in a large sauté pan over high heat. Add the onions and ginger, and sauté for 2 minutes, or until just wilted. Add the pickled mustard greens and edamame. Cover with the stock and simmer for 10 minutes. Stir in the cornstarch slurry and simmer for another 5 minutes, or until just thickened. Remove from the heat. Add the lime juice, white pepper, and the remaining 1 teaspoon sesame oil. Add salt to taste.

To make the filling, blanch the eggplant for 1 minute in salted water (see page 223). Drain.

Place a large sauté pan or wok over high heat and add the canola oil. When very hot and almost starting to smoke, add the onions and garlic. Sauté for 1 minute. Add the black beans, ginger, and pepper flakes. Follow with the mushrooms and eggplant. Sauté for 2 to

3 minutes, until the eggplant is just soft. Add the tomato paste, Sucanat, tamari, and sesame oil. Toss well. Sauté for 1 minute, or until the sauce thickens and glazes the eggplant and mushrooms.

To make the crêpes, preheat the oven to 200°F. Combine the rice flour, cornstarch, egg replacer, salt, scallions, and sesame seeds in a mixing bowl. In another bowl, combine the sesame oil with the soy milk. Slowly whisk 3/4 cup of the soy milk mixture into the dry ingredients. Use more soy milk as needed to make a pancake-like batter.

Place a large nonstick skillet over medium-high heat. Brush the bottom with a thin coating of vegetable oil. Ladle 1/3 cup of the batter into the center of the skillet. Tilt the skillet to distribute the batter to form a 6- to 7-inch crêpe. Cook the crêpe for 1 1/2 minutes, or until the edges start to brown. Flip the crêpe, and cook for 30 seconds.

Transfer the crêpe to a large plate. Cover with a damp kitchen towel and keep warm in the oven until all of the crêpes are done. Repeat with the remaining batter until you have 6 crêpes total.

To serve, spoon 1/3 cup of the edamame sauce onto the center of each plate. Place 1 crêpe over the sauce and fill with 1 cup of the eggplant filling. Add up to one-sixth of the basil leaves. Fold the crêpe over. Drizzle the plate with 1 tablespoon of the kecap manis. Sprinkle the top of the crêpe with equal amounts of peanuts, scallions, and enoki mushrooms.

NUTRITIONAL INFORMATION

PER CUP FILLING: 170 calories (20% from fat), 5.1 g protein, 33 g carbohydrate, 4.3 g fat, 0 mg cholesterol, 517 mg sodium, 5.5 g fiber

PER 1/3 CUP SAUCE: 133 calories (46% from fat), 9.6 g protein, 9.4 g carbohydrate, 7.3 g fat, 0 mg cholesterol, 2 mg sodium, 2.4 g fiber

PER CRÊPE: 179 calories (12% from fat), 3.7 g protein, 3.5 g carbohydrate, 2.8 g fat, 0 mg cholesterol, 125 mg sodium, 2.3 g fiber

KOREAN-STYLE BARBECUED TEMPEH *over*
RICE NOODLE SALAD *with* CITRUS *and* KIMCHEE

SERVES 6

I hope you find our version of a Korean barbecue sauce as addictive as I do. In the sauce, we try to approximate kotochang, a Korean sweet and spicy chile paste, with dried Korean chiles, sweet miso, and a combination of paprika and cayenne pepper. Pair this dish with a crisp, dry beer. E.T.

KOREAN BARBECUE SAUCE

2 teaspoons Spanish paprika
1/2 teaspoon cayenne pepper
3 tablespoons white miso
2 tablespoons toasted sesame oil
2 teaspoons sesame seeds
5 cloves garlic, minced
2 tablespoons peeled and minced fresh ginger
1/2 bunch scallions, white part only, minced
1/4 cup tamari
2 tablespoons unrefined sugar
1 cup vegetable stock (page 205) or water
2 teaspoons cornstarch, dissolved in 1/4 cup water

RICE NOODLE SALAD WITH
CITRUS AND KIMCHEE

1 (16-ounce) package rice vermicelli, or cooked soba or udon noodles
1 1/2 cups peeled and supremed orange, grapefruit, and lime segments (see page 222)
1 cup kimchee, drained and julienned
1 cup cucumber, peeled, seeded, and julienned
1 cup mung bean sprouts
1/2 bunch scallions, green part only, thinly sliced
1/2 bunch fresh cilantro leaves
Juice of 2 limes
2 tablespoons tamari
1 teaspoon toasted sesame oil

SAUTÉED BABY BOK CHOY

2 teaspoons vegetable oil
1/2 yellow onion, thinly sliced
1 clove garlic, minced
1 teaspoon peeled and minced fresh ginger

12 (2- to 3-inch long) baby bok choy leaves, halved lengthwise
1/2 teaspoon salt
1/2 teaspoon toasted sesame oil
Sesame seeds, toasted (see page 223; optional)

1 recipe baked marinated tempeh (page 211)
2 tablespoons sesame seeds, toasted (see page 223), for garnish
1/4 cup loosely packed fresh cilantro leaves, for garnish
1/2 cup peeled and supremed citrus segments (see page 222), for garnish

To make the barbecue sauce, place the paprika and cayenne pepper in a small bowl and mix in the white miso to make a Korean chile paste. (Store refrigerated indefinitely).

Heat the sesame oil and sesame seeds in a saucepan over medium heat. Toast the sesame seeds in the oil for 1 minute, stirring often. Add four-fifths of the minced garlic, and the ginger and scallions. Sauté for 2 minutes, or until starting to brown. Add the Korean chile paste mixture, tamari, sugar, and stock. Simmer for 15 minutes. Add the cornstarch slurry to thicken. Remove from the heat and add the remaining minced garlic. Let cool to room temperature. (Store refrigerated for up to 2 weeks.)

To make the noodle salad, bring 2 quarts water to a boil in a saucepan. Place the noodles in a large bowl. Cover with the boiling water and let sit for 10 minutes, or until al dente. Drain and let cool under cold water. Drain well.

In a large mixing bowl, combine the citrus, kimchee, cucumber, bean sprouts, scallions, cilantro, lime juice, tamari, and sesame oil. Add the rice noodles and toss well. Reserve until needed.

To make the bok choy, place a skillet or wok over high heat. When very hot, add the oil, and then the onions, garlic, and ginger. Sauté for 30 seconds, or until lightly browned. Add the bok choy and salt.

Sauté, tossing the mixture often, for 2 minutes, or until the bok choy just begins to wilt. Add the sesame oil and sesame seeds, and toss. Transfer the bok choy to a platter. Keep warm.

To make the tempeh, preheat the grill or broiler. Place the barbecue sauce in a large baking dish. Add the tempeh and cover with barbecue sauce. Marinate for 20 minutes. Grill or broil the tempeh for 2 minutes per side, or until the sauce caramelizes on the tempeh. Remove from the heat. Slice the tempeh diagonally into 1/2-inch-wide pieces.

To serve, mound one-sixth of the rice noodle salad in the center of each large dinner plate. Fan the tempeh slices over the noodle salad. Place 4 pieces of the bok choy around the plate. Drizzle the whole dish with 2 to 3 tablespoons of the remaining sauce. Garnish with equal amounts of toasted sesame seeds, cilantro, and citrus segments.

NUTRITIONAL INFORMATION

PER SERVING BARBECUED TEMPEH: 261 calories (35% from fat), 22 g protein, 21 g carbohydrate, 11 g fat, 0 mg cholesterol, 205 mg sodium, 3.7 g fiber

PER SERVING NOODLE SALAD: 301 calories (4% from fat), 12 g protein, 64 g carbohydrate, 1.4 g fat, 0 mg cholesterol, 1025 mg sodium, 2.9 g fiber

PER SERVING BOK CHOY: 33 calories (50% from fat), 1.3 g protein, 3.3 g carbohydrate, 2.1 g fat, 0 mg cholesterol, 199 mg sodium, 1 g fiber

PER 2 TABLESPOONS BARBECUE SAUCE: 38 calories (49% from fat), 1.1 g protein, 3.7 g carbohydrate, 2.1 g fat, 0 mg cholesterol, 370 mg sodium, 0.3 g fiber

THE ASIAN NAPOLEON

SERVES 6

Here's a Millennium signature. It's kind of a dissected Thai coconut curry showcasing contrasts in flavors and textures. Vegetables are seared in a sweet sesame sauce and layered between crisp sweet and spicy sesame-phyllo wafers over fragrant jasmine rice atop a tart but rich Kaffir lime and coconut sauce. Add some aromatic mint and basil and some crunchy sprouts and you have an exciting yet elegant dish. Try pairing with a dry or off-dry Riesling or Gerwürztraminer. You'll have some sesame sauce left over; save it for other Asian-inspired dishes. E.T.

SESAME SAUCE

1^1/$_2$ cups water
1 apple, cored and diced
^{1}/$_4$ cup plus 2 teaspoons sesame seeds, toasted
  (see page 223)
2 cloves garlic, minced
^{1}/$_4$ teaspoon crushed red pepper flakes
1 tablespoon fermented black beans
1 tablespoon peeled coarsely chopped fresh ginger
2 tablespoons Sucanat (see page 224) or brown sugar
1 tablespoon rice vinegar
1 tablespoon sesame oil
^{1}/$_3$ cup soy sauce
1 Kaffir lime leaf

KAFFIR LIME–COCONUT SAUCE

3 tablespoons peeled and coarsely chopped fresh
  ginger
^{1}/$_2$ yellow onion, coarsely chopped
2 lemongrass stalks, coarsely chopped
Juice of 3 limes
2 teaspoons minced lime zest
^{1}/$_2$ jalapeño chile, seeded
1 tablespoon white miso
2 teaspoons unrefined sugar
^{1}/$_2$ teaspoon salt
1 cup rice milk
1 (14-ounce) can coconut milk
1 tablespoon cornstarch, dissolved in 3 tablespoons
  cold water
2 fresh or frozen Kaffir lime leaves, chiffonade

NAPOLEON SPROUT MIX

^{1}/$_2$ head radicchio, chiffonade
1 carrot, peeled and shredded or chiffonade
^{1}/$_4$ cup loosely packed daikon sprouts
^{1}/$_4$ cup loosely packed sunflower sprouts

PHYLLO WAFERS

^{1}/$_4$ cup whole sesame seeds
^{1}/$_4$ cup ground sesame seeds
1 tablespoon whole black sesame seeds
^{1}/$_4$ cup Sucanat (see page 224)
^{1}/$_4$ teaspoon cayenne pepper
^{1}/$_4$ teaspoon salt
6 (13 by 18-inch) sheets phyllo dough
Canola or light vegetable oil

JASMINE RICE

2 teaspoons canola oil
^{1}/$_2$ cup diced yellow onion
^{1}/$_4$ teaspoon salt
^{1}/$_4$ cup unsweetened coconut flakes
1^1/$_2$ cups jasmine rice
1^3/$_4$ cups boiling water

VEGETABLE MIXTURE

Canola or light vegetable oil
1 red onion, thinly sliced
^{1}/$_4$ pound Japanese eggplant, thinly sliced on the
  diagonal
4 ounces oyster mushrooms
^{1}/$_2$ pound asparagus, sliced into 1-inch-long pieces on
  the diagonal
^{1}/$_2$ pound small florets cauliflower or broccoli
^{1}/$_4$ pound snap peas or snow peas, stemmed
3 to 4 ounces smoked baked tofu (page 221) or firm
  tofu, cut into small dice

2 tablespoons mint leaves, chiffonade, for garnish
2 tablespoons Thai basil leaves, chiffonade, for garnish

To make the sesame sauce, heat 1 cup of the water over medium heat, and add the apple. Simmer for 10 minutes, or until soft. Transfer the apple and its cooking liquid to a blender and add ^{1}/$_4$ cup of the sesame seeds, the garlic, pepper flakes, black beans, ginger, Sucanat, vinegar, sesame oil, soy sauce, the remaining 1/2 cup water, and the lime leaf. Blend until smooth. Place the sauce in a bowl and stir in the remaining 2 teaspoons sesame seeds. (Store, covered, in the refrigerator for up to 1 week.)

To make the lime sauce, place the ginger, onions, lemongrass, lime juice and zest, jalapeño, miso, sugar, salt, and rice milk in a blender. Blend until smooth. Place this mixture in a saucepan and add the coconut milk. Bring to a boil. Decrease the heat to medium-low and simmer for 15 minutes, or until reduced by one-third. Slowly whisk in the cornstarch mixture, adding only enough to thicken to the consistency of heavy cream. Remove from the heat, let cool slightly, and then strain through a chinois or fine-mesh strainer into another saucepan. Add the Kaffir lime leaves. (Store, covered, in the refrigerator for up to 4 days).

To make the sprout mix, combine all of the ingredients together in a bowl.

To make the phyllo wafers, preheat the oven to 350°F. Cover a baking sheet with parchment paper. Combine the whole sesame seeds, ground sesame seeds, black sesame seeds, Sucanat, cayenne pepper, and salt in a small bowl.

Place 2 sheets of phyllo dough over the parchment, and brush with the oil. Sprinkle the oiled phyllo liberally with the sesame mix until the mixture fully covers the phyllo. Place 2 more sheets of phyllo over the first 2 sheets. Brush with oil, and repeat with the sesame mix. Repeat the process with 2 more sheets of phyllo. Cut the phyllo in half lengthwise, and then cut each half in half again lengthwise. Cut the phyllo strips in thirds down their length for a total of 12 squares. Bake in the oven for 10 minutes, or until golden. Let cool to room temperature.

To make the rice, preheat the oven to 350°F. Heat the canola oil in an ovenproof saucepan over medium heat. Add the onions and salt and sauté for 6 minutes, or until translucent. Add the coconut and the rice.

Sauté, stirring constantly, to toast the rice for 2 minutes. Add the boiling water, and cover the saucepan. Place the saucepan in the oven for 15 minutes to bake the rice. (Alternatively, cover and simmer over medium-low heat for 15 minutes.) Remove from the oven and let steam, still covered, for 10 minutes. Fluff the rice with a fork. Transfer to a baking pan to cool.

To make the vegetable mixture, put a dash of canola oil in a very large sauté pan or wok (or use two smaller pans or woks) over high heat. Add the onions, eggplant, and mushrooms and sauté for 1 minute. Add the asparagus, cauliflower, peas, and tofu, and sauté, tossing the vegetables often, for 2 to 3 minutes, until the vegetables are crisp-tender. Add 3/4 cup of the sesame sauce and sauté for 1 minute, or until the sauce glazes onto the vegetables.

Warm the coconut sauce and jasmine rice.

To serve, ladle 4 tablespoons of the lime sauce on the bottom of each dinner plate. Pack 1 cup of the rice into a 1-cup mold and unmold it in the center of the plate. Top with 1 phyllo wafer. Place one-sixth of the vegetable mixture over the phyllo wafer. Sprinkle with some of the chopped mint and basil and top with a second phyllo wafer. Top with some of the sprout mix.

NUTRITIONAL INFORMATION

PER ASSEMBLED NAPOLEON: 604 calories (12% from fat), 16.6 g protein, 85 g carbohydrate, 28.1 g fat, 0 mg cholesterol, 451 mg sodium, 6.6 g fiber

PER CUP RICE: 205 calories (12% from fat), 3.7 g protein, 40 g carbohydrate, 2.8 g fat, 0 mg cholesterol, 91 mg sodium, 1.2 g fiber

PER 1/4 CUP LIME SAUCE: 84 calories (63% from fat), 1 g protein, 7.3 g carbohydrate, 6.3 g fat, 0 mg cholesterol, 114 mg sodium, 0.4 g fiber

PER 2 TABLESPOONS SESAME SAUCE: 24 calories (39% from fat), 0.9 g protein, 3.7 g carbohydrate, 1.4 g fat, 0 mg cholesterol, 224 mg sodium, 0.5 g fiber

PER 2 PHYLLO SQUARES: 175 calories (46% from fat), 3.5 g protein, 20 g carbohydrate, 9.3 g fat, 0 mg cholesterol, 172 mg sodium, 0.6 g fiber

CELERY ROOT RAVIOLI STUFFED *with* BEETS *and* MATSUTAKE MUSHROOMS *in a* LOBSTER MUSHROOM CRÈME

SERVES 4

This is a fun dish from a fall Aphrodisiac Dinner. Instead of pasta, we use thin sheets of celery root to create translucent ravioli. Matsutakes and lobster mushrooms are certainly not easy to find, so feel free to try other mushrooms (such as shiitakes, oyster mushrooms, or chanterelles). E.T.

LOBSTER MUSHROOM CRÈME

2 tablespoons extra virgin olive oil
2 leeks, white part only, thinly sliced
8 ounces lobster mushrooms, thinly sliced
1/4 teaspoon fresh thyme
1/2 teaspoon Spanish paprika
1/4 teaspoon ground nutmeg
2 tablespoons dry sherry
1 cup vegetable stock (page 205) or mushroom stock (page 206)
1 1/2 cups cashew cream (page 212)
1 teaspoon nutritional yeast (see page 224)
1/2 teaspoon salt, plus more as needed
1/2 teaspoon shredded lemon zest
Freshly ground white pepper

CELERY ROOT RAVIOLI

4 red beets, peeled and coarsely chopped
2 teaspoons extra virgin olive oil
6 shallots, white and green parts, minced
2 tablespoons dry sherry
1/2 cup vegetable stock (page 205)
8 ounces matsutake mushrooms, cut into small dice
1 teaspoon all-purpose flour
1/4 teaspoon ground nutmeg
Salt and freshly ground black pepper
3 large celery root bulbs
1 tablespoon cornstarch, dissolved in 2 tablespoons water
Olive oil for brushing

HERB SALAD

1/2 cup loosely packed fresh chervil leaves
1/2 cup baby arugula or micro greens
2 tablespoons loosely packed fresh tarragon leaves

1/2 bunch chives, cut into 2-inch lengths
2 teaspoons toasted walnut oil or olive oil
1 teaspoon sherry vinegar
Salt

1/4 cup pine nuts, toasted (see page 222), for garnish

To make the crème, place a saucepan over medium heat and add the olive oil. Add the leeks and cook for 10 minutes, or until soft. Add the mushrooms and continue to cook for 5 minutes. Stir in the thyme, paprika, and nutmeg. Add the sherry and stir to scrape up the browned bits from the bottom of the saucepan. Add the stock, cashew cream, yeast, salt, and zest. Simmer for 2 minutes, or until just thickened. Add salt and white pepper to taste.

To make the ravioli, preheat the oven to 350°F. Place the beets in a food processor fitted with the metal blade, and pulse until minced. Place a large skillet over medium heat and add the olive oil. Add the shallots, and cook, stirring often, for 10 minutes, or until lightly caramelized. Add the sherry and stir to scrape up the browned bits from the bottom of the pan. Add the beets, followed by the stock. Cover, and simmer for 10 minutes. Add the mushrooms and simmer, uncovered, for 10 minutes, or until the pan is dry. Stir in the flour, followed by the nutmeg and salt and pepper to taste. Remove from the heat. The filling should be dry.

Line a baking sheet with parchment paper or silpat. Peel the celery root and square the sides. Using a mandoline, slice the celery root very thin. You will need 24 slices, plus extra in case some tear. Place the slices on the baking sheet. Cover with another piece of parchment or silpat and bake for 10 minutes, or until just soft and flexible. Let cool to room temperature.

Line two baking pans with parchment and coat lightly with oil. Increase the oven temperature to 450°F. For each ravioli, place about 1 tablespoon of the filling in the center of a slice of celery root. Brush the edges with a bit of the cornstarch slurry, place a slice of celery root over the filling, and press together. Repeat with the remaining slices to make 12 ravioli. Place the ravioli on the two baking pans. Brush the tops of each ravioli with oil. Bake for 10 minutes, or until the edges brown slightly. Remove from the heat.

To make the salad, combine the chervil, arugula, tarragon, and chives. Dress with the oil and vinegar. Add salt to taste.

To serve, ladle ¹/₄ cup of the crème on each plate. Place 3 ravioli over the sauce. Place one-quarter of the herb salad in the center of the ravioli. Sprinkle the plate with 1 tablespoon of the toasted pine nuts.

NUTRITIONAL INFORMATION

PER SERVING: 237 calories (68% from fat), 8.2 g protein, 18.4 g carbohydrate, 13.8 g fat, 0 mg cholesterol, 228 mg sodium, 4.1 g fiber

PER ¹/₄ CUP CRÈME: 61 calories (75% from fat), 1.1 g protein, 2.4 g carbohydrate, 4.7 g fat, 0 mg cholesterol, 160 mg sodium, 0.6 g fiber

PER SERVING SALAD: 32 calories (61% from fat), 1.2 g protein, 2.4 g carbohydrate, 2.5 g fat, 0 mg cholesterol, 5 mg sodium, 0.7 g fiber

ROOT VEGETABLE RAVIOLI *with* PORTOBELLO MUSHROOM PÂTÉ *and* SWEET PEPPER–OLIVE TAPENADE

SERVES 6

This colorful, elegant, and satisfying raw dish works well as an entrée or as an appetizer. We've used paper-thin slices of celery root, rutabaga, parsnip, carrot, Chioggia and gold beet, and strawberry daikon with stunning results. The garnishes make it a visually attractive dish as well. For shredding the beets, we like to use a Japanese vegetable stringer, which makes striking thin, long ribbons. E.T.

PORTOBELLO MUSHROOM PÂTÉ

1 1/2 cups walnuts
16 ounces portobello mushrooms, stemmed and thinly sliced
1/2 cup thinly sliced red onions
1 clove garlic, minced
2 teaspoons barley miso
3 tablespoons extra virgin olive oil
1 teaspoon minced fresh rosemary
1/4 teaspoon dried thyme
1/8 teaspoon ground nutmeg
Salt and freshly ground black pepper

SWEET PEPPER–OLIVE TAPENADE

1 cup finely diced sweet peppers (such as red, yellow, and purple peppers)
1 cup finely diced pitted kalamata olives
1 teaspoon grated lemon zest
Juice of 1/2 lemon
1/4 cup minced chives or scallions, green part only
1 teaspoon minced fresh oregano
2 teaspoons minced fresh tarragon
Freshly ground black pepper

ROOT VEGETABLE PASTA

2 root vegetables (such as parsnips, celery root, gold beets, and strawberry daikon), peeled and squared off to 2 inches in diameter
2 teaspoons extra virgin olive oil
Juice of 1/2 lemon
1/4 teaspoon salt
1/8 teaspoon freshly ground black pepper

LEMON-DILL CASHEW CREAM

1/2 cup unsalted cashews
2/3 cup water, plus more as needed
Juice of 1 lemon
2 teaspoons white miso
2 tablespoons minced fresh dill

2 ripe avocados, peeled, pitted, and cut into small dice, tossed with 2 teaspoons freshly squeezed lemon juice
1/2 cup shredded gold or Chioggia beets
1 bunch fresh chervil (optional)
1 (4-ounce) package enoki mushrooms, for garnish
3 teaspoons white truffle oil, for garnish
2 teaspoons minced chives or scallions, green part only, for garnish

To make the pâté, place the walnuts in a bowl and cover with lukewarm water (below 118°F). Soak for at least 4 hours at room temperature, or refrigerate overnight.

Place the mushrooms, onions, garlic, miso, and oil in a bowl and toss to coat. Cover and marinate for 2 hours.

Drain the walnuts and place them in a food processor fitted with the metal blade. Add the mushroom mixture and the rosemary, thyme, and nutmeg. Process until the mixture resembles a smooth paste. Add salt and black pepper to taste. (Store refrigerated, in an airtight container, for up to 4 days.)

To make the tapenade, place the peppers, olives, lemon zest, lemon juice, chives, oregano, and tarragon in a bowl and toss together. Add pepper to taste.

To make the pasta sheets, using a mandoline, slice the root vegetables into paper-thin sheets; you will need 60 sheets for 6 servings. Toss the root vegetable sheets in a bowl with the olive oil, lemon juice, salt, and pepper. Marinate for 30 minutes.

(continued)

ROOT VEGETABLE RAVIOLI, *continued*

To make the cream, combine all of the ingredients in a blender. Blend until smooth, adding additional water if needed to thin to the texture of heavy cream.

To serve, drizzle 3 tablespoons of the lemon-dill cream over the bottom of each plate. Place 5 root vegetable pasta sheets around the perimeter of the plate. Place 1 heaping teaspoon of the mushroom pâté in the center of each sheet. Place another sheet over the pâté. Top each ravioli with about 1/2 teaspoon of the tapenade. Place one-sixth of the avocado in the center of the plate. Top with a small tuft of the shredded beets, followed by a small tuft of chervil. Place a portion of the enoki mushrooms standing in the center of the avocado. Drizzle with 1/2 teaspoon truffle oil, and sprinkle the whole plate with chives.

NUTRITIONAL INFORMATION

PER SERVING: 276 calories (65% from fat), 5.5 g protein, 15.2 g carbohydrate, 23.9 g fat, 0 mg cholesterol, 556 mg sodium, 3.9 g fiber

PER 2 TABLESPOONS PÂTÉ: 106 calories (75% from fat), 2.3 g protein, 4.7 g carbohydrate, 9.5 g fat, 0 mg cholesterol, 72 mg sodium, 1.1 g fiber

PER 1/4 CUP TAPENADE: 23 calories (62% from fat), 0.3 g protein, 2.2 g carbohydrate, 1.8 g fat, 0 mg cholesterol, 148 mg sodium, 0.7 g fiber

PER 3 TABLESPOONS CREAM: 102 calories (65% from fat), 3 g protein, 6.6 g carbohydrate, 8.1 g fat, 0 mg cholesterol, 108 mg sodium, 1.2 g fiber

Portobello Carpaccio *over* Carrot *and* Parsnip Fettuccine *with* Raw Pumpkin Seed–Ancho Chile Pesto

SERVES 8

Recently, more and more of our diners have asked for totally raw dishes. This is one of my favorites. The portobellos are so rich that you will want to serve them on their own as an appetizer. For soy sauce, we use Oshawa brand nama shoyu, which is cold-fermented and therefore raw. You'll need to allow a couple of hours of advance planning to marinate the portobellos, soak the pumpkin seeds, and rehydrate the chiles. E.T.

PORTOBELLO CARPACCIO

3 large portobello mushrooms, stemmed
1 clove garlic, minced
2 teaspoons peeled and minced fresh ginger
1/4 teaspoon freshly ground black pepper
2 tablespoons extra virgin olive oil
2 tablespoons soy sauce

CARROT AND PARSNIP FETTUCCINE

2 large carrots, peeled
2 large parsnips, peeled
1 tablespoon extra virgin olive oil or a raw nut oil
   (such as almond or walnut oil)
Juice of 1/2 lemon
1/4 teaspoon salt
Freshly ground black pepper

PUMPKIN SEED–ANCHO CHILE PESTO

1 cup soaked pumpkin seeds (see page 222)
2 dried ancho chiles, seeded and rehydrated (see page
   222), soaking liquid reserved
2 tablespoons extra virgin olive oil
1 clove garlic, minced
1/2 teaspoon ground cumin
Juice of 1 lime
1/2 bunch cilantro leaves
1/2 teaspoon salt, plus more as needed

2 cups Exotic Mushroom Ceviche (page 35) or a
   favorite raw salsa
Cilantro leaves, for garnish
6 tablespoons sprouted quinoa (see page 223), beans,
   lentils or chickpeas, for garnish

To make the carpaccio, slice the mushrooms on the diagonal as thinly as possible (about 1/8 inch). Place the mushroom slices in a large baking dish. Sprinkle with the garlic, ginger, black pepper, olive oil, and soy sauce and cover with plastic wrap. Place another baking dish over the plastic wrap, and weight it down with cans, a brick, or a container full of water. Marinate at room temperature for 2 hours. After 2 hours, remove the mushrooms from the accumulated liquid and discard the liquid.

To make the fettuccine, with a vegetable peeler, peel the carrot and parsnip into as thin ribbons as possible. Place in a bowl and toss with the olive oil, lemon juice, salt, and pepper to taste. Marinate for 30 minutes.

To make the pesto, place the soaked pumpkin seeds, rehydrated chiles, oil, garlic, cumin, and lime juice in a food processor fitted with the metal blade. Process until smooth, adding the reserved chile soaking water as needed to make a thin paste. Add the cilantro and salt and process until just incorporated, with bits of cilantro still visible. Transfer to a bowl, and add salt to taste.

To serve, toss the fettuccine with 1 cup of the pesto. Divide among 8 dinner plates or pasta bowls. Top each serving with a portion of mushroom carpaccio fanned or mounded over the fettuccine. Place 1 teaspoon of the pesto over the mushrooms. Scatter some mushroom ceviche around the plate. Sprinkle with cilantro leaves and sprouted quinoa.

NUTRITIONAL INFORMATION

PER SERVING: 149 calories (40% from fat), 3.9 g protein, 19.9 g carbohydrate, 7.2 g fat, 0 mg cholesterol, 451 mg sodium, 8 g fiber

PER TABLESPOON PESTO: 50 calories (30% from fat), 2 g protein, 7.4 g carbohydrate, 1.8 g fat, 0 mg cholesterol, 123 mg sodium, 4.7 g fiber

CREOLE SAUTÉED MUSHROOMS *and* KIDNEY BEANS *over* PECAN DIRTY RICE

SERVES 6

This is one of my favorite recipes, with its rich and complexly spicy Creole sauce. It's really all about the sauce! We have made countless variations on this dish—from adding seitan sausage and root vegetables to coating tofu or tempeh medallions with the sauce.

We bake this dirty rice—as well as most of our rices and grains—in the oven to guarantee even cooking. On the stovetop, heat emanates from the bottom of the pan, making the grains cook unevenly and possibly scorching the bottom of the pan. E.T.

CREOLE SAUCE

1/4 cup extra virgin olive oil
1/4 cup all-purpose flour
2 cups 1/4-inch-diced celery
2 cups 1/4-inch-diced carrots
1 red onion, cut into 1/4-inch dice
4 cloves garlic, minced
1 1/2 teaspoons dried thyme
2 bay leaves
1 teaspoon espresso grounds
2 teaspoons Spanish paprika
1/3 teaspoon cayenne pepper, plus more as needed
1 teaspoon dried oregano
2 teaspoons nutritional yeast (see page 224)
2 cups dry red wine
1/2 teaspoon freshly ground black pepper, plus more as needed
1/4 cup tomato paste
3 cups mushroom stock (page 206)
1 tablespoon balsamic vinegar
1 tablespoon tamari
Salt

PECAN DIRTY RICE

2 teaspoons olive oil
1/2 red onion, cut into 1/4-inch dice
1 clove garlic, minced
1/2 cup pecans, toasted (see page 222) and coarsely chopped
1/4 teaspoon dried thyme

1/4 teaspoon ground cinnamon
1/4 teaspoon ground allspice
Pinch of freshly ground black pepper
1/2 teaspoon salt
1 cup brown basmati rice
1 1/2 cups water

BRAISED KALE

1/2 teaspoon salt
2 bunches Red Russian or Lacinato kale, washed, stemmed, and cut into 1-inch-wide strips
2 teaspoons extra virgin olive oil
1 yellow onion, halved crosswise and then sliced into thin crescents
2 cloves garlic, minced
2 teaspoons umeboshi vinegar

CREOLE SAUTÉED MUSHROOMS

2 teaspoons extra virgin olive oil
2 cloves garlic, minced
8 ounces cremini mushrooms, halved
8 ounces shiitake mushrooms, stemmed and halved
8 ounces oyster mushrooms
1/4 teaspoon salt, plus more as needed
1 1/2 cups cooked kidney beans
Cayenne pepper

Non-Macho Cornbread (page 218)
6 lemon wedges, for garnish
12 chive sprigs, plus 2 tablespoons chopped chives, for garnish
1/2 cup pecans, toasted (see page 222) and coarsely chopped

To make the sauce, begin with a roux. Heat 3 tablespoons of the olive oil in a small sauté pan over low heat. Whisk in the flour. Simmer for about 20 minutes, whisking almost constantly, to make a deep nutbrown roux. Remove from the heat. Let cool to close to room temperature before using.

Heat the remaining tablespoon olive oil in a heavybottomed saucepan over medium heat. Add the celery, carrots, onion, and garlic, and sauté for 10 to

15 minutes, until soft and starting to brown. Add the thyme, bay leaves, espresso, paprika, cayenne pepper, and oregano. Sauté, stirring often, for 2 minutes to toast the spices. Add the yeast, and then add the wine and stir to scrape up the browned bits from the bottom of the pan. Add the black pepper, tomato paste, stock, vinegar, and tamari. Decrease the heat to medium-low, and simmer for 15 minutes, or until reduced by one-third. Slowly whisk in the roux, decrease the heat to low, and continue to simmer for another 10 minutes, or until thickened. Remove from the heat. Add salt, black pepper, and cayenne pepper to taste.

To make the rice, preheat the oven to 350°F. Heat the olive oil in an ovenproof saucepan over medium heat. Add the onions and garlic, and sauté for 5 minutes, or until the onions are soft. Add the pecans, thyme, cinnamon, allspice, pepper, and salt. Sauté for 1 minute. Add the rice, and sauté for 2 minutes, stirring often, to toast the rice. Add the water and bring to a boil.

Cover the saucepan and place in the oven. Bake for 30 minutes, or until the liquid is absorbed and the rice is al dente. (Alternatively, cover and simmer over low heat for 30 minutes.) Remove from the oven and let steam still covered, for 10 minutes. Fluff the rice with a fork. Serve or keep covered until needed.

To make the kale, bring 1 gallon water to a boil in a large stockpot. Add the salt. Place the kale in the boiling water and blanch for 3 to 7 minutes, depending on the variety, until just tender (see page 223). Drain the kale in a colander. If not using immediately, rinse with cold water.

Heat a large sauté pan over high heat and add the olive oil. When the oil is hot, add the onions and garlic and sauté for 2 minutes, or until just softened. Add the drained kale and the vinegar and sauté for 2 minutes, or until heated through. Remove from the heat.

To make the mushrooms, place a large saucepan over medium-high heat and add the olive oil. Add the garlic and sauté for 1 minute, or until just starting to brown. Add the cremini, shiitake, and oyster mushrooms and the salt. Sauté for 4 minutes, or until the mushrooms are just softened. Add the kidney beans and the Creole sauce and heat through. Add salt and cayenne pepper to taste.

To serve, for each serving, place a ring of kale around the inside perimeter of a large shallow bowl, such as a pasta bowl. Follow with a ring of rice. Fill the center of the bowl with a portion of the Creole mushroom mixture. Place a wedge of cornbread and a wedge of lemon on the side. Sprinkle the plate with some chopped chives and pecans. Put 2 chive sprigs upright in the center.

NUTRITIONAL INFORMATION

PER SERVING MUSHROOMS: 372 calories (25% from fat), 11 g protein, 50 g carbohydrate, 13 g fat, 0 mg cholesterol, 158 mg sodium, 9.5 g fiber

PER SERVING RICE: 190 calories (35% from fat), 3.4 g protein, 27.8 g carbohydrate, 7.7 g fat, 0 mg cholesterol, 161 mg sodium, 1.6 g fiber

PER SERVING KALE: 58 calories (27% from fat), 2.4 g protein, 9.3 g carbohydrate, 2 g fat, 0 mg cholesterol, 533 mg sodium, 1 g fiber

ASIAN-STYLE SMOKED TOFU
and MARINATED CABBAGE LAVASH

SERVES 4

This addictively good and intensely flavored sandwich is our take on a wrap. Use lavash flatbread or even large tortillas. For convenience, use pre-prepared smoked or baked tofu. This recipe calls for Chinese fermented tofu with chile. Chile is traditionally used in pork roast marinades, and it adds a pungency to the tofu. We like Dragonfly brand's chile, available in most Asian markets. E.T.

MARINATED CABBAGE

2 cups thinly shredded Chinese or green cabbage
1 carrot, peeled and shredded
1/2 red onion, thinly sliced
1 Japanese cucumber or English cucumber, seeded and thinly sliced (optional)
2 teaspoons sesame seeds, toasted (see page 223)
2 teaspoons unrefined sugar or agave nectar (see page 224)
2 tablespoons rice vinegar
1/2 teaspoon salt

SMOKED TOFU

2 tablespoons tamari
2 tablespoons agave nectar (see page 224) or rice syrup
3 tablespoons sesame oil
1 teaspoon Chinese fermented tofu with chile (optional)
1 clove garlic, minced
1 teaspoon peeled and minced fresh ginger
Freshly ground black pepper
1 pound smoked baked tofu (page 211)

2 large lavash rolls, or 4 tortillas
2 cups assorted sprouts (such as clover, onion, and daikon sprouts)
1/4 cup Thai or Italian basil chiffonade
1/2 cup Creamy Wasabi Dressing (page 52)

To make the cabbage, combine all of the ingredients in a mixing bowl. Marinate for 30 minutes. Squeeze out the excess moisture from the cabbage, or place in a strainer to let the marinated cabbage dry.

To make the tofu, in a mixing bowl, whisk together the tamari, agave nectar, sesame oil, tofu, garlic, ginger, and black pepper. Immerse the tofu in the mixture to coat. Marinate for 10 minutes.

Preheat the broiler. Line a baking sheet with parchment paper. Place the tofu on the pan, and spoon some marinade on each piece. Broil for 2 minutes per side, or until the glaze caramelizes and adheres to the tofu. Remove from the heat and let cool. Slice the tofu thinly.

To assemble the sandwiches, place 1 lavash roll on a flat surface. At the bottom of the roll, place about one-half of the marinated cabbage, followed by half of the sprout mixture. Sprinkle with the basil. Place half of the tofu slices on top of the basil. Spread 1/4 cup of the wasabi dressing on the remaining lavash. Fold the ends of the lavash in, and roll burrito style. Slice in half. Repeat with the remaining ingredients to make another lavash. Cut in half, and serve one half lavash per person.

NUTRITIONAL INFORMATION

PER SERVING: 255 calories (60% from fat), 10.5 g protein, 29.5 g carbohydrate, 12.8 g fat, 0 mg cholesterol, 645 mg sodium, 3.7 g fiber

OYSTER MUSHROOM *and* TOFU RÉMOULADE POORBOY

SERVES 4

This amazing poorboy is our take on the New Orleans sandwich—again, another favorite from our Southern Comfort Dinner menu. For significantly lower fat, try grilling or broiling the mushrooms with a bit of the tamari and lemon instead of dry-frying them. E.T.

TOFU RÉMOULADE

1 cup tofu aïoli (page 213)

¹/₄ cup minced roasted red pimientos or red bell peppers (see page 222)

1 tablespoon minced pepperoncini

2 tablespoons minced cornichons

Tabasco sauce or a favorite hot sauce, as needed

OYSTER MUSHROOMS

1 cup breadcrumbs (page 222)

1¹/₂ cups all-purpose flour

1 teaspoon dried thyme

¹/₄ teaspoon cayenne pepper

¹/₄ teaspoon freshly ground black pepper

2 teaspoons salt

1 cup soy milk

¹/₄ cup tofu aïoli (page 213), or ¹/₄ cup tofu purée mixed with 2 teaspoons water

8 ounces oyster mushrooms

Canola or vegetable oil

2 cups shredded romaine lettuce

¹/₂ red onion, sliced paper-thin

Juice of 1 lemon

2 teaspoons extra virgin olive oil (optional)

¹/₃ teaspoon dried oregano

Salt and freshly ground black pepper

2 large sweet or sour French rolls, sliced open

1 or 2 tomatoes, thinly sliced

To make the rémoulade, combine all of the ingredients in a mixing bowl. (Store refrigerated for up to 4 days.)

To make the mushrooms, in a mixing bowl, combine the breadcrumbs, flour, thyme, cayenne pepper, black pepper, and salt. Mix well. In a separate bowl, combine the soy milk and aïoli. Place a 2-quart saucepan over medium-high heat and add at least 2 inches of oil. Heat to 350°F.

Dredge the oyster mushrooms in the flour mixture and dip them in the soy milk mixture. Return them to the flour mixture and coat well. In batches, deep-fry the mushrooms in the oil for 2 minutes, or until golden brown. Remove with a slotted spoon and drain on paper towels.

To make the lettuce mixture, combine the lettuce, red onion, lemon, juices, olive oil, and oregano in a bowl. Add salt and pepper to taste.

To assemble the sandwiches, open the French rolls and place half of the lettuce mixture on the bottom of each roll. Spread the tofu rémoulade evenly over the top half. Place the sliced tomatoes over the lettuce and the oyster mushrooms over the tomatoes. Place the top halves of the rolls over mushrooms and cut each sandwich in half. Serve one half per person.

NUTRITIONAL INFORMATION

PER SERVING: 533 calories (32% from fat), 17.1 g protein, 77 g carbohydrate, 17.5 g fat, 0 mg cholesterol, 1409 mg sodium, 4.6 g fiber

PER 2 TABLESPOONS RÉMOULADE: 29 calories (41% from fat), 2.9 g protein, 3.6 g carbohydrate, 1.9 g fat, 0 mg cholesterol, 229 mg sodium, 0.5 g fiber

AFRICAN TEFF CAKES *with* FAVA–WILD MUSHROOM WAT *and* CARROT-CHILE CHUTNEY

SERVES 6

Paul Rose, a favorite line cook, showed up one day with a bag of teff and said "Let's play!" This wild and popular dish was the result. Teff, the smallest whole grain, originates in Africa. It is available in health food stores. The cakes are accompanied by our rendition of wat, an African stew that is typically seasoned with Berber spices. B.E.

CARROT-CHILE CHUTNEY

1 teaspoon olive oil
1/2 teaspoon whole mustard seeds
1 habanero, Thai, or Scotch Bonnet chile, plus more as needed, seeded and minced
2 tablespoons champagne vinegar
1 1/2 tablespoons Florida Crystals (see page 224)
2 large carrots, peeled and cut into 1/4-inch dice
1/2 teaspoon ground cinnamon
1/2 cup fresh carrot juice
1/2 teaspoon salt

TEFF CAKES

4 cups water
1 teaspoon salt
2 cups whole teff
2 teaspoons olive oil

FAVA–WILD MUSHROOM WAT

2 teaspoons cumin seeds
1 teaspoon coriander seeds
1 (1/2-inch) cinnamon stick
1/2 teaspoon fenugreek seeds
1/4 teaspoon hulled cardamom seeds
1/4 teaspoon ground nutmeg
2 whole cloves
2 teaspoons olive oil, or vegetable stock (page 205) for oil free
2 red onions, cut into small dice
2 cloves garlic, minced
1 carrot, peeled and diced
1 (1/2-inch) piece fresh ginger, peeled and minced
1/2 teaspoon spearmint tea

1/2 teaspoon crushed red pepper flakes
3 cups chopped assorted wild mushrooms (such as morels, chanterelles, or other spring mushrooms)
1 cup vegetable stock (page 205) or water, as needed
3 cups fresh fava beans, shelled and peeled

1/2 cup cucumber raita (page 214)

To make the chutney, heat the olive oil in a heavy-bottomed saucepan over medium-high heat. Add the mustard seeds and sauté for 45 seconds, or until the seeds begin to pop. Add the chile, vinegar, Florida Crystals, carrots, cinnamon, carrot juice, and salt. Cook over high heat, stirring often, for 5 to 7 minutes, until the liquid is reduced to syrup and the carrots are soft. Let cool. (Store refrigerated for up to 1 week.)

To make the teff, bring the water and salt to a boil. Whisk in the teff. Cook, whisking often, for 15 minutes, or until a thick porridge forms. Spread the teff evenly on a baking sheet to a depth of 1/2 inch. Let cool to room temperature.

To cook the teff, preheat the broiler. Cut the teff into 18 even triangles and brush lightly with olive oil. Heat the triangles under the broiler for 5 minutes, or until toasted and browned. Keep warm.

To make the wat, place a saucepan over medium heat. Add the cumin, coriander, cinnamon stick, fenugreek, cardamom, nutmeg, and cloves and toast, stirring frequently, for 2 minutes, or until aromatic. Grind in a coffee grinder.

In a heavy-bottomed saucepan, heat the olive oil over medium heat. Add the onions and garlic and sauté for 10 minutes, or until they begin to caramelize. Add the carrots, ground spices, the ginger, spearmint tea, and pepper flakes. Cook over medium heat for 3 minutes, or until the carrots are just soft. Add the mushrooms, and sauté for 5 minutes, or until they lose their water. They should release a fair amount of liquid; if they don't, add 1 cup light vegetable stock or

(continued)

AFRICAN TEFF CAKES, *continued*

water. Add the favas. Simmer for 10 minutes, or until the favas are tender and most of the liquid has evaporated. Serve immediately, as the fresh favas will not retain their color for long.

To serve, arrange 3 toasted teff on each plate in a pinwheel. Spoon the wat in the center, and garnish evenly with the raita and carrot chutney.

NUTRITIONAL INFORMATION

PER 3 TEFF CAKES: 169 calories (10% from fat), 6 g protein, 33 g carbohydrate, 2.1 g fat, 0 mg cholesterol, 249 mg sodium, 6 g fiber

PER 1/2 CUP WAT: 139 calories (8% from fat), 9.4 g protein, 24 g carbohydrate, 1.4 g fat, 0 mg cholesterol, 10 mg sodium, 9 g fiber

PER 1/4 CUP CHUTNEY: 45 calories (17% from fat), 0.7 g protein, 9 g carbohydrate, 1 g fat, 0 mg cholesterol, 176 mg sodium, 1.7 g fiber

SLOPPY JOSE

SERVES 6

This is a longtime staff-meal favorite. We decided to name it after Jose "King of all Busboys" Maldonado, as a consolation for the Dallas Cowboys' losing season(s). It's perhaps the most decadent thing in the book, and the messiest!

The tomato sauce used in the Sloppy Jose mixture is a Millennium staple. Save the leftover sauce or whip up a new batch to use with our fresh pasta (page 208). B.E.

TOMATO SAUCE

2 teaspoons extra virgin olive oil
2 cloves garlic, minced
4 shallots, minced
2 teaspoons capers
1/4 teaspoon crushed red pepper flakes (optional)
1/2 teaspoon dried oregano
1/4 teaspoon ground fennel seed
1/4 cup Chianti
1 (16-ounce) can diced tomatoes
1/2 teaspoon salt, plus more as needed
1 tablespoon minced fresh basil leaves
Freshly ground black pepper

SLOPPY JOSE

2 teaspoons canola oil
1 red onion, cut into 1/4-inch dice
2 cloves garlic, minced
1 tablespoon Sucanat (see page 224)
1 tablespoon chile powder
1/4 teaspoon crushed red pepper flakes
1/2 teaspoon salt
1/4 teaspoon freshly ground black pepper
24 ounces tempeh or extra firm tofu, crumbled
   (1 1/2 cups)
2 teaspoons balsamic vinegar
1 tablespoon tamari
Vegetable stock (page 205) or water

Millennium Focaccia (page 217)
Lettuce
Tomatoes
Onions
Pickles

To make the tomato sauce, place a saucepan over medium heat and add the oil. Add the garlic and shallots and sauté for 5 minutes, or until translucent. Add the capers, pepper flakes, oregano, and fennel. Sauté for 30 seconds, or until fragrant. Add the wine and stir to scrape up the browned bits from the bottom of the pan. Add the tomatoes and salt. Decrease the heat to low and simmer for 20 minutes, or until slightly thickened. Add the basil, and season with salt and pepper to taste. (Store refrigerated for up to 5 days.)

To make the Sloppy Jose mixture, place a heavy skillet over medium-high heat and add the oil. Add the onions, garlic, Sucanat, chile powder, pepper flakes, salt, and black pepper. Sauté for 1 to 2 minutes, until the onions are soft. Add the tempeh, and cook, stirring constantly, for 2 minutes. Add 1/2 cup of the tomato sauce, the balsamic, and tamari. Stir to combine, and cook over low heat for 10 minutes, or until thick. If the mixture is too thick, add a little vegetable stock or to reach the desired consistency.

To assemble the sandwiches, cut the focaccia into 6 sandwich-sized pieces and then into sandwich halves, and toast. Spoon the tempeh mixture over the bottom halves of the bread. Add the lettuce, tomato, onions, and pickles as desired, and cover with the top piece of focaccia.

NUTRITIONAL INFORMATION

PER SERVING: 539 calories (20 from fat), 21 g protein, 61 g carbohydrate, 13.6 g fat, 0 mg cholesterol, 1081 mg sodium, 4.8 g fiber

CAJUN-CRUSTED TEMPEH *with* LEMON-CAPER-DILL CREAM *and* BRAISED COLLARD GREENS

SERVES 6

Blackening doesn't do for tempeh what it does for fish, but this Cajun cornmeal crust combines the best of all worlds. The lemon-dill sauce is a perfect foil, and the pecan rice is ooo-eee *good! Pour a glass of Beaujolais, cook up some greens, and enjoy! B.E.*

LEMON-CAPER-DILL CREAM SAUCE

1/2 teaspoon olive oil

1 yellow onion, halved crosswise and then sliced into thin crescents

1/2 teaspoon salt, plus more as needed

1 cup dry white wine

1 cup unsalted cashews

3 cups vegetable stock (page 205)

1 teaspoon nutritional yeast (see page 224)

3 tablespoons freshly squeezed lemon juice

2 teaspoons capers

1/4 teaspoon freshly ground white pepper

1 tablespoon chopped fresh dill

CAJUN-CRUSTED TEMPEH

1 cup cornmeal

1/2 cup Hungarian paprika

2 teaspoons garlic powder

2 teaspoons onion powder

1 teaspoon fresh thyme

1 teaspoon fresh oregano

1 teaspoon chile powder

2 teaspoons salt

1/2 teaspoon freshly ground black pepper

1/2 teaspoon ground nutmeg

1/2 teaspoon cayenne pepper

1/4 cup tofu aïoli (page 213)

1/2 cup soy milk

6 (4-ounce) pieces baked marinated tempeh (page 211)

Canola or grapeseed oil

BRAISED COLLARD GREENS

2 tablespoons olive oil

1 red onion, thinly sliced

2 cloves garlic, minced

1 large bunch collard greens, cut into 1-inch-wide
  strips
$^1/_2$ cup water or vegetable stock (see page 205)
2 tablespoons balsamic vinegar
$^1/_2$ teaspoon salt

3 cups Pecan Dirty Rice (page 148)

To make the cream, heat the olive oil in a saucepan over medium heat. Add the onions and salt and cook for 3 to 5 minutes, until transparent. Add the wine and simmer for 5 to 7 minutes, or until reduced by one-third.

In a blender, blend the cashews, stock, and yeast until smooth. Whisk the cashew mixture into the wine and onions and cook for 2 minutes, or until the cashew milk thickens into a rich sauce. Stir in the lemon juice, capers, pepper, and dill. Add salt to taste.

To make the tempeh, combine the cornmeal, paprika, garlic powder, onion powder, thyme, oregano, chile powder, salt, pepper, nutmeg, and cayenne pepper in a bowl. In another bowl, combine the aïoli and soy milk.

Cut the tempeh into triangles or fingers, and dredge from the dry to the wet ingredients and back to the dry. Heat the oil in a frying pan over medium-high heat. Fry 1 or 2 pieces of tempeh at a time for

1 to 2 minutes per side, or until dark brown. Repeat with the remaining tempeh pieces. Drain well on paper towels. Keep warm.

To make the collard greens, preheat the oven to 350°F. Place a sauté pan over medium heat and add the olive oil. Add the onion and garlic and sauté for 10 minutes, or until lightly caramelized. Transfer to a deep ovenproof baking dish and fill with the greens, water, vinegar, and salt. Cover and bake for 30 minutes, or until the greens are very soft.

To serve, place $^1/_2$ cup of the rice in the center of each plate. Place 2 tablespoons of the cream at the front of the plate. Fan a potion of the tempeh over the sauce, and place some collard greens on the side.

NUTRITIONAL INFORMATION

PER 6 OUNCES TEMPEH: 397 calories (35% from fat), 25 g protein, 44 g carbohydrate, 16 g fat, 0 mg cholesterol, 642 mg sodium, 7.2 g fiber

PER 2 TABLESPOONS CREAM: 23 calories (63% from fat), 0.5 g protein, 1.3 g carbohydrate, 1.4 g fat, 0 mg cholesterol, 21 mg sodium, 0.2 g fiber

PER SERVING COLLARD GREENS: 81 calories (48% from fat), 1.8 g protein, 9.6 g carbohydrate, 4.8 g fat, 0 mg cholesterol, 177 mg sodium, 3.9 g fiber

FAUXLET AU POIVRE *with* SYRAH JUS, CHICORY *and* SMOKED CHERRIES, *and* ROASTED POTATOES *and* ROOTS

SERVES 6

Let this be a lesson: be careful about the jokes you crack; they may just stick around to haunt you. Yes, we coined the word fauxlet. *It is a subtle play on* "faux fillet." *For the "meat" in this fauxlet, we often use tempeh, but the recipe also works well with marinated seitan or smoked portobellos.*

For the assorted roasted roots, you have a lot to choose from: celery root, parsnip, turnip, burdock, salsify, sweet potato, yam, carrots, beets of varieties other than red, and daikon. At Millennium, we roast the potatoes and roots for this dish separately to account for the different cooking times. You may choose to simply roast them together; in small amounts, the variance in cooking times is not as much of a factor. B.E.

HORSERADISH CREAM

1/4 cup unsalted whole cashews or cashew butter
1 1/2 teaspoons peeled and grated fresh horseradish
1 teaspoon white wine vinegar
Salt
3/4 cup water
1 teaspoon miso

SYRAH REDUCTION

3 tablespoons olive oil
2 tablespoons all-purpose flour
3 cups Syrah
1 cup roasted vegetable dark stock (page 207)
1 cup tawny port
1 teaspoon tamari
1 teaspoon balsamic vinegar
Salt and freshly ground black pepper

ROASTED POTATOES AND ROOTS

2 small potatoes (such as Yellow Finn, German Butterball, or red-skinned), cut into 1-inch dice
3 to 4 cups assorted root vegetables (such as parsnip, rutabega, and celery root), cut into bite-sized pieces
4 teaspoons olive oil
1 teaspoon salt

1/2 teaspoon freshly ground black pepper
2 pinches of minced fresh rosemary

ONION-CHERRY-CHICORY MIX

1 tablespoon olive oil
1 cup small onions (such as shallots or cipollini), peeled and thinly sliced
2 tablespoons dried cherries, reconstituted in lukewarm water for 20 minutes
Salt and freshly ground black pepper
3 to 4 cups loosely packed assorted chicory lettuces or bitter greens (such as radicchio, escarole, frisée, arugula, and dandelion), washed and trimmed to bite size

FAUXLET AU POIVRE

1/2 cup breadcrumbs (page 222)
1 teaspoon dried thyme
2 teaspoons freshly ground black pepper
1 teaspoon salt
Pinch of ground nutmeg
2 1/2 cups all-purpose flour
1 cup tofu aïoli (page 213)
1 1/2 cups plain soy milk
6 (4-ounce) pieces baked marinated tempeh (page 211), halved diagonally
Canola oil

1/4 cup tarragon oil (see page 215), for garnish

To make the horseradish cream, blend all of the ingredients together until very smooth. (Store refrigerated for up to 4 days.)

To make the Syrah reduction, begin with a roux. Heat the olive oil in a small sauté pan over low heat. Whisk in the flour. Simmer for about 20 minutes, whisking almost constantly, to make a deep nut-brown roux. Remove from the heat. Let cool to close to room temperature before using.

Combine the Syrah, stock, port, tamari, and vinegar in a saucepan over medium heat. Simmer for 15 minutes, or until reduced by one-half. Whisk in the roux. Add salt and pepper to taste.

To roast the potatoes and roots, preheat the oven to 450°F. Toss the potatoes, root vegetables, olive oil, salt, pepper, and rosemary together in a bowl and place on a baking sheet. Roast for 20 to 30 minutes, until caramelized on the outside and soft all the way through.

To make the chicory mix, heat the olive oil in a large sauté pan over medium-high heat. Add the onions and cherries and salt and pepper to taste. Cook for 15 to 20 minutes, until caramelized. Stir in the chicories. Cook until warmed through, and immediately remove from the heat.

To make the fauxlets, combine the breadcrumbs, thyme, pepper, salt, nutmeg, and 1 cup of the flour in a bowl. In a second bowl, place the remaining 1 1/2 cups flour. In a third bowl, combine the aïoli and soy milk.

Dredge each triangle of tempeh in the plain flour, then dip in the aïoli mixture, and then dredge in the breadcrumb mixture. Place a sauté pan over medium-high heat, and add enough canola oil to come 1/2 inch up the side. When the oil is shimmering, fry the fauxlets in batches for 1 to 2 minutes per side, until brown. Drain on paper towels.

To serve, divide the roasted potatoes and roots in the center of each plate, top with equal amounts of the chicory mix, and wedge 2 tempeh triangles into the mix. Drizzle Syrah reduction around the plate, followed by 2 teaspoons of the tarragon oil. Drizzle horseradish cream over the tempeh.

NUTRITIONAL INFORMATION

PER 4 OUNCES TEMPEH: 243 calories (24% from fat), 14 g protein, 32 g carbohydrate, 6.8 g fat, 0 mg cholesterol, 396 mg sodium, 3.1 g fiber

PER 1/4 CUP REDUCTION: 61 calories (45% from fat), 0.4 g protein, 4.2 g carbohydrate, 1.7 g fat, 0 mg cholesterol, 69 mg sodium, 0 g fiber

PER SERVING POTATOES AND ROOTS: 63 calories (45% from fat), 1.1 g protein, 9.6 g carbohydrate, 4.8 g fat, 0 mg cholesterol, 177 mg sodium, 3.9 g fiber

PER SERVING CHICORY MIX: 41 calories (31% from fat), 1 g protein, 6.5 g carbohydrate, 1.5 g fat, 0 mg cholesterol, 88 mg sodium, 1.4 g fiber

PER TABLESPOON HORSERADISH CREAM: 12 calories (65% from fat), 0.4 g protein, 0.8 g carbohydrate, 1 g fat, 0 mg cholesterol, 14 mg sodium, 0.1 g fiber

FEIJOADA *with* CRISPY YUCA CAKES

SERVES 6

This version of the classic stew—a recipe that owes its existence to former intern and employee Sylvia Chan, a native Brazilian—uses chile and bell pepper meats and smoked apples and is served with yuca (cassava) cakes to allude to the traditional cassava flour. ℬ.ℰ.

YUCA CAKES

1 large yuca root, peeled and shredded
3 tablespoons fresh chives
1 teaspoon salt
1/2 teaspoon freshly ground black pepper
3 tablespoons cornstarch or tapioca flour
1 tablespoon canola oil, plus 1 cup for frying

FEIJOADA

1 teaspoon olive oil
1 red onion, diced
2 celery stalks, diced
3 scallions, white and green parts, chopped
3 cloves garlic, minced
Peel of 1 orange, coarsely chopped
1 teaspoon cumin seeds, toasted (see page 223)
1/2 teaspoon ground nutmeg
1/2 teaspoon ground cinnamon
1 teaspoon salt
1/2 teaspoon freshly ground black pepper
1/8 teaspoon cayenne pepper
1 tablespoon tamari
2 cups dried black beans, soaked and cooked with
    1 bay leaf (see page 220), drained with liquid
    reserved
1 to 3 red bell peppers, roasted, peeled, seeded, and
    cut into large dice
1 to 3 poblano chiles, or 1 to 3 green peppers plus
    1 jalapeño chile, roasted, peeled, seeded, and cut
    into large dice
1/2 cup smoked (see page 219, optional) reconstituted
    dried apple, diced
1/4 cup fresh cilantro, stemmed and coarsely chopped

Braised collard greens (page 157)

To make the yuca cakes, combine the yuca, chives, salt, pepper, cornstarch, and 1 tablespoon of the canola oil to form a stiff, firm dough. (You may need to process a portion of the mixture in a blender and recombine it to facilitate the binding.) Form the mixture into 6 patties. Heat the remaining oil in a sauté pan over medium-high heat. Fry the patties in batches for 1 to 2 minutes per side, until crisp. Drain well on paper towels. Keep warm until ready to serve. (Alternatively, for lower fat, preheat the oven to 350°F. Brush the cakes with soy milk and bake for 30 to 35 minutes, until firm.)

To make the feijoada, heat the olive oil in a large pot over medium-high heat. Add the onions, celery, scallions, and garlic. Sauté for 3 to 5 minutes, until soft. Add the orange peel, cumin, nutmeg, cinnamon, salt, pepper, cayenne pepper, and tamari. Toast for 1 minute. Add the beans and just enough of the cooking liquid to cover. Bring the stew to a boil. Decrease the heat and simmer for 15 to 20 minutes, letting the flavors mingle. Stir in the red bell peppers, poblanos, apples, and cilantro. Simmer for 5 minutes, or until heated through.

To serve, divide the feijoada among 6 soup bowls or deep pasta dishes. Place a portion of the collard greens in the center and a yuca cake on top of the greens.

NUTRITIONAL INFORMATION

PER CAKE: 126 calories (48% from fat), 1.4 g protein, 15 g carbohydrate, 7 g fat, 0 mg cholesterol, 317 mg sodium, 0.2 g fiber

PER SERVING FEIJOADA: 319 calories (73% from fat), 16 g protein, 62 g carbohydrate, 2.3 g fat, 0 mg cholesterol, 516 mg sodium, 14 g fiber

SMOKED TEMPEH *and* EGGPLANT MUFFALETTA *with* OLIVE *and* CUCUMBER RELISH

SERVES 6

This sandwich was inspired by the olive-enriched New Orleans classic. More than a sandwich, it is a hearty meal in itself, and it often finds its way into our Southern Comfort Dinners. Choose an especially good crusty sourdough. B.E.

SMOKED TEMPEH AND EGGPLANT

2 (16-ounce) tempeh pieces
1 globe eggplant, sliced into $1/2$-inch rounds
3 teaspoons salt
1 teaspoon coarsely ground black pepper
4 cloves garlic, minced
1 teaspoon ground cinnamon
$1/2$ teaspoon ground cloves
$1/2$ teaspoon ground allspice
1 tablespoon tamari
2 tablespoons balsamic vinegar
2 teaspoons Sucanat (see page 224)
$2/3$ cup vegetable stock (page 205) or water

OLIVE AND CUCUMBER RELISH

1 cup pitted kalamata or other pitted black olives, minced
1 cucumber, peeled, seeded, and minced
6 pickled okra pods, minced (optional)
1 teaspoon olive oil
1 tablespoon capers
2 teaspoons garlic powder

$1/4$ cup olive oil
$1/4$ cup nutritional yeast (see page 224)
3 (8-inch) round sourdough bread rolls, sliced open
2 tablespoons Dijon mustard
2 tomatoes, thinly sliced
1 small red onion, thinly sliced
2 cups arugula, loosely packed

To make the eggplant, combine all of the ingredients in a large bowl and marinate at room temperature for 1 hour.

Preheat the oven to 350°F. Smoke the tempeh and eggplant (see page 219) and then return them to the marinade. Transfer to a baking sheet and bake for 45 minutes, or until the tempeh and eggplant absorb most of the marinade. Remove the tempeh and slice thinly.

To make the relish, combine all of the ingredients in a medium bowl. Let sit for 10 minutes.

To assemble the sandwiches, preheat the broiler. Combine the olive oil and yeast in a small bowl to form a paste. Spread the paste on the bread, and toast in the broiler for 1 minute, or until golden and bubbly.

Evenly distribute the tempeh and eggplant across the slices. Spread relish on the bottom halves of the sandwiches and mustard on the tops. Return the sandwiches to the broiler, and toast, open faced, for 1 to 2 minutes, until the mustard begins to dry.

To serve, dress the sandwich halves with tomatoes, onions, and arugula. Place the halves together and cut the sandwiches into quarters. Serve 2 quarters per person.

NUTRITIONAL INFORMATION

PER SERVING: 500 calories (30% from fat), 34.5 g protein, 42 g carbohydrate, 23 g fat, 0 mg cholesterol, 1370 mg sodium, 8.7 g fiber

PER $1/4$ CUP RELISH: 36 calories (57% from fat), 0.6 g protein, 3.7 g carbohydrate, 2 g fat, 0 mg cholesterol, 174 mg sodium, 0.7 g fiber

HUITLACOCHE-POLENTA ROULADES *with* CHOCOLATE MOLE *and* CARROT-HABANERO SAUCE

SERVES 12

Huitlacoche is also known as the Mexican truffle. It is a pungent, inky black mushroom that grows on corn. Farmers know it as corn smut and often discard the delicacy. If I could only make one contribution to the culinary world, I would like to reclaim the reputation of this incredible mycelium. Its flavor is the best of my two favorite foods—corn and mushrooms—and its aroma and character add a depth of flavor to a myriad of dishes. Look for it at specialty markets, or consult your local corn farmer.

The tamales I ate growing up in Texas inspired this dish. The term mole *refers to the traditional method of preparing the sauce in a* molcajete y tejolete, *a Mexican version of the mortar and pestle. Here, some traditional ingredients are combined with some "tricks," such as adding complexity of flavor with caramelized onions, dried mushrooms, and toasted flour. This is also an excellent sauce for enchiladas or stuffed peppers. Be sure to handle the habaneros with gloves, especially if you have sensitive skin. B.E.*

CHOCOLATE MOLE

3 dried porcini mushrooms ($^1/_2$ cup, loosely packed)
3 cups hot vegetable stock (page 205)
1 teaspoon sesame oil
1 red onion, thinly sliced
2 cloves garlic, minced
1 teaspoon Sucanat (see page 224)
1 teaspoon salt
1 dried guajillo chile, toasted (see page 222) and seeded
1 dried ancho chile, toasted (see page 222) and seeded (optional)
1 dried pasilla chile, toasted (see page 222) and seeded
$^1/_4$ teaspoon ground nutmeg
$^1/_4$ teaspoon ground cinnamon
1 tablespoon tamari
2 ounces bittersweet chocolate
3 tablespoons creamy peanut butter
2 tablespoons corn flour, toasted until almost burnt (see page 223)

CARROT-HABANERO SAUCE

1 cup fresh carrot juice
1 peeled and chopped boiled carrot, cooled
$^1/_2$ habanero chile, plus more as needed
Juice of 1 lime
$^1/_2$ teaspoon sherry vinegar or apple cider vinegar
2 teaspoons canola oil
2 teaspoons olive oil
$^1/_2$ teaspoon salt

SOFT POLENTA

4 cups salted water
1 cup polenta or corn grits
2 tablespoons cashew butter
3 cloves garlic, roasted (page 224)
2 teaspoons nutritional yeast (see page 224)
1 teaspoon salt
$^1/_4$ teaspoon freshly ground black pepper

HUITLACOCHE FILLING

2 teaspoons Dijon mustard
3 tablespoons agave nectar (see page 224)
3 tablespoons tamari
1 teaspoon olive oil
12 ounces frozen tofu, thawed and cut into small dice
16 ounces assorted fresh mushrooms (such as cremini, chanterelles, and shiitakes), chopped
1 red onion, smoked (see page 219) and cut into $^1/_4$-inch dice
Kernels from 1 ear corn
1 cup huitlacoche
1 teaspoon olive oil
$^1/_2$ teaspoon whole cumin seeds
$^1/_2$ teaspoon chile powder
$1^1/_2$ teaspoons salt
1 teaspoon Sucanat (see page 224)

16 (13 by 18-inch) sheets whole-wheat phyllo dough
$^1/_4$ cup canola oil
2 bunches braised kale (page 148)
White truffle oil, for garnish

To make the mole, place the porcini in the stock. Let steep for 10 minutes. Strain and reserve the liquid.

Place a heavy saucepan over medium heat and add the sesame oil. Add the onions, garlic, Sucanat, and salt, and cook, stirring often and scraping the bottom of the pan for the rich bits that accumulate there, for 15 minutes, or until caramelized. When the onions are dark, add the guajillo, ancho, and pasilla chiles, and the nutmeg, cinnamon, and tamari. Stir for 1 minute. Add the reserved porcini stock and bring to a simmer. Whisk in the chocolate, peanut butter, and toasted flour, stirring until the chocolate has melted. Blend the sauce with a handheld immersion blender, or let cool and blend in the blender in batches. Keep warm.

To make the carrot-habanero sauce, in a blender, mix the carrot juice, carrots, habanero, lime juice, and vinegar. When this is smooth, slowly add the canola and olive oils. Add the salt.

To make the polenta, bring the water to a boil in a large saucepan. Whisk in the polenta, decrease the heat to low, and stir constantly for 10 minutes, or until the polenta is thick and pulls away from the sides of the saucepan. Remove from the heat. Stir in the cashew butter, garlic, yeast, salt, and pepper. Let cool.

To make the filling, preheat the oven to 450°F and preheat the broiler. Combine the mustard, agave nectar, tamari, and olive oil in a mixing bowl. Baste the tofu by dipping it in the marinade or brushing the marinade on with a pastry brush. Bake for 10 minutes, or until the tofu absorbs the marinade. Broil for 3 to 5 minutes, until dry. Set aside and let cool.

In a large bowl, combine the mushrooms, onions, corn, huitlacoche, olive oil, cumin, chile powder, salt, and Sucanat. Toss to coat. Spread on a baking sheet, and broil, turning every 5 minutes, for 20 minutes, or until evenly roasted. Crumble the tofu over the roasted vegetables. Let cool.

To make the roulades, on a clean surface, spread one layer of 2 sheets of phyllo. Brush lightly with canola oil. Place a second layer of 2 more sheets of phyllo on top of the first and brush with oil. Cut the layered sheets crosswise into 3 equal rectangles.

On the lower half of each rectangle, place 3 tablespoons of the polenta and ¼ cup of the filling. Fold the top half of the rectangle over the filling and seal the sides (the roulade should resemble a tamale). Place seam side down on a baking sheet. Repeat the process with the remaining phyllo and filling to make 12 roulades. Bake for 15 minutes, or until brown.

To serve, pour ¼ cup of the mole on each plate. Place some of the kale in the center and lean 1 roulade against it. Drizzle 1 tablespoon of the habanero sauce around the plate and drizzle truffle oil on the roulade.

NUTRITIONAL INFORMATION

PER ROULADE: 209 calories (29% from fat), 7.5 g protein, 33 g carbohydrate, 5 g fat, 0 mg cholesterol, 786 mg sodium, 4.2 g fiber

PER ¼ CUP MOLE: 138 calories (45% from fat), 4.1 g protein, 15 g carbohydrate, 7 g fat, 0 mg cholesterol, 357 mg sodium, 3.4 g fiber

PER TABLESPOON HABANERO SAUCE: 16 calories (59% from fat), 0.2 g protein, 1.6 g carbohydrate, 1.2 g fat, 0 mg cholesterol, 63 mg sodium, 0.4 g fiber

Black Chanterelles en Papillote *with* Toasted Barley Risotto, Beet-Cabernet Truffle Foam, *and* Braised Celery Hearts

SERVES 6

This dish was created to pair with the excellent Cabernets of Heitz Cellars for a dinner in fall 1999. The foam, a bit of fun we had exploring the concept of textures on the plate, was a surprising hit! The black chanterelles should explode with rich aromas when the paper is torn at the table. They are available in late fall and throughout the winter from specialty grocers.

To emphasize the presence of barley in the risotto, we garnish it with roasted specialty barley. We use Crystal malt because it's a sweeter roast, with a nice, nutty, toasty flavor. Crystal malt is sold in most home-brew supply stores.

You will need a foaming device to make the foam. If you do not own a whipping siphon or an Espuma (a canister device that uses nitrous oxide cartridges to make whipped cream), simply omit the agar and present the beet-Cabernet reduction as a sauce. B.E.

BEET-CABERNET TRUFFLE FOAM

3 cups Cabernet
1 red beet, peeled and diced (about 1 cup)
$1/2$ teaspoon salt
2 teaspoons balsamic vinegar
Pinch of freshly ground black pepper
1 tablespoon agar (see page 224)
1 teaspoon truffle oil

TOASTED BARLEY RISOTTO

8 to 10 cups vegetable stock (page 205)
1 teaspoon nutritional yeast (see page 224)
$1/4$ ounce dried wild mushrooms (such as porcini or chanterelles)
1 teaspoon salt
1 teaspoon canola oil
1 large yellow onion, diced
1 fennel bulb, cored and diced
1 carrot, peeled and diced
2 cloves garlic, minced
$1/4$ teaspoon ground nutmeg

$1/4$ teaspoon freshly ground white pepper
$1^{1}/2$ cups pearled barley, toasted (see page 221)

BLACK CHANTERELLES EN PAPILLOTE

12 ounces black chanterelles
16 ounces assorted fresh mushrooms (such as cremini or chanterelles), coarsely chopped
1 teaspoon canola oil
$1/2$ teaspoon salt
$1/4$ teaspoon freshly ground black pepper
$1/2$ teaspoon Sucanat (see page 224)
2 tablespoons tamari
2 shallots, minced

BRAISED CELERY HEARTS

$1/2$ teaspoon canola oil
1 large bunch celery
2 large leeks, white parts only, trimmed and thinly sliced
2 cloves garlic, minced
$1/2$ teaspoon fresh thyme
$1/2$ teaspoon salt
$1/4$ teaspoon freshly ground black pepper
1 teaspoon Florida Crystals (see page 224)

$3/4$ cup cashew cream (page 212)
Salt
1 tablespoon roasted specialty barley, for garnish

To make the foam, in a saucepan, combine the Cabernet, beets, salt, vinegar, and black pepper over medium heat. Cook for 20 minutes, or until reduced to 2 cups. Whisk in the agar and simmer for 10 minutes, stirring well. Transfer the mixture to a blender and purée. Strain. Refrigerate for 2 hours, or until set. Add the truffle oil. Using a whipping siphon, whip the mixture according to the manufacturer's directions.

To make the risotto, place a 2-quart saucepan over medium-high heat and add the stock, yeast, dried mushrooms, and salt. Bring to a boil. Decrease the heat to low and simmer for 15 minutes, or until the mushrooms have reconstituted. Drain and mince the mushrooms, reserving the stock.

Place a large, heavy-bottomed skillet or Dutch oven over medium heat, and add the canola oil. Add the onions, fennel, carrots, garlic, minced mushrooms, nutmeg, and white pepper, and cook for 10 minutes, or until the vegetables are just soft. Add the toasted barley and stir to coat. Add the hot stock, one ladleful at a time, stirring constantly and letting each ladleful be absorbed before adding the next. Cook for 15 to 20 minutes, including the stock absorption time, until the barley is just al dente. Remove from heat, whether or not all of the stock has been added.

To make the chanterelles en papillote, preheat the oven to 350°F. Tear open the chanterelles to reveal the insides. With a damp kitchen towel, brush out any dirt or pine needles that may have accumulated there. Toss the mushrooms, oil, salt, pepper, Sucanat, tamari, and shallots together in a bowl.

Divide the mixture evenly among 6 pieces of parchment paper. Fold each piece of parchment into a pouch, crimping the ends well so that it will not come open during baking. Bake for 20 minutes.

To make the celery hearts, preheat the oven to 350°F. Remove the outer stalks from the celery, juice them in a vegetable juicer, and set aside. Trim the tender inner stalks and cut into 2-inch lengths. Heat the canola oil in a skillet with a tight-fitting lid over medium-high heat. Add the celery hearts, leeks, garlic, thyme, salt,

pepper, Florida Crystals, and celery juice and bring to a boil. Cook for 3 to 5 minutes, until warmed through. Cover and braise for 20 minutes, or until the celery is very soft. Remove the celery from the liquid and place in a bowl. Cook the liquid over medium heat for 5 minutes, or until reduced to a syrupy consistency. Drizzle over the celery.

To serve, stir the cashew cream into the risotto. Add salt to taste, and warm through.

Distribute the warmed barley risotto among 6 plates. Place 1 papillote pouch next to the risotto on each plate. Place some of the celery hearts and liquid around the risotto. Place 1 tablespoon of the foam next to the papillote and sprinkle the plate with barley. At the table, slit open the top of each pouch, so that your guests may remove the filling onto the risotto.

NUTRITIONAL INFORMATION

PER POUCH CHANTERELLES: 198 calories (6% from fat), 6.8 g protein, 47 g carbohydrate, 1.6 g fat, 0 mg cholesterol, 335 mg sodium, 7 g fiber

PER SERVING RISOTTO: 247 calories (6% from fat), 6.4 g protein, 47 g carbohydrate, 1.5 g fat, 0 mg cholesterol, 341 mg sodium, 10 g fiber

PER TABLESPOON FOAM: 6 calories (28% from fat), 0.1 g protein, 0.7 g carbohydrate, 0.1 g fat, 0 mg cholesterol, 46 mg sodium, 0.1 g fiber

PER SERVING CELERY HEARTS: 45 calories (12% from fat), 1.5 g protein, 9.7 g carbohydrate, 0.7 g fat, 0 mg cholesterol, 290 mg sodium, 2.9 g fiber

STUFFED POBLANO CHILES *over* FORBIDDEN BLACK RICE RISOTTO *with* ROASTED CORN–AVOCADO ABDI

SERVES 6

This dish is not for the timid! It is inspired by Caribbean cuisine, with jerked tempeh, plantains, and fiery habanero chiles, although the risotto suggests the flavors of Mexican mole sauce. If you cannot find Lotus Foods forbidden black rice (see page 22), try mixing two parts arborio rice to one part Thai black or purple rice.

The inspiration for the "abdi" salsa came from a cookbook I used to own. I have no idea where the word abdi *came from. Abdi is a common first name in the Middle East and India, so I suppose the recipe may have been created originally by or for someone of that name. I guess the main reason we like the name is because people ask us, "Why do you call it abdi?" B.E.*

JERK MARINADE

2 teaspoons olive oil
1/2 red onion, thinly sliced
1 clove garlic
1/2 serrano chile
2 tablespoons Sucanat (see page 224)
1/4 cup balsamic vinegar
1/4 cup tamari
1/2 bunch cilantro
1 teaspoon dried thyme
1/4 teaspoon ground cloves
1/2 teaspoon ground allspice
1/4 teaspoon ground nutmeg
1/2 cup vegetable stock (page 205) or water

ROASTED CORN–AVOCADO ABDI

1 red onion, cut into 1/4-inch dice
1 carrot, peeled and cut into 1/4-inch dice
Kernels from 1 ear corn
4 to 6 kumquats, sliced, or 4 to 6 orange segments
1 cucumber, peeled, seeded, and cut into 1/4-inch dice
1 teaspoon dried oregano, toasted (see page 223)
1 teaspoon allspice berries, toasted (see page 223) and ground
1/4 bunch cilantro, stemmed and finely chopped

FORBIDDEN BLACK RICE RISOTTO

2 tablespoons olive oil
1 red onion, cut into small dice
1 carrot, peeled and cut into small dice
1 celery stalk, cut into small dice
2 cloves garlic, minced
2 teaspoons curry powder
2 teaspoons ancho or guajillo chile powder
1 teaspoon ground cinnamon
1 1/2 ounces unsweetened chocolate
1 1/2 cups forbidden black rice
3 1/2 cups vegetable stock (page 205)
1/2 cup cashew cream (page 212)
Salt

TEMPEH-PEPPER RAGOÛT

16 ounces tempeh, cut into 1-inch dice
1/4 cup canola oil
1 red onion, cut into large dice
1 carrot, peeled and cut into 1/2-inch dice
1 celery stalk, cut into 1/2-inch dice
2 cloves garlic, minced
3 to 4 red, yellow, purple, and green peppers, cut into large dice
1 medium-ripe plantain, peeled and diced
2 teaspoons chile powder
1 teaspoon whole cumin seeds
Vegetable stock (page 205)
Salt and freshly ground black pepper

Juice of 1 lime
1/2 habanero chile, seeded, plus more as needed
1 avocado, peeled, pitted, and diced
Salt
6 poblano chiles
6 cilantro sprigs, for garnish

To make the marinade, place a saucepan over medium heat and add the olive oil. Add the onion and sauté for 10 minutes, or until caramelized. Transfer to a blender and add the remaining ingredients. Blend on low to form a thick, smooth paste.

(continued)

STUFFED POBLANO CHILES, *continued*

To make the abdi, preheat the broiler. Place the corn on baking sheet and broil for 5 minutes, or until some of the kernels start to brown.

Mix the onions, carrots, corn, kumquats, cucumber, oregano, allspice, and cilantro in a bowl and set aside.

To make the risotto, place a deep skillet over medium-high heat and add the oil. Add the onions, carrots, celery, and garlic, and sauté for 5 minutes, or until soft. Add the curry, chile powder, cinnamon, chocolate, and rice and stir well. Stir in the stock. Cover and simmer for 45 minutes. Remove the lid and simmer, stirring often, for 5 to 10 minutes, until the liquid is absorbed. Stir in the cashew cream, and add salt to taste. Remove from the heat.

To make the ragoût, preheat the broiler. Put half of the jerk marinade in a bowl and stir in 2 tablespoons of the canola oil and the tempeh. Place the tempeh on a baking sheet and broil for 10 minutes, or until dry and browned.

Heat the remaining 2 tablespoons canola oil in a large skillet over medium-high heat. Add the onions, carrots, celery, and garlic, and sauté for 5 minutes, or until just soft. Add the peppers, plantain, chile powder, cumin, and the remaining jerk marinade and sauté for 10 minutes, or until the peppers are soft. Add the stock, if needed, to prevent scorching. Remove from the heat, and add the tempeh. Season with salt and pepper to taste.

To make the chiles, preheat the oven to 400°F. Place the chiles on a baking sheet and roast for 20 minutes. Remove from the oven, slit the chiles lengthwise, and remove the seeds and membrane. Fill each chile with about 1 cup of the ragoût and return to the oven. Bake for 20 minutes, or until heated through.

To finish the abdi, in a blender, blend the lime juice and habanero with 1/4 cup of the abdi mix. Combine with the rest of the abdi. Gently stir in the avocado and add salt to taste.

To serve, place a equal mounds of the risotto on each plate. Top with a chile, and surround with some of the abdi. Garnish with a cilantro sprig.

NUTRITIONAL INFORMATION

PER STUFFED CHILE: 330 calories (39% from fat), 17 g protein, 36.8 g carbohydrate, 15 g fat, 0 mg cholesterol, 42 mg sodium, 7.6 g fiber

PER 2 TABLESPOONS MARINADE: 14 calories (3.2% from fat), 0.6 g protein, 2.9 g carbohydrate, 0.1 g fat, 0 mg cholesterol, 252 mg sodium, 0.2 g fiber

PER SERVING ABDI: 125 calories (36% from fat), 2.8 g protein, 18 g carbohydrate, 5.4 g fat, 0 mg cholesterol, 15 mg sodium, 4.5 g fiber

PER SERVING RISOTTO: 315 calories (35% from fat), 7.8 g protein, 46 g carbohydrate, 12.9 g fat, 0 mg cholesterol, 30 mg sodium, 5.7 g fiber

DESSERTS

rtful, elegant desserts that are rich and satisfying without eggs, butter, or cream? Some might laugh at the prospect, but pastry chef Amy Pearce proves the possibilities on a nightly basis—from the decadence of white chocolate mousse and peanut butter cannoli, to the elegance of caramelized fig cake with lemon anglaise; from adventurous adaptations of classics like German chocolate cake and Key lime pie, to an innovative and exotic flan made from candy cap mushrooms. Simple cookies, luxurious chocolate truffles, and vibrant sorbets round out this section, along with tips, pointers, and suggestions on the hows and whys of vegan desserts and pastries. These desserts dispel the myth that vegan desserts have to be stodgy and lackluster as they showcase pure, vibrant flavor with irristable presenations of decadent delight.

Walnut Macaroons ❦ 190

Chocolate Biscotti ❦ 191

German Chocolate Cake ❦ 193

Bittersweet Truffles ❦ 195

Earl Gray Truffles ❦ 195

Strawberry, Rose, and Rhubarb Soup ❦ 196

Almond Sherbet ❦ 198

Cinnamon Sherbet ❦ 198

Espresso-Raspberry Sorbet ❦ 199

Hard Apple Cider Sorbet ❦ 199

Peppermint-Chocolate Sorbet ❦ 200

Pineapple–Passion Fruit Sorbet ❦ 200

Pear-Cardamom Sorbet ❦ 201

Coconut Sorbet ❦ 201

APPLE QUINCE CHERRY STRUDEL

SERVES 4

*For those who have not had quince, now is the time
to try it. The crunchy phyllo and the juicy fruit on the
inside will make this dessert an instant hit. We prefer
Fuji apples, for their sweet taste. Serve with Cinnamon Sherbet (page 198). A.P.*

1 large quince, diced (2 cups)
Juice of 1 orange
Chopped zest of 1 orange
1 tablespoon light agave nectar (see page 224)
1/2 teaspoon ground cardamom
1/2 teaspoon ground cinnamon, plus 1 pinch
1 to 2 apples, peeled and diced (3/4 cup)
3 tablespoons plus 1 1/2 teaspoons Florida Crystals (see
   page 224)
1 1/2 teaspoons arrowroot
1/2 cup coarsely chopped dried cherries
5 (13 by 18-inch) sheets phyllo dough
6 tablespoons canola oil

To make the strudel, preheat the oven to 400°F. In a
bowl, toss the quince with the orange juice and zest,
agave, cardamom, and 1 pinch of the cinnamon. Turn
out onto a baking sheet, and bake for 8 minutes, or
until the quince is cooked through but still holds
its shape.

Remove from the oven, and let cool in the same bowl.
Add the apples, 1 1/2 teaspoons of the Florida Crystals,
the arrowroot, and the cherries to the quince, and mix
to combine.

In a separate bowl, mix the remaining 1/2 teaspoon
cinnamon and the remaining 3 tablespoons Florida
Crystals.

Place a piece of parchment paper on a work surface.
Lay 1 sheet of phyllo on top of the parchment. Place
the short side of the phyllo toward you. Brush the
phyllo with oil, and then sprinkle some of the
cinnamon-sugar mixture over the surface. Place the
second phyllo sheet on top of the first. Brush with oil,
and sprinkle with some of the cinnamon-sugar. Repeat
with the remaining 3 sheets of phyllo and the remaining oil and cinnamon-sugar, until all 5 sheets of phyllo
are stacked on top of each other. Carefully roll the
bottom half of the phyllo up to meet the top, pressing
the filling in to make 1 even log. Use the parchment
to lift the log to a clean baking sheet. Bake for
20 minutes, or until deep golden brown.

To serve, cut into 4 equal portions, place on dessert
plates, and serve hot.

NUTRITIONAL INFORMATION

PER SERVING: 512 calories (38% from fat), 3.2 g protein,
78 g carbohydrate, 22 g fat, 0 mg cholesterol,
118 mg sodium, 6.2 g fiber

PEAR-HUCKLEBERRY TRIFLE

SERVES 6

Growing up, I often made trifle with my grand-mother. Ladyfingers, canned cherries, and instant pudding layered in a crystal trifle bowl made a beautiful dessert. Here, I remake that trifle in true Millennium style, using the finest pears, wild huckleberries, and cashews served in a wine glass. If you can't find fresh huckleberries, frozen huckleberries or blueberries will do. A.P.

PEAR MOUSSE

6 to 8 Bartlett or French butter pears, peeled, cored, and cut into large dice (about 4 cups)

$3/4$ cup plus 2 tablespoon white grape juice

1 cup unsalted cashew pieces

6 tablespoons Florida Crystals (see page 224)

$1/2$ vanilla bean, split and seeds reserved

$3/4$ teaspoon agar powder (see page 224)

Pinch of salt

$2^1/2$ tablespoons arrowroot, dissolved in $1/4$ cup water

6 ounces extra firm silken tofu

HUCKLEBERRY SAUCE

$1^1/2$ cups fresh huckleberries

1 cup white grape juice

$1/4$ cup Florida Crystals (see page 224)

$1^1/2$ teaspoons freshly squeezed lemon juice

1 tablespoon arrowroot, dissolved in 2 tablespoons water

CASHEW CRUMBS

1 cup unsalted cashew pieces

Chopped zest of 1 lemon

$1^1/2$ cups all-purpose flour

$1/4$ teaspoon baking soda

$1/4$ teaspoon salt

2 tablespoons freshly squeezed lemon juice

$1/3$ cup pure maple syrup

$1/3$ cup canola oil

$1/2$ teaspoon pure vanilla extract

2 Bartlett or French butter pears, peeled and cut into small dice, plus extra slices for garnish

To make the mousse, place the pears, grape juice, cashews, Florida Crystals, vanilla bean and seeds, agar, and salt in a saucepan. Stir to mix, cover, and cook over medium heat for 20 minutes, or until the pears are soft and appear slightly translucent. Stir the arrowroot slurry into the pear mixture. Remove from the heat and let cool for 10 minutes. Remove the vanilla bean and place the pear mixture and tofu in a blender. Blend until completely smooth. Pour into a shallow metal pan and let cool in the refrigerator for $1^1/2$ to 2 hours, until firm.

To make the sauce, combine the huckleberries, grape juice, Florida Crystals, and lemon juice in a small saucepan. Place over medium heat and bring to a simmer. Simmer for 8 minutes, or until the berries have released their juices and appear slightly plump. Stir the arrowroot slurry into the berry mixture, continuing to simmer. Stir for 1 minute, or until the sauce thickens. Refrigerate for 15 minutes, or until cool.

To make the crumbs, preheat the oven to 350°F. Cover a baking pan with parchment paper. In the bowl of a food processor fitted with the metal blade, grind the cashews and lemon zest for 1 to 2 minutes, until fine. Place the crumbs in a bowl. Sift the flour, baking soda, and salt into the bowl, and stir to mix.

In a separate bowl, whisk the lemon juice, maple syrup, oil, and vanilla. Pour the wet ingredients into the cashew crumb mixture and mix well to make the dough. Using your hands, break the dough into pieces and spread on the prepared pan. Bake for 10 minutes. Remove from the oven and stir the dough around with a metal spatula to make crumbs. Return the pan to the oven and bake for another 10 minutes. Remove from the oven again, and stir the dough around to make crumbs, breaking up large pieces of dough to make the mixture as uniform as possible. Return to the oven and bake for another 5 to 10 minutes, for a total baking time of 25 to 30 minutes, until the dough appears lightly brown and crumb-like. Let cool.

(continued)

PEAR-HUCKLEBERRY TRIFLE, *continued*

To assemble the trifles, fit a pastry bag with a round tip and fill the bag with the pear mousse. For each serving, pipe a layer of mousse into the bottom of an 8-ounce wine glass. Top with 1 or 2 tablespoons of huckleberry sauce followed by about 3 tablespoons of the cashew crumbs and about 2 tablespoons of diced pears. Repeat until the wine glass is full, finishing with a layer of crumbs. Garnish with pear slices. Repeat with 5 more wine glasses. Chill before serving.

NUTRITIONAL INFORMATION

PER TRIFLE: 528 calories (46% from fat), 8.7 g protein, 67 g carbohydrate, 23 g fat, 0 mg cholesterol, 136 mg sodium, 6 g fiber

PER ¼ CUP MOUSSE: 86 calories (30% from fat), 1.6 g protein, 15 g carbohydrate, 3 g fat, 0 mg cholesterol, 16 mg sodium, 1.7 g fiber

PER 2 TABLESPOONS SAUCE: 31 calories (2% from fat), 0.2 g protein, 8 g carbohydrate, 0.1 g fat, 0 mg cholesterol, 1 mg sodium, 0.4 g fiber

PER 2 TABLESPOONS CRUMBS: 98 calories (51% from fat), 1.7 g protein, 10.6 g carbohydrate, 5.7 g fat, 0 mg cholesterol, 34 mg sodium, 0.6 g fiber

CARAMELIZED FIG CAKE *with* LEMON ANGLAISE

SERVES 8

I have made many variations on the upside-down cake, but this one is by far my favorite. It is super moist and has an elusive lemon flavor accented by the sherry.

In the uncommon event that there is any of this yummy lemon sauce left over, you can freeze it to make an excellent sorbet. To make sorbet from a full recipe of sauce, just add 2 more tablespoons of agave nectar, and freeze when cool. A.P.

LEMON ANGLAISE SAUCE

1 cup soy milk
1/2 (14-ounce) can coconut milk
1/4 cup light agave nectar (see page 224)
Grated zest of 1 lemon
1/4 teaspoon pure vanilla extract
1/4 teaspoon lemon extract
2 teaspoons freshly squeezed lemon juice
1 1/2 teaspoons arrowroot
Pinch of turmeric
Pinch of salt

CARAMELIZED FIG CAKE

1 1/2 tablespoons Sucanat (see page 224)
3 cups fresh black Mission figs, stemmed and thinly sliced
1/4 cup blanched sliced almonds
1 cup unbleached white flour
1/4 cup whole-wheat pastry flour
1 1/2 teaspoons baking powder
1/4 teaspoon baking soda
1/4 teaspoon egg replacer (see page 224)
1/4 teaspoon salt
1/2 cup almond milk
5 tablespoons light agave nectar (see page 224)
3 tablespoons canola oil, plus more as needed
1 1/2 teaspoons pure vanilla extract
1/4 teaspoon almond extract
1 1/2 tablespoons freshly squeezed lemon juice
1 1/2 tablespoons dry sherry
Finely chopped zest of 1 lemon

To make the sauce, whisk all of the ingredients together in a small saucepan until the arrowroot is dissolved. Place over medium heat, and simmer for about 7 minutes. The mixture does not need to boil.

Remove from heat, and let the lemon zest steep in the sauce for 10 minutes. Strain through a fine-mesh strainer. Let cool, uncovered, in the refrigerator. (Store, covered, in the refrigerator for up to 1 week.)

To make the cake, brush a 9-inch round cake pan with canola oil and line it with parchment paper. Sprinkle the Sucanat onto the parchment and top with the sliced figs, fanning them out decoratively.

Preheat the oven to 350°F. Using a spice grinder, grind the almonds to a meal. Place in a bowl. Sift the white flour, pastry flour, baking powder, baking soda, egg replacer, and salt into the bowl.

In a separate bowl, whisk the almond milk, agave, canola oil, vanilla extract, almond extract, lemon juice, sherry, and lemon zest. Pour the wet ingredients into the almond mixture, and whisk just until smooth.

Pour the mixture on top of the figs in the prepared pan. Carefully smooth out the batter with a spatula (be careful not to disturb the fan of figs on the bottom of the pan). Bake for 35 to 45 minutes, until the top is lightly browned and a toothpick or small knife inserted in the center of the cake comes out clean. Let cool in the pan. (Store, wrapped tightly, in the refrigerator for up to 2 days. After 2 days, you will need to toast it for the best flavor.)

To serve, cut the cake into 8 pieces. Spoon some lemon sauce on each dessert plate, and place a slice of warm cake on top.

NUTRITIONAL INFORMATION

PER SLICE FIG CAKE: 228 calories (30% from fat), 3.5 g protein, 38 g carbohydrate, 8 g fat, 0 mg cholesterol, 174 mg sodium, 4.4 g fiber

PER 1/4 CUP SAUCE: 75 calories (56% from fat), 1.1 g protein, 8 g carbohydrate, 5.2 g fat, 0 mg cholesterol, 29 mg sodium, 0.4 g fiber

CARROT CAKE *with* CANDIED WALNUTS

SERVES 10

This is my take on traditional carrot cake. The candied walnuts are easy and elegant. Try adding different spices or using different nuts, such as hazelnuts or pecans.

The frosting may fool you into believing it's cream cheese! This frosting is a revelation in the art of vegan cake making. Not only is it yummy, but it can be piped into decorations. Eric describes it as "the best vegan frosting I've ever had." The recipe calls for soy milk powder and coconut oil, which are both available in health food stores. To measure the coconut oil, you need to place the whole jar in hot water until the oil is liquid. If you prefer a clean, speckle-free frosting, use lemon extract instead of zest. A.P.

COCONUT CREAM FROSTING

2 (14-ounce) cans coconut milk
1/4 cup soy milk
1 cup soy milk powder
1 cup Florida Crystals (see page 224)
1/2 teaspoon agar powder (see page 224)
1/4 cup coconut oil
2 teaspoons freshly squeezed lemon juice
1 1/2 tablespoons finely chopped lemon zest, or 1 teaspoon pure lemon extract (optional)

CANDIED WALNUTS

Canola oil
2 cups water
2 cups Florida Crystals (see page 224)
1/4 teaspoon ground cinnamon
Pinch of salt
2 cups walnuts

CARROT CAKE

1 whole nutmeg
1/2 teaspoon whole cloves
1/2 teaspoon whole white peppercorns
1 1/2 teaspoons ground cinnamon
1 1/2 teaspoons ground ginger
1/2 teaspoon mustard powder
2 1/2 cups all-purpose flour
1 tablespoon baking powder
1/4 teaspoon baking soda
1/2 teaspoon salt
1/2 cup canola oil, plus more as needed
1 cup pure maple syrup
1 1/2 teaspoons freshly squeezed lemon juice
3/4 cup soy milk
1 teaspoon pure vanilla extract
1 large carrot, peeled and shredded (1 1/2 cups)
1/2 cup finely chopped fresh pineapple
3/4 cup walnuts, finely chopped

To make the frosting, in a saucepan, whisk together the coconut milk, soy milk, soy powder, Florida Crystals, and agar. Make sure there are no lumps, and then stir in the coconut oil. Place over medium heat. Bring to a boil, stirring and scraping the bottom of the saucepan every minute or two.

Whisk in the lemon juice and zest. After the mixture comes to a boil, pour into a shallow pan with high sides. Let cool in the refrigerator for 4 hours, or until the frosting is firm enough to pipe.

To make the candied walnuts, preheat the oven to 350°F. Prepare a baking sheet by brushing it with canola oil and lining it with parchment paper. Stir the water, Florida Crystals, cinnamon, and salt together in a saucepan over high heat. Cover and bring to a boil. Add the nuts. Decrease the heat to medium, and uncover. Boil, stirring occasionally, for 20 minutes, or until the bubbles in the syrup are thick. Strain over the sink so the liquid drains away. Spread the nuts onto the baking sheet in a single layer. Bake for 15 minutes, or until golden brown. (Store, tightly covered, for up to 2 weeks.)

To make the cake, preheat the oven to 350°F. Brush three 8-inch cake pans with canola oil and line with parchment paper.

Place the nutmeg, cloves, and peppercorns in a spice grinder, and grind until fine. Sift with the cinnamon, ginger, mustard powder, flour, baking powder, baking soda, and salt in a large bowl.

In a separate bowl, whisk the $^1/_2$ cup canola oil, the maple syrup, lemon juice, soy milk, and vanilla. Pour the wet ingredients into the spice mixture, and whisk until mixed. Using a rubber spatula, fold in the carrots, pineapple, and nuts, just to combine. Pour directly into the prepared pans, and bake for 40 to 45 minutes, or until a small knife inserted in the center of the cake comes out clean. Let cool completely on a rack before frosting.

Remove the cakes from the pans, and discard the parchment paper. Place one layer of cake on a serving plate. Use a serrated knife to cut the top off the cake, making it level. Repeat with the other two layers.

Top the first layer of cake with $^1/_2$ cup of frosting. Using an offset metal spatula or a butter knife, spread the frosting, going all the way to the edges of the cake before lifting the spatula. Top with the next layer of cake and repeat. Top with the final layer, and frost, also covering the sides of the cake thickly enough so that no cake shows through. Place the leftover frosting in a pastry bag fitted with a fluted tip and pipe the frosting decoratively on the cake. Top with candied walnuts.

To serve, cut the cake into 10 slices, and place each slice on a dessert plate with $^1/_4$ cup candied walnuts.

NUTRITIONAL INFORMATION

PER SERVING CAKE: 548 calories (46% from fat), 9.5 g protein, 63 g carbohydrate, 30 g fat, 0 mg cholesterol, 144 mg sodium, 2.9 g fiber

PER $^1/_4$ CUP CANDIED WALNUTS: 386 calories (40% from fat), 7 g protein, 51 g carbohydrate, 18 g fat, 0 mg cholesterol, 31 mg sodium, 1.6 g fiber

KEY LIME TART

SERVES 6 TO 8

Growing up in Alabama and spending many summers in Florida, I got my share of Key lime pie. Key limes have a very distinct flavor, much more floral than the limes we normally find in grocery stores. I felt compelled to make a vegan version that stands up to the traditional. For body and color, I use avocado, which carries the flavor of the Key lime well. The filling makes an excellent spread for toast or a dip for fresh fruit, and the flavors go well with our Coconut Sorbet (page 201). My southern kin would be downright proud of the new, vegan Key lime tart.

Sascha Weiss, who wrote the dessert recipes for The Millennium Cookbook, *originally created this white chocolate mousse recipe—but I have changed it significantly. It's so yummy that people hardly believe it's vegan. We use the peanut butter variation in Paulo's Cannoli (see page 186). The recipe will make about 3 1/2 cups, so save the leftover mousse to use in Napoleons, trifles, cakes, or as a dip for sliced fruit.*

I feel I should add a few notes about this temperamental mousse. If it is not set up when removed from the refrigerator, let it sit out at room temperature for 20 to 30 minutes. If for some reason the stars of white chocolate are not in alignment and it still does not set up, it probably was not cool enough before blending. If this is the case, you can save it by melting down 2 ounces of cocoa butter, and blending it with the mousse. Refrigerate overnight again. Persevere! It's worth it. A.P.

WHITE CHOCOLATE MOUSSE

3 cups soy milk
12 ounces cocoa butter, chopped into pieces
3/4 cup plus 2 tablespoons Florida Crystals (see page 224)
1 tablespoon pure vanilla extract

MANGO SAUCE

1 mango, peeled, pitted, and diced (1 cup)
1/2 cup white grape juice

2 tablespoons agave nectar (see page 224)
Juice of 1/2 lime (2 teaspoons)

TART SHELL

3/4 cup unbleached white flour
1/3 cup whole-wheat pastry flour
1/8 teaspoon salt
1/8 teaspoon baking soda
1/2 cup raw unsalted pistachios, finely ground in a spice mill
1 tablespoon poppy seeds
1/4 cup canola oil
1/4 cup pure maple syrup
1/2 teaspoon pure vanilla extract

AVOCADO–KEY LIME FILLING

3/4 cup white grape juice or water
1 tablespoon agar flakes (see page 224)
1 1/2 tablespoon kudzu powder, dissolved in 1/4 cup water
2 ounces silken tofu
7 tablespoons fresh or bottled Key lime juice
1/2 cup mashed avocado
Pinch of salt
1/2 cup Florida Crystals (see page 224)
1/4 teaspoon pure vanilla extract

1 teaspoon poppy seeds, for garnish
2 tablespoons chopped raw unsalted pistachios, for garnish
4 strawberries, hulled and sliced, for garnish

To make the mousse, place 1 cup of the soy milk in a 2-cup measuring cup. Add the cocoa butter until the contents reach 1 3/4 cups.

Place a saucepan, filled halfway with water, over low heat. Place a small metal bowl on top of the saucepan, without touching the simmering water, to create a double boiler. Add the soy milk–cocoa butter mixture, the remaining soy milk, the Florida Crystals, and the vanilla. Stir for 10 minutes, or until everything is melted and heated through.

(continued)

Let cool to at most 100°F (this is very important!). When cool, blend for 2 minutes.

Pour the mousse into a storage container, and let cool at room temperature for 15 minutes. Refrigerate overnight to set up.

To make the mango sauce, place all of the ingredients in a blender and blend until smooth. (Store, covered, in the refrigerator for up to 4 days).

To make the tart shell, preheat the oven to 350°F. Oil six 4-inch round tart pans or one 9-inch tart pan, and line with parchment paper. Sift the white flour, pastry flour, salt, and baking soda in a bowl. Stir the pistachios and poppy seeds into the flour mixture.

In a separate bowl, whisk together the oil, maple syrup, and vanilla. Pour the wet into the dry ingredients, and mix to make a dough. Place the dough in the tart pan(s), and cover with plastic wrap. Using the plastic wrap, begin pushing down the dough with your hands. Push the dough around the sides of the tart pan(s) and on the bottom to a uniform thickness to allow for even baking. When the dough is pressed evenly, discard the plastic wrap, and prick the bottom of the tart shell(s) a few times with a fork. Bake the small tart shells for 18 to 22 minutes or the single large shell for 25 to 28 minutes, until lightly browned. Let cool. (Store, unfilled and wrapped, at room temperature for up to 5 days.)

To make the filling, place the grape juice and agar in a small saucepan. Soak for 10 minutes.

Place the saucepan over low heat and bring to a simmer. Simmer, stirring occasionally, for 10 minutes, or until the agar flakes have dissolved. Stir in the kudzu slurry, and continue cooking for 3 minutes, or until thick.

Pour the mixture into a blender. Add the tofu, Key lime juice, avocado, salt, Florida Crystals, and vanilla. Blend until smooth. Pour the mixture into a 9-inch loaf pan and place in the refrigerator. Let cool for 1 hour, or until the mixture hardens. When cool, place in a food processor fitted with the metal blade. Process until there are no lumps. (Store refrigerated for up to 5 days.)

When ready to eat, spread the filling into the cooled tart shell(s), and refrigerate for 1 hour to overnight.

To serve, place 1 small tart on each plate or cut the large tart into 8 slices and place each on a dessert plate. Place a dollop of white chocolate mousse on top, and sprinkle with poppy seeds and pistachios. Garnish the plate with mango sauce and strawberries.

NUTRITIONAL INFORMATION

PER SLICE: 275 calories (58% from fat), 4.2 g protein, 20 g carbohydrate, 12.7 g fat, 0 mg cholesterol, 59 mg sodium, 2.3 g fiber

PER 2 TABLESPOONS MOUSSE: 94 calories (75% from fat), 1 g protein, 4.8 g carbohydrate, 8 g fat, 0 mg cholesterol, 18 mg sodium, 0.3 g fiber

PER 2 TABLESPOONS MANGO SAUCE: 47 calories (1.5% from fat), 0.3 g protein, 13.1 g carbohydrate, 0.1 g fat, 0 mg cholesterol, 1 mg sodium, 0.7 g fiber

APPLE CAKE *and* CANDY CAP FLAN

SERVES 9

This dessert was a delicious finale to one of our famous Exotic Mushroom Dinners, where yes, everything did have mushrooms in it. Candy caps (Lactarius fragilis) are often used in desserts because they have a sweet yet earthy quality, reminiscent of maple syrup. Unforunately, they're only grown in the Pacific Northwest; we get ours through a mushroom supplier called Wine Forest, which is based in Napa, California. Seek them out—you won't be disappointed! A.P.

APPLE CAKE

1/4 cup whole oats
2 tablespoons dried candy cap mushrooms
1 Fuji or Granny Smith apple, shredded
1/4 cup plus 1 tablespoon Sucanat (see page 224)
2 cups unbleached white flour
1/2 teaspoon ground cinnamon
Pinch of ground cloves
1 teaspoon baking powder
1 teaspoon baking soda
1/4 teaspoon salt
1/4 cup canola oil, plus more as needed
3/4 cup pure maple syrup
1/4 cup soy milk
2 teaspoons freshly squeezed lemon juice
1 cup dried apples, coarsely chopped

CANDY CAP FLAN

1 (14-ounce) can coconut milk
1 1/2 cups soy milk
1 cup water
1/2 cup Florida Crystals (see page 224)
Pinch of salt
2 teaspoons agar powder (see page 224)
1/2 teaspoon freshly squeezed lemon juice
1 cup dried candy cap mushrooms

1 Fuji or Granny Smith apple, sliced into fans, for garnish

To make the cake, preheat the oven to 350°F. Brush a 9 by 9-inch square cake pan with canola oil and line with parchment paper.

Using a coffee grinder, grind the oats and dried mushrooms to a powder. Place in a bowl. Add the apple, oats, and mushrooms to the bowl. Sift the Sucanat with the flour, cinnamon, cloves, baking powder, baking soda, and salt into the bowl.

In a separate bowl, whisk together 1/4 cup canola oil, the maple syrup, soy milk, and lemon juice. Pour the wet ingredients into the apple-mushroom mixture, and stir until mixed. Fold in the dried apples.

Pour into the prepared pan, and flatten the batter with a spatula. Bake for 35 to 45 minutes, until a small knife inserted in the center of the cake comes out clean. Let cool in the pan for 10 minutes, and then turn out onto a cooling rack. (Store refrigerated, in an airtight container, for up to 3 days. After 3 days, you will need to toast it for the best flavor.)

To make the flan, whisk the coconut milk, soy milk, water, Florida Crystals, salt, agar, and lemon juice together in a saucepan until everything is dissolved. Place over medium heat and bring to a boil. Boil for 5 to 7 minutes, until the soy and coconut milks and agar are incorporated. Remove from the heat.

Whisk in the dried candy caps, cover, and let steep for 15 minutes. Strain the mixture through a fine-mesh sieve into the 9 by 9-inch pan, squeezing all of the liquid out of the mushrooms. Discard the mushrooms. Let the flan mixture cool in the refrigerator for 1 hour, or until set.

To serve, remove the parchment paper from the cake, and cut it into 9 even squares. Place each square of cake on a dessert plate. Using a small metal spatula, cut the flan into 9 even squares, and place a square on each slice of cake. Garnish with a fan of apple slices.

NUTRITIONAL INFORMATION

PER SLICE APPLE CAKE: 320 calories (19% from fat), 4.1 g protein, 62 g carbohydrate, 7 g fat, 0 mg cholesterol, 245 mg sodium, 3.7 g fiber

PER SLICE FLAN: 164 calories (58% from fat), 2.3 g protein, 15 g carbohydrate, 11 g fat, 0 mg cholesterol, 39 mg sodium, 1 g fiber

CARDAMOM-PERSIMMON FLAN *with* DRIED FRUIT COMPOTE

SERVES 6

This is my version of the traditional flan. It demands the Hachiya variety of persimmon, which is extremely sweet and turns to mush when ripe. The dried fruit compote, the perfect companion to this flan, is also wonderful with creamy sorbets or waffles. A.P.

DRIED FRUIT COMPOTE

1/4 cup dried cherries

1/4 cup golden raisins

1/4 cup dried apricots, sliced

1/4 cup dried black Mission figs, stemmed and
   quartered

2 cups Gewürztraminer

2 cinnamon sticks

1/2 cup Florida Crystals (see page 224)

CARDAMOM-PERSIMMON FLAN

2 large Hachiya persimmons, quartered

1/2 cup rice milk

1 cup coconut milk

3 tablespoons Florida Crystals (see page 224)

1/2 teaspoon agar powder (see page 224)

Pinch of salt

2 tablespoons pure maple syrup

1 1/2 teaspoons freshly squeezed lemon juice

1/2 teaspoon ground cardamom

1 tablespoon arrowroot, dissolved in 2 tablespoons
   cold water

To make the compote, place all of the ingredients in a saucepan over low heat, and bring to a simmer. Cover and simmer for 10 minutes, or until reduced slightly. Let cool. (Store refrigerated, in an airtight container, for up to 1 month.)

To make the flan, place six 4-ounce ramekins on a sided baking sheet. Using a spoon, scoop the pulp away from the skin of the quartered persimmons. Discard the skin. Blend the pulp in a blender until smooth. Measure out 1 cup.

Whisk the rice milk, coconut milk, Florida Crystals, agar, salt, maple syrup, lemon juice, and cardamom together in a saucepan over medium heat. Bring to a boil. Remove the flan mixture from the heat. Stir the arrowroot slurry and then whisk it into the hot liquid. Divide the flan mixture into the ramekins, and refrigerate for 2 hours, or until set.

Using a sharp knife, cut around the edges of the ramekins to loosen the flan. Invert onto a plate, jiggling slightly if it sticks.

To serve, place each flan on a dessert plate with 1/4 cup of the compote.

NUTRITIONAL INFORMATION

PER SLICE FLAN: 183 calories (45% from fat), 1.2 g protein, 25 g carbohydrate, 9.9 g fat, 0 mg cholesterol, 54 mg sodium, 0.9 g fiber

PER 1/4 CUP COMPOTE: 138 calories (0.9% from fat), 0.4 g protein, 14 g carbohydrate, 0.1 g fat, 0 mg cholesterol, 1 mg sodium, 0.8 g fiber

JASMINE TEA POACHED PEARS *with* POMEGRANATE SAUCE

SERVES 6

This dessert is very light and elegant. Use a firm variety of pears, such as Bosc or Bartlett—best if deliciously ripe! Jasmine pearls, available in Chinese tea markets or herb stores, are simply a jasmine flower that amazingly opens up when exposed to hot water. Watch out! The pomegranate sauce has zip. The color is incredible, especially served next to pears and a scoop of Almond Sherbet (page 198). The Knudsen brand of pomegranate juice is available at most health food stores, but if you can't find any, try substituting raspberry nectar.
J.P.

POMEGRANATE SAUCE

1 1/2 cups pomegranate juice (see page 224)
1 cup water
1/8 teaspoon guar gum
1 cup Florida Crystals (see page 224)
1 1/2 tablespoons arrowroot, dissolved in 3 tablespoons water

POACHED PEARS

12 cups water
1 vanilla bean, split in half and seeds reserved
1 cup loose jasmine tea
1 tablespoon jasmine pearls (optional)
1 cup Florida Crystals (see page 224)
6 ripe Bosc or Bartlett pears, peeled, cored, and seeded

To make the sauce, stir the pomegranate juice, water, guar gum, and the Florida Crystals together in a small saucepan over high heat. Cook for 25 to 27 minutes, until reduced by half. Remove from the heat, and immediately stir in the arrowroot slurry. Refrigerate until ready to use. (Store refrigerated for up to 2 weeks.)

To make the pears, place a large soup pot over high heat, and add the water and vanilla bean. Bring to a boil. Whisk in the tea, jasmine pearls, and Florida Crystals. Turn off the heat, and let steep for 6 to 7 minutes (not more, or it may become bitter).

Strain the tea and return to the pot. Bring to a simmer, and add the pears to poach. Place a piece of parchment paper on top of the pears while they are poaching (this acts as a weight and helps keep the color uniform). Poach for 6 to 8 minutes for ripe pears (10 to 12 minutes for less ripe pears), until easily pierced with a paring knife but still holding shape. Remove the pears with a slotted spoon, and let the liquid and pears cool separately. (Store the pears in the liquid, covered, in the refrigerator for up to 5 days.) If you want to poach more pears, reuse the liquid only once.

To serve, place 1 pear on each plate, and drizzle with 1/4 cup of the pomegranate sauce.

NUTRITIONAL INFORMATION

PER SERVING: 252 calories (0.7% from fat), 0.8 g protein, 63 g carbohydrate, 0.7 g fat, 0 mg cholesterol, 22 mg sodium, 3.9 g fiber

COCONUT-PISTACHIO CUSTARD *with* FIGS *in* MARSALA

SERVES 9

This dessert has an array of textures: creamy, crunchy, and moist. The figs in Marsala really send it over the top. For a dramatic touch, drizzle a few drops of pistachio oil, which you can find in specialty food stores, on the plate. A.P.

COCONUT CUSTARDS

1 cup rice milk
1 (14-ounce) can light coconut milk
1 teaspoon agar powder (see page 224)
Pinch of salt
1/4 teaspoon freshly squeezed lime juice
6 tablespoons Florida Crystals (see page 224)
1/2 vanilla bean
1 1/2 tablespoons arrowroot
1/4 cup water
2 tablespoons rose water

PISTACHIO CAKE

1 cup unbleached all-purpose flour
1 teaspoon baking powder
1/4 teaspoon baking soda
4 teaspoons semolina flour
1/4 cup raw unsalted pistachios, finely ground in a coffee grinder
1/4 teaspoon salt
1/2 cup Florida Crystals (see page 224)
1/4 cup unrefined corn oil
1/2 cup soy milk
2 tablespoons freshly squeezed lemon juice
2 tablespoons pure maple syrup

PISTACHIO LACE COOKIES

2 tablespoons canola oil
1 1/2 tablespoons rice syrup
3 tablespoons pure maple syrup
1/4 cup plus 1 teaspoon all-purpose flour
3/4 teaspoon cornstarch
Pinch of salt
2 tablespoons coarsely chopped raw unsalted pistachios

FIGS IN MARSALA

1 cup dried black Mission figs (about 1/2 pound), stemmed and quartered
2 cups Marsala
Zest of 1 lemon
1 teaspoon pure vanilla extract
1/4 cup pomegranate juice (see page 224)
1/2 cup water
1/2 cup Florida Crystals (see page 224)

Pistachio oil, for garnish

To make the custard, whisk the rice milk, coconut milk, agar, salt, lime juice, and Florida Crystals together in a heavy-bottomed saucepan. Use a paring knife, split the vanilla bean in half lengthwise and scrape out the inside. Put the pod and seeds in a saucepan over medium heat. Bring to a boil, then decrease the heat to low. Cook for 10 minutes.

Dissolve the arrowroot in the water and rose water in a small bowl. Whisk the arrowroot slurry into the custard mixture until thickened. Strain, and portion into nine 4-ounce ramekins. Refrigerate for 2 hours, or until set.

To make the cake, preheat the oven to 350°F. Oil a 9 by 9-inch square or 8-inch round pan, and line the bottom with parchment paper. Sift the all-purpose flour, baking powder, baking soda, semolina flour, pistachios, salt, and Florida Crystals into a bowl.

In a separate bowl, whisk the corn oil, soy milk, lemon juice, and maple syrup together. Pour the wet ingredients into the pistachio mixture, and whisk until combined and thick. Pour the batter into the prepared pan, and bake for 25 to 30 minutes, until a small knife inserted in the center of the cake comes out clean. Let cool.

To make the cookies, preheat the oven to 350°F. Line a baking sheet with parchment paper. Whisk the oil and the rice syrup and maple syrup together in a bowl. Sift the flour, cornstarch, and salt into the bowl with the syrups. Add the nuts, and whisk well.

Spoon 2 tablespoons of batter for each cookie, spaced 4 inches apart, onto the baking sheet to make about 9 cookies. Bake for 7 minutes. Rotate the tray and bake for 6 minutes, or until brown and bubbly. Let cool on the tray. (Store, in airtight container, for up to 4 days.)

To make the figs, place a saucepan over low heat, and add all of the ingredients. Cover and simmer for 15 minutes, or until the figs are very soft.

To serve, cut rounds out of the cake using a 2$^1/_2$-inch round cutter, or cut into 9 wedges. Place a round of cake on each plate, and place a cookie on top. Using a paring knife, cut around the edges of each ramekin to loosen the custards. Place a custard on top of the cake and cookie. Place $^1/_4$ cup of the figs in Marsala on the plate and drizzle a few drops of pistachio oil around the plate.

NUTRITIONAL INFORMATION

PER CUSTARD: 164 calories (54% from fat), 1.1 g protein, 18 g carbohydrate, 10 g fat, 0 mg cholesterol, 44 mg sodium, 0.2 g fiber

PER ROUND CAKE: 189 calories (38% from fat), 2.7 g protein, 26 g carbohydrate, 8.2 g fat, 0 mg cholesterol, 130 mg sodium, 1.0 g fiber

PER COOKIE: 53 calories (64% from fat), 0.8 g protein, 4.1 g carbohydrate, 3.9 g fat, 0 mg cholesterol, 26 mg sodium, 0.3 g fiber

PER $^1/_4$ CUP FIGS: 83 calories (2% from fat), 0.5 g protein, 16 g carbohydrate, 0.2 g fat, 0 mg cholesterol, 3 mg sodium, 1.4 g fiber

PAULO'S CANNOLI

SERVES 6

One day I turned to Paul Rose, one of our well-rounded chefs at Millennium, for inspiration as to what dessert to make. He replied, "Something with peanut butter!" My White Chocolate Mousse (page 179) was already a big hit, so I decided to take his advice and try out a peanut butter variation, which I still make to this day.

Making the cannoli shells requires some practice, so I've written the shell batter recipe with the assumption that you'll have to sacrifice a few in the learning process. But don't throw the broken shells away! They make a delightful snack. A.P.

PEANUT BUTTER MOUSSE

1 recipe White Chocolate Mousse (page 179)
$1/2$ cup smooth or chunky peanut butter
3 tablespoons pure maple syrup
$1/8$ teaspoon salt

CANNOLI SHELLS

2 tablespoons peanuts
$1^1/2$ cups all-purpose flour
2 tablespoons unsweetened cocoa powder
$1/4$ teaspoon salt
$3/4$ cup Florida Crystals (see page 224)
$1/4$ teaspoon egg replacer (see page 224)
$1/8$ teaspoon guar gum
$1/2$ cup water
$1/4$ cup canola or grapeseed oil, plus more as needed
$1/2$ cup soy milk
1 tablespoon pure maple syrup
$1^1/2$ teaspoon pure vanilla extract

2 blood oranges, segmented and juice reserved
2 tablespoons agave nectar (see page 224)
2 tablespoons cacao nibs, for garnish

To make the peanut butter mousse, follow the White Chocolate Mousse recipe, but blend in the peanut butter, maple syrup, and salt before letting the mousse set overnight.

To make the shells, preheat the oven to 350°F. Toast the peanuts in the oven for 5 to 7 minutes, until lightly brown. Grind them in a food processor fitted with the metal blade for 30 seconds, or until coarsely chopped.

In a bowl, sift the flour, cocoa powder, salt, and Florida Crystals.

Place the egg replacer, guar gum, water, $1/4$ cup of the oil, the soy milk, maple syrup, and vanilla in a blender. Blend on high speed for 1 minute, or until thoroughly emulsified. Add the wet ingredients into the dry ingredients, and whisk until smooth.

Brush a baking sheet with canola oil and then line it with a sheet of parchment paper. Using an offset metal spatula, spread about $1/2$ teaspoon of the batter in a circle on the parchment. It should be 2 to 3 inches in diameter and about $1/16$ inch thin. Repeat with the remaining batter until baking sheet is full (4 to 6 shells). Sprinkle the ground peanuts over the shells and bake for 7 minutes. Rotate the tray, and bake for 3 or 4 minutes, until the shells look dry but are still malleable. Loosen the cannoli using the metal spatula.

To assemble the shells, wearing oven mitts, wrap a shell around the handle of a whisk and hold for 2 or 3 seconds, until set. Slide the cannoli off the whisk handle and let cool. Repeat for the remaining cannoli. Work quickly so that the shells don't harden before you can shape them; if they do begin to harden, place them back in the oven for 2 minutes at a time.

Place the mousse in a pastry bag fitted with the star tip, and pipe the mousse into each cannoli.

To serve, toss the blood orange segments, reserved juice, and agave in a small bowl. Evenly distribute the fruit and liquid among 6 dessert plates. Place 2 cannoli on each plate, and sprinkle with cacao nibs.

NUTRITIONAL INFORMATION

PER 2 CANNOLI: 260 calories (70% from fat), 3 g protein, 21 g carbohydrate, 18.6 g fat, 0 mg cholesterol, 54 mg sodium, 1 g fiber

TAPIOCA PUDDING

SERVES 6

I was never a tapioca fan until we made this pudding, which became an instant hit at the restaurant. Place a scoop of our Pineapple–Passion Fruit Sorbet (page 200) on top, and enjoy! A.P.

4 3/4 cups rice milk
1 (14-ounce) can coconut milk
1/2 vanilla bean, split and scraped
6 tablespoons Florida Crystals (see page 224)
Pinch of salt
1/2 cup tapioca pearls
1/4 cup cold water

2 kiwi fruits, peeled and diced
1 mango, peeled and diced

To make the pudding, in a saucepan, stir together 4 cups of the rice milk with the coconut milk, vanilla bean, Florida Crystals, and salt over high heat. Bring to a boil, and then whisk in the tapioca pearls. Decrease the heat to medium-low, and simmer, stirring occasionally, for 25 minutes, or until the tapioca pearls are nearly transparent.

Add the remaining 3/4 cup rice milk. Simmer for an additional 10 minutes. Add the cold water to shock the tapioca. Return to a boil, and boil for 1 to 2 minutes, until all of the tapioca pearls are completely clear. (Store, covered, in the refrigerator for up to 7 days.)

To serve, divide the kiwi and mango into 6 serving bowls. Divide the tapioca pudding evenly among the bowls.

NUTRITIONAL INFORMATION

PER SERVING: 368 calories (40% from fat), 2.7 g protein, 54 g carbohydrate, 17 g fat, 0 mg cholesterol, 115 mg sodium, 2 g fiber

SPICY GINGER COOKIES

These cookies were a knockout at the Millennium 2001 New Year's Eve extravaganza. Try making a sandwich with two cookies and the Cinnamon Sherbet (page 198) or the Coconut Sorbet (page 201) and freezing it for a most excellent "ice cream" sandwich. A.P.

6 tablespoons pure maple syrup

2 tablespoons dark molasses

1/4 cup canola oil

1 1/2 tablespoons freshly squeezed grapefruit or orange juice

1 1/2 teaspoons grated grapefruit or orange zest

1 (3-inch) piece fresh ginger, peeled and grated (2 tablespoons)

1 1/2 cups whole-wheat pastry flour

2 tablespoons Sucanat (see page 224)

1/4 teaspoon baking soda

1/4 teaspoon ground cinnamon

1/8 teaspoon freshly ground white pepper

Pinch of ground cloves

1/4 teaspoon salt

6 pieces crystallized ginger, chopped

Preheat the oven to 350°F. Line a baking sheet with parchment paper. Place the maple syrup, molasses, canola oil, juice, zest, and ginger in a blender, and blend well.

Sift the flour, Sucanat, baking soda, cinnamon, white pepper, cloves, and salt in a bowl. Pour the ginger mixture into the dry ingredients, and mix well to create a smooth batter.

Using a spoon, scoop about 2 tablespoons batter onto the prepared baking sheet for each cookie. Top each cookie with some of the crystallized ginger, and flatten it slightly. Bake for 15 to 20 minutes, until light brown around the edges. Serve. (Store in an airtight container for up to 1 week or store frozen, in an airtight container, for up to 3 weeks.)

NUTRITIONAL INFORMATION

PER COOKIE: 135 calories (30% from fat), 2.1 g protein, 22 g carbohydrate, 4 g fat, 0 mg cholesterol, 68 mg sodium, 1.9 g fiber

WALNUT MACAROONS

MAKES 12 COOKIES

Coconut is obviously one of our favorite ingredients at Millennium, as these very "Amy-style" macaroons demonstrate. For the sweet potato, you will need only a small piece of potato; shred the required amount using the smallest side of a box grater. A.P.

2 tablespoons peeled and shredded sweet potato
$1/2$ cup unsweetened, shredded coconut
$1/2$ cup walnuts, coarsely chopped
$1/4$ cup Sucanat (see page 224)
Pinch of salt
2 tablespoons rice flour
$1/8$ teaspoon egg replacer (see page 224)
$1/8$ teaspoon dark molasses
$1^1/2$ teaspoons pure vanilla extract
1 teaspoon coconut oil (see page 176)
$1/4$ cup boiling water

Preheat the oven to 350°F. Line a baking sheet with parchment paper.

Place the sweet potato, coconut, nuts, Sucanat, salt, rice flour, and egg replacer in a bowl. Using your hands, toss well, making sure the potato does not lump up. Make a well in the center of the dry ingredients. In the well, place the molasses, vanilla, and coconut oil. Slowly add the boiling to dissolve the molasses and soften the coconut. Still using your hands, mix until all of the ingredients are incorporated.

Using a spoon, drop about 2 tablespoons of the batter onto the baking sheet for each macaroon. Lightly press them down with the palm of your hand to flatten. Bake for 20 minutes, or until lightly brown. You may need to bake them in two batches, depending on the size of your baking sheet. Let cool on the baking sheet, and then serve. (Store in an airtight container for up to 5 days.)

NUTRITIONAL INFORMATION

PER COOKIE: 76 calories (55% from fat), 1.6 g protein, 7.4 g carbohydrate, 4 g fat, 0 mg cholesterol, 1 mg sodium, 0.8 g fiber

CHOCOLATE BISCOTTI

MAKES 12 BISCOTTI

Chocolate, chocolate, and nuts. Need I say more? Oh, and whiskey. My personal preference is Jim Beam. The biscotti use cacao nibs, the very essence of chocolate—simply the roasted cacao bean. Look for them in specialty food stores. A.P.

1 cup all-purpose flour

1 tablespoon plus 1 teaspoon Florida Crystals (see page 224), plus extra for dusting

1 tablespoon unsweetened cocoa powder

$1/2$ teaspoon baking powder

$1/8$ teaspoon baking soda

$1/8$ teaspoon salt

$1/2$ cup walnuts, coarsely chopped

$2 1/4$ teaspoons cacao nibs

2 ounces bittersweet chocolate bar, chopped, or $1/4$ cup chocolate chips

2 pitted prunes

2 tablespoons canola oil, plus more as needed

2 tablespoons soy milk

$1/4$ cup pure maple syrup

2 tablespoons whiskey

$1/4$ teaspoon pure vanilla extract

Preheat the oven to 350°F. Oil a 9 by 13-inch baking pan with canola oil and line it with parchment paper. In a bowl, sift the flour, Florida Crystals, cocoa, baking powder, baking soda, and salt. Stir in the nuts, cacao nibs, and chocolate.

Place the prunes in another bowl. Bring $1/2$ cup water to a boil, and pour over the prunes. Let the prunes soak for 5 minutes to soften. Drain.

Place the softened prunes with the canola oil, soy milk, maple syrup, whiskey, and vanilla in a blender. Blend well. Stir into the chocolate mixture to form a dough.

Sprinkle some Florida Crystals on the baking pan, and then place the dough on it. Roll it into a log the length of the baking pan and 2 inches wide, sprinkling more Florida Crystals on the dough as needed to prevent it from sticking to your hands. Bake for 30 minutes, or until firm to the touch but cooked through.

Remove from the oven. Let cool for 10 minutes on a cooling rack. Refrigerate for 2 hours to cool completely, allowing for nice, neat slices.

Preheat the oven to 250°F. Line a baking pan with parchment paper. Using a serrated knife, slice the log into $1/4$-inch-wide biscotti. Place the biscotti on the pan, and return it to the oven for 10 minutes. Remove from the oven, and flip over the biscotti so that the sides dry out evenly. Return to the oven, and bake for 7 minutes, or until dry. Let cool to room temperature and serve. (Store, in a tightly covered container, for up to 2 weeks. If the biscotti become moist, preheat the oven to 250°F, and bake for 5 minutes to dry them out.)

NUTRITIONAL INFORMATION

PER BISCOTTI: 149 calories (48% from fat), 3 g protein, 16 g carbohydrate, 8 g fat, 0 mg cholesterol, 50 mg sodium, 1.6 g fiber

GERMAN CHOCOLATE CAKE

SERVES 4

Another decadent pleasure: here we have the seductive flavors of the German chocolate cake, coconut flakes, rich macadamia nuts, hazelnuts, and gooey date caramel. If blanched hazelnuts are not available, use unblanched nuts, removing as much skin as possible. Serve with a scoop of our Coconut Sorbet (page 201) and garnish with chocolate cigars, available in most specialty chocolate stores. A.P.

CHOCOLATE CAKE

1/4 cup unsweetened cocoa powder
1 cup all-purpose flour
1 1/2 teaspoons baking powder
1/2 teaspoon baking soda
1/4 teaspoon salt
1/4 teaspoon egg replacer (see page 224)
1 1/2 teaspoons ground espresso beans
1/2 cup plus 2 tablespoons brewed coffee
4 ounces silken tofu
1 cup plus 2 tablespoons pure maple syrup
1/2 cup canola oil
1 1/2 teaspoons pure vanilla extract
1/2 teaspoon apple cider vinegar
1 1/2 teaspoons coffee extract or coffee liqueur

CARAMEL-NUT FILLING

3/4 cup macadamia nuts, plus more for garnish
3/4 cup blanched hazelnuts
1 cup soy milk
1/2 cup rice milk
3/4 cup shredded unsweetened coconut, plus more for garnish
3/4 cup Sucanat (see page 224)
Pinch of agar powder (see page 224)
1 tablespoon arrowroot
1/2 teaspoon pure vanilla extract

DATE CARAMEL

4 Deglet Noor dates, or 2 Medjool dates, pitted
1 cup Florida Crystals (see page 224)
1 cup water
1/4 cup agave nectar (see page 224)

2 kumquats, thinly sliced, for garnish
8 chocolate cigars, for garnish

To make the chocolate cake, preheat the oven to 350°F. Oil a 9 by 13-inch pan, and line it with parchment paper. Sift the cocoa powder, flour, baking powder, baking soda, salt, egg replacer, and espresso in a bowl.

In a blender, combine the coffee, tofu, maple syrup, canola oil, vanilla, vinegar, and coffee extract. Blend until smooth. Pour the wet ingredients into the cocoa mixture and whisk until smooth (some small lumps are okay). Pour the batter into the prepared pan and spread evenly. Bake for 10 minutes. Rotate the tray and bake for 10 minutes, or until the cake pulls away from the sides of the pan and a small knife inserted in the center of the cake comes out clean. Let cool in the pan.

To make the filling, decrease the oven temperature to 325°F. Spread the macadamia nuts and hazelnuts on a baking sheet, and toast in the oven for 8 to 10 minutes, until light brown. Remove from the oven and let cool. Pulse the nuts in a food processor fitted with the metal blade four or five times, until coarsely ground.

Place the nuts, soy milk, rice milk, coconut, Sucanat, agar, arrowroot, and vanilla in a saucepan, and whisk until smooth. Heat the mixture over medium heat, whisking continuously, for 7 to 10 minutes, until very hot but not boiling. Pour into a shallow pan to cool.

To make the caramel, soak the dates in hot tap water for 10 minutes. Meanwhile, place the Florida Crystals and water in a small saucepan over medium-high heat and bring to a boil. Decrease the heat to low and simmer for 12 to 15 minutes, until the bubbles in the syrup are thick.

Remove the dates from the water and transfer to a blender. Add the agave and Florida Crystal syrup. Transfer the mixture to a blender and blend for 1 minute, or until smooth. Let cool at room temperature.

(continued)

GERMAN CHOCOLATE CAKE, *continued*

(Store at room temperature for up to 1 month. If the caramel crystalizes, cook over low heat until the crystals dissolve.)

To assemble and serve, using a 2$\frac{1}{2}$-inch round biscuit cutter or glass tumbler, cut 12 rounds out of the chocolate cake. Place 1 round on a dessert plate. Using a small ice cream scoop, top with 2 tablespoons of the filling. Repeat, creating 2 more layers of cake and filling. Set a few whole macadamia nuts on top, and sprinkle with shredded coconut. Dot the plate with caramel sauce, and garnish with kumquat slices and chocolate cigars.

NUTRITIONAL INFORMATION

PER SERVING CAKE: 581 calories (49% from fat), 6.7 g protein, 64 g carbohydrate, 34 g fat, 0 mg cholesterol, 226 mg sodium, 4.5 g fiber

PER 2 TABLESPOONS DATE CARAMEL: 65 calories (1% from fat), 0 g protein, 17 g carbohydrate, 0.2 g fat, 0 mg cholesterol, 1 mg sodium, 0.2 g fiber

Amy Pearce

BITTERSWEET CHOCOLATE TRUFFLES

MAKES 16 TRUFFLES

Our chocolate truffles will silence anyone who doubts the decadence of dairy-free chocolate. For the bittersweet chocolate, we prefer the organic Green & Black's brand or Scharffen Berger. A.P.

6 ounces bittersweet chocolate bar, chopped into
   2-inch pieces
$1/4$ cup soy milk
$1/4$ cup port or orange liqueur
$1/4$ teaspoon chile powder (optional)
$1/4$ cup dried cherries, finely chopped (optional)
2 tablespoons unsweetened cocoa powder

Place a saucepan, filled halfway with water, over low heat. Place a small metal bowl on top of the saucepan, without touching the simmering water, to create a double boiler. Add the chocolate, soy milk, port, chile powder, and cherries to the bowl. After a few minutes, whisk well with a wire whip for 30 seconds, or until the chocolate and soy are well incorporated and the mixture is uniformly melted. Refrigerate for 2 hours, or until firm.

Place the cocoa powder in a small, clean bowl. Using a melon baller or a tablespoon measure, scoop the truffle mix into balls. Roll the balls in the cocoa powder, using a spoon or with your hands. Serve immediately, or wrap and save for later. (Store in the refrigerator for up to 2 weeks.)

NUTRITIONAL INFORMATION

PER TRUFFLE: 69 calories (67% from fat), 1.4 g protein, 5.1 g carbohydrate, 6 g fat, 0 mg cholesterol, 2 mg sodium, 2.1 g fiber

EARL GREY TEA TRUFFLES

MAKES 16 TRUFFLES

These tasty truffles have a hint of tea. Be sure to use good-quality bittersweet chocolate, such as Green & Black's or Scharffen Berger. A.P.

6 ounces bittersweet chocolate bar, chopped into
   2-inch pieces
$1/2$ cup soy milk
2 tablespoons loose Earl Grey tea
2 tablespoons unsweetened cocoa powder

Place a saucepan, filled halfway with water, over low heat. Place a small metal bowl on top of the saucepan, without touching the simmering water, to create a double boiler. Add the chocolate to the bowl.

Pour the soy milk into another small saucepan over low heat, and bring to a simmer. Add the tea, cover, remove from the heat, and steep for 10 minutes. Strain the tea directly into the bowl of chocolate using a fine-mesh strainer. Be sure to squeeze out all of the liquid, using a rubber spatula. Discard the tea. Whisk well with a wire whip for 30 seconds, or until the mixture is uniformly melted. Refrigerate for 2 hours, or until firm.

Place the cocoa powder in a small, clean bowl. Using a melon baller or a tablespoon measure, scoop the truffle mix into balls. Roll the balls in the cocoa powder, using a spoon or with your hands. Serve immediately, or wrap and save for later. (Store in the refrigerator for up to 2 weeks.)

NUTRITIONAL INFORMATION

PER TRUFFLE: 60 calories (72% from fat), 1.5 g protein, 3.7 g carbohydrate, 6.1 g fat, 0 mg cholesterol, 3 mg sodium, 2 g fiber

STRAWBERRY, ROSE, *and* RHUBARB SOUP

SERVES 4

This fresh and fruity dessert soup provides a nice balance of sweet and tart. The sweetness of the strawberries and rose water is accentuated by the tartness of the rhubarb and orange. Rose water can be found in Middle Eastern and Indian markets, as it is a popular flavoring in those cuisines, traditionally used in baklava or custards. The flavors in this go well with our Pear-Cardamom Sorbet (page 201). Ȿ.P.

2 rhubarb stalks, sliced into 1-inch pieces (1 cup)

1/2 cup plus 2 tablespoons Florida Crystals (see page 224)

2 tablespoons freshly squeezed orange juice

1 cup water

2 teaspoons rose water

1 1/2 teaspoons arrowroot, dissolved in 2 tablespoons water

1 1/2 cups chopped strawberries

2 tablespoons grated orange zest or fresh mint chiffonade, for garnish

To make the soup, preheat the oven to 425°F. Toss the rhubarb, 1/2 cup of the sugar, and the orange juice together in a bowl. Pour the mixture onto a baking pan and bake for 10 minutes, or until the rhubarb is cooked through but still retains its shape. Let cool to room temperature.

In a saucepan, combine the water, the remaining 2 tablespoons sugar, and the rose water over medium heat. Bring to a simmer. Slowly whisk in the arrowroot slurry, and continue to cook, without boiling, for 2 to 3 minutes total, until the liquid becomes clear. Remove from the heat, and stir in the strawberries and rhubarb mixture. Refrigerate for 2 hours, or until well chilled.

To serve, divide the soup among 4 soup bowls, and garnish with orange zest.

NUTRITIONAL INFORMATION

PER SERVING: 149 calories (1.7% from fat), 0.7 g protein, 36 g carbohydrate, 0.3 g fat, 0 mg cholesterol, 4 mg sodium, 1.8 g fiber

ALMOND SHERBET

MAKES 1 QUART

Serve this sherbet with Jasmine Tea Poached Pears (page 183) for a decadent yet light and refreshing dessert. The almond milk is available at health food stores. A.P.

1 quart almond milk
3/4 cup Florida Crystals (see page 224) or agave nectar (see page 224)
1 teaspoon pure vanilla extract
1/4 teaspoon almond extract
1/4 teaspoon guar gum
Pinch of salt

Whisk all of the ingredients together in a bowl until the Florida Crystals are dissolved. Transfer to an ice cream maker, and freeze according to the manufacturer's instructions. (Store frozen, in an airtight container, for up to 2 weeks. If the sherbet becomes icy, defrost and refreeze it.)

NUTRITIONAL INFORMATION

PER 1/2 CUP: 108 calories (10% from fat), 0 g protein, 23 g carbohydrate, 1.3 g fat, 0 mg cholesterol, 79 mg sodium, 0 g fiber

CINNAMON SHERBET

MAKES 1 QUART

This is the perfect accompaniment to the Apple Quince Cherry Strudel (page 171). It is so easy to prepare, though, that you'll want to have it all by itself. A.P.

2 cups soy milk
2 cups rice milk
3/4 cup Florida Crystals (see page 224) or agave nectar (see page 224)
1 tablespoon pure vanilla extract
1/4 teaspoon guar gum
Pinch of salt
1/2 teaspoon ground cinnamon

Vigorously whisk all of the ingredients in a bowl until the Florida Crystals are dissolved. Transfer to an ice cream maker, and freeze according to the manufacturer's instructions. (Store frozen, in an airtight container, for up to 2 weeks. If the sherbet becomes icy, defrost and refreeze it.)

NUTRITIONAL INFORMATION

PER 1/2 CUP: 127 calories (11% from fat), 1.9 g protein, 26 g carbohydrate, 1.6 g fat, 0 mg cholesterol, 59 mg sodium, 0.8 g fiber

ESPRESSO-RASPBERRY SORBET

MAKES 1 QUART

The raspberry and coffee flavors in this sorbet make an interesting combination and an unexpected delight! A.P.

2 cups soy milk
2 cups coconut milk
1 1/2 cups whole coffee beans
1/2 cup plus 2 tablespoons light agave nectar (see page 224)
1 (10-ounce) package frozen raspberries (1 1/2 cups), or 10 ounces fresh raspberries
Pinch of salt
1 1/2 teaspoons coffee liqueur

Whisk the soy milk, coconut milk, coffee beans, agave, raspberries, and salt together in a saucepan. Bring to a boil over medium heat, whisking occasionally. Cover, remove from the heat, and let steep for 10 to 15 minutes. Strain the sorbet through a fine-mesh strainer, pressing with a rubber spatula to exude all the juices. Let cool completely, then add the liqueur.

Transfer to an ice cream maker, and freeze according to the manufacturer's instructions. (Store frozen, in an airtight container, for up to 2 weeks. If the sorbet becomes icy, defrost and refreeze it.)

NUTRITIONAL INFORMATION

PER 1/2 CUP: 236 calories (53% from fat), 3.4 g protein, 27 g carbohydrate, 15 g fat, 0 mg cholesterol, 46 mg sodium, 2.6 g fiber

HARD APPLE CIDER SORBET

MAKES 1 QUART

If you like hard apple cider, you'll love this sorbet. Use a sweet apple such as a Fuji or a Braeburn for the best flavor. A.P.

3 apples (about 1 1/2 pounds total), peeled, cored, and diced in large pieces
1 (12-ounce) bottle hard apple cider
1/3 cup water
1/4 cup light agave nectar (see page 224)
1 cinnamon stick
Pinch of salt
1 1/4 teaspoons freshly squeezed lemon juice
2 tablespoons pure maple syrup

Place the apples in a saucepan, and add all but 1/3 cup of the cider, along with the water, agave nectar, cinnamon stick, salt, lemon juice, and maple syrup. Cover and simmer over low heat for 20 minutes, or until the apples are soft. Let sit, still covered, for 5 minutes.

Remove the cinnamon stick, and tranfer the mixture to a blender. Blend until smooth. Let cool completely, and add the remaining 1/3 cup cider.

Transfer to an ice cream maker, and freeze according to the manufacturer's instructions. (Store frozen, in an airtight container, for up to 1 week. If the sorbet becomes icy, defrost and refreeze it.)

NUTRITIONAL INFORMATION

PER 1/2 CUP: 112 (2.3% from fat), 0.2 g protein, 30 g carbohydrate, 0.3 g fat, 0 mg cholesterol, 36 mg sodium, 1.7 g fiber

PEPPERMINT-CHOCOLATE SORBET

MAKES 1 QUART

Use only the freshest organic peppermint for this sorbet. Its subtle mint and chocolate aromas will have you addicted in no time. A.P.

3 ounces bittersweet chocolate, melted
1 cup rice milk
2^1/$_2$ cups soy milk
3 tablespoons unsweetened cocoa powder
^{3}/$_4$ cup light agave nectar (see page 224)
Pinch of salt
^{3}/$_4$ teaspoon guar gum

1 cup chopped fresh peppermint (about 1 bunch)

Line a small baking sheet with parchment paper. Pour the melted chocolate onto the parchment paper, and spread as thinly as possible with an offset metal spatula or a knife. Refrigerate until needed.

Blend the rice milk, soy milk, cocoa powder, agave, salt, and guar gum in a blender. Place in a small saucepan, and bring to a simmer over medium heat. Add the peppermint and remove from the heat. Cover and let steep for 10 to 15 minutes. Strain, squeezing the mint leaves well to extract the flavor, and let cool. Transfer to an ice cream maker, and freeze according to the manufacturer's instructions.

Remove the chocolate from the parchment paper. Be careful not to touch it with your fingers as it will melt on contact. Using a knife, break the chocolate into bite-sized pieces. Fold the chocolate into the frozen sorbet. (Store frozen, in an airtight container, for up to 3 weeks. If the sorbet becomes icy, defrost and refreeze it.)

NUTRITIONAL INFORMATION

PER ^{1}/$_2$ CUP: 176 calories (33% from fat), 4.1 g protein, 32 g carbohydrate, 7 g fat, 0 mg cholesterol, 55 mg sodium, 4.1 g fiber

PINEAPPLE–PASSION FRUIT SORBET

MAKES 1 QUART

Exotic and tropical, passion fruits have an elusive, tart, floral flavor. The color of the juice inside is an opaque, bright orange, unlike any other fruit. The skin is usually a dark purple and is wrinkled when ripe. For an elegant presentation, serve scoops of the frozen sorbet in the leftover passion fruit skins. A.P.

13 fresh passion fruits, halved
2 cups diced pineapple (about ^{1}/$_2$ of a large fruit)
6 tablespoons agave nectar (see page 224)
Juice of ^{1}/$_2$ lime
Pinch of salt

Using a small spoon, scoop the flesh of the passion-fruit into a blender. Pulse only a few times, just to loosen the flesh from the seeds without pulverizing them. Strain through a fine-mesh strainer, and measure out ^{1}/$_3$ cup juice. Rinse any remaining seeds out of the blender.

Place the passion fruit juice, pineapple, agave, lime juice, and salt in the blender. Blend for 1 minute.

Transfer to an ice cream maker, and freeze according to the manufacturer's instructions. (Store frozen, in an airtight container, for up to 2 weeks. If the sorbet becomes icy, defrost and refreeze it.)

NUTRITIONAL INFORMATION

PER ^{1}/$_2$ CUP: 60 calories (2% from fat), 0.2 g protein, 17 g carbohydrate, 0.2 g fat, 0 mg cholesterol, 30 mg sodium, 0.6 g fiber

PEAR-CARDAMOM SORBET

MAKES 3 CUPS

French butter pears absolutely must be used when in season. These pears are very aromatic and have an excellent texture when cooked down. The ground cardamom adds an exotic twist. Substitute ground nutmeg for an equally aromatic quality. *A.P.*

4 French butter pears, peeled and diced (4 cups total)
6 tablespoons agave nectar (see page 224)
$^1/_2$ cup water
$1^1/_2$ tablespoons freshly squeezed lemon juice
$^1/_2$ cup almond milk
$^1/_4$ teaspoon ground cardamom
Pinch of salt

Place the pears, agave, and water in a small saucepan over medium heat. Cover and simmer for 12 to 15 minutes, until the pears are soft and appear slightly translucent. Transfer to a blender, and add the lemon juice, almond milk, cardamom, and salt. Blend until smooth. Let cool slightly before freezing.

Transfer to an ice cream maker, and freeze according to the manufacturer's instructions. (Store frozen, in an airtight container, for up to 2 weeks. If the sorbet becomes icy, defrost and refreeze it.)

NUTRITIONAL INFORMATION
PER $^1/_2$ CUP: 102 calories (4% from fat), 0.4 g protein, 28 g carbohydrate, 0.6 g fat, 0 mg cholesterol, 41 mg sodium, 2.3 g fiber

COCONUT SORBET

MAKES 3 CUPS

This simple coconut sorbet is always a favorite at the restaurant. Served with German Chocolate Cake (page 193), it is downright decadent. It also makes a wonderful "ice cream" sandwich filling for Spicy Ginger Cookies (page 189).

Try these flavor options for a simple twist on this delicious sorbet: For coconut-cardamom sorbet, add $^1/_4$ teaspoon freshly ground cardamom to the mixture before warming. For coconut–rose water sorbet, add $2^1/_2$ teaspoons rose water to the sorbet just before freezing. For coconut-huckleberry sorbet, place $^1/_2$ cup fresh or frozen huckleberries with 1 tablespoon additional agave nectar in a small saucepan over low heat, and cook for about 7 minutes, to create a sauce; let cool, and fold into the frozen sorbet to create a marbled look. *A.P.*

1 (14-ounce) can coconut milk
$^1/_2$ cup water
$^1/_2$ cup light agave nectar (see page 224)
Pinch of guar gum
Pinch of salt
$^1/_2$ vanilla bean

Whisk the coconut milk, water, agave nectar, guar gum, and salt in a small saucepan. Split the vanilla bean in half with a sharp knife. Scrape out the seeds, and place the seeds and the pod in the pot with the coconut milk mixture. Bring just to a simmer over medium heat. Let cool. Strain out the vanilla pod, and discard.

Transfer to an ice cream maker, and freeze according to the manufacturer's instructions. (Store frozen, in an airtight container, for up to 3 weeks. If the sorbet becomes icy, defrost and refreeze it.)

NUTRITIONAL INFORMATION
PER $^1/_2$ CUP: 216 calories (62% from fat), 1.5 g protein, 19.7 g carbohydrate, 15 g fat, 0 mg cholesterol, 50 mg sodium, 0.3 g fiber

BASICS

This chapter contains staples you'll see in many of our recipes. Most of the recipes are essential to our dishes—vegetable stocks, fresh pasta, seitan sausage, baked tofu, chipotle paste. You can substitute commercially available products to save time for some ingredients, such as stocks or marinated tempeh and seitan, but these simple recipes are worth preparing just to add to your food skills and knowledge—and they're great to store and keep on hand, as we do in our kitchen.

VEGETABLE STOCK

MAKES 3 QUARTS

Vegetable stocks are the foundation for many of our soups, sauces, and entrées. We make them every day with the vegetable trimmings we have saved from the previous day. Our stocks vary with the seasons, although onions, garlic, tomato, carrot, and celery are regular ingredients.

This recipe is a good starting point for any number of variations. It is assertive as a basic stock, but can be modified with vegetables, herbs, and spices to accent the flavors in a specific dish. Look at the key flavor notes in a recipe and try to mirror them in your stock. For example, if a sauce contains ginger, add a tablespoon or two of ginger to the stock to give the sauce more ginger backbone. Or, for an asparagus soup, consider using a stock containing asparagus to enhance the flavor (although it probably wouldn't taste good in anything else).

A few words of caution: Stay away from cruciferous vegetables like broccoli, kale, various greens, and the cabbage family; they tend to lend an unpleasant sulfurous, or "skunky," quality to a stock. Also, avoid using too many onion peels, which, when used in quantity, make a stock bitter.

Stocks freeze quite well. Prepare a large batch, portion it into smaller increments (a quart or so), and freeze until you need a batch. E.T.

6 quarts cold water
4 yellow onions, halved
4 cloves garlic
4 carrots, peeled and coarsely chopped
2 celery stalks
2 to 4 tomatoes
1/2 pound button mushrooms, with or without stems
2 bay leaves
6 allspice berries
4 parsley sprigs
1 (2-inch) piece kombu sea vegetable
1/2 teaspoon dried thyme, or 1/2 bunch fresh thyme stems
1/2 teaspoon dried rosemary, or 3 fresh rosemary stems
4 peppercorns
1/2 teaspoon grated lemon zest (optional)
Assorted vegetables of choice (such as root vegetables, fennel bulb, corn, wild mushrooms, and basil stems)

Combine all of the ingredients in a large pot over medium-high heat and bring to a boil. Decrease the heat to medium-low and simmer for 1 hour, or until reduced by one-third. Strain. (Store refrigerated for up to 4 days or frozen for up to 2 months.)

NUTRITIONAL INFORMATION

PER CUP: 20 calories (0% from fat), 0 g protein, 5 g carbohydrate, 0 g fat, 0 mg cholesterol, 25 mg sodium, 0 g fiber

ASIAN VEGETABLE STOCK

MAKES 3 QUARTS

This aromatic Asian inspired stock has top notes of anise, lemongrass, and Kaffir lime. Follow the vegetable stock recipe (page 205), omitting the thyme and rosemary, and adding:

4 stalks lemongrass, crushed or coarsely chopped
1/2 cup coarsely chopped fresh ginger
1 cup shiitake mushroom stems
1 teaspoon Szechuan peppercorns
1 bunch cilantro stems
1 bunch basil stems
1 whole star anise pod
2 Kaffir lime leaves (optional)

Combine all of the ingredients in a large pot over medium-high heat and bring to a boil. Decrease the heat to medium-low and simmer for 1 hour, or until reduced by one-third. Strain. (Store refrigerated for up to 4 days or frozen for up to 2 months.)

NUTRITIONAL INFORMATION

PER CUP: 18 calories (0% from fat), 0 g protein, 2 g carbohydrate, 0 g fat, 0 mg cholesterol, 21 mg sodium, 0 g fiber

MUSHROOM STOCK

MAKES 3 QUARTS

You can improvise a bit with this versatile stock, depending on the season and on the mushrooms in your dish. Each mushroom adds its own character to the stock. Fresh porcini are available in the fall; substitute dried porcini during the rest of the year. Black chanterelles, available in winter, make for a rich, earthy stock, as do morels, which are available in the spring. Follow the vegetable stock recipe (page 205), adding:

8 ounces button or cremini mushrooms
2 ounces dried porcini mushrooms
4 ounces shiitake stems
1 tablespoon nutritional yeast (see page 224)
1 teaspoon tamari

Combine all of the ingredients in a large pot over medium-high heat and bring to a boil. Decrease the heat to medium-low and simmer for 1 hour, or until reduced by one-third. Strain. (Store refrigerated for up to 4 days or frozen for up to 2 months.)

NUTRITIONAL INFORMATION

PER CUP: 22 calories (0% from fat), 0.4 g protein, 2 g carbohydrate, 0 g fat, 0 mg cholesterol, 30 mg sodium, 0 g fiber

ROASTED VEGETABLE DARK STOCK

MAKES 2 QUARTS

This rich and hearty stock has an incredible depth of flavor that lingers on the palate. It will make the difference between a good sauce and an extraordinary one, so it's well worth the time to prepare it. For a vegan demi-glace (a thick concentrate that can be used as the base for a rich sauce), cook the finished stock over medium-low heat for 1 to 1¹/2 hours, or until reduced to 1 cup. E.T.

4 to 6 red onions, halved
2 leeks, white and green parts, sliced
4 to 6 cloves garlic
4 carrots, peeled and coarsely chopped
1 cup shiitake stems
8 ounces button mushrooms
2 cups dry red wine
1 tablespoon olive oil
6 quarts cold water
1 tablespoon nutritional yeast (see page 224)
1 teaspoon ground coffee
2 teaspoons tamari
2 bay leaves
6 allspice berries
$^{1}/_{2}$ teaspoon dried thyme, or $^{1}/_{2}$ bunch thyme sprigs
    or stems
$^{1}/_{2}$ teaspoon dried rosemary, or 3 rosemary stems

Preheat the oven to 400°F. Toss the onions, leeks, garlic, carrots, shiitakes, and button mushrooms with 1 cup of the wine and the oil. Transfer to a roasting or baking pan and roast for 45 minutes to 1 hour, stirring the vegetables after 30 minutes, until well browned.

Transfer the vegetables to a large pot and add the water, the remaining 1 cup wine, the nutritional yeast, coffee, tamari, bay leaves, allspice, thyme, and rosemary. Bring to a boil over medium-high heat. Decrease the heat to medium-low and simmer for 1$^{1}/_{2}$ hours, or until reduced by one-half, skimming the top occasionally to remove oil and impurities from the roasting process. Strain. (Store refrigerated for up to 4 days or frozen for up to 2 months.)

NUTRITIONAL INFORMATION

PER CUP: 17 calories (26% from fat), 0 g protein, 3 g carbohydrate, 0.5 g fat, 0 mg cholesterol, 25 mg sodium, 0 g fiber

FRESH PASTA

MAKES 1 POUND (SERVES 6)

Fresh pasta is a great deal easier to make than you may think. For an extra 15 minutes of work, you can turn an ordinary noodle dish into a gourmet experience. Many cookbooks have pages devoted to the intricate steps involved in making perfect pasta. I, however, am amazed and overjoyed at imperfect pasta. Big rough-hewn noodles cut with a pizza roller, or clumsy hand-cut raviolis boiled for 5 minutes and tossed with olive oil, garlic, salt, and pepper—in my mind, these make a perfect meal.

Our recipe is simple. For most pasta all you need is semolina flour, salt, and water. The ratio is four parts flour to one part water, and this is true across the board. For a recipe starting with 2 cups flour, you'll need 1/2 teaspoon salt. If you want to make stuffed pasta, such as ravioli, you should also add 1 teaspoon olive oil to help the pasta stick to itself.

For variations on the dough, substitute one-quarter to one-half of the flour with other finely milled flours, such as buckwheat, whole-wheat pastry, corn, or rice. You can also add fresh or dried herbs, spices, or spice mixes, or replace the water with a fresh juice. Some of our most successful experiments have involved essential oil of lemongrass, steeped saffron threads, and dried, powdered porcini mushrooms.

The long kneading times called for in many non-vegan recipes are generally necessary to distribute and activate the binding of the egg yolks. In eggless pasta, this step becomes superfluous. For wide noodles, you just need a little time, a large flat surface, and a rolling pin. A pasta roller machine is a wise invest-ment if you want to play with pasta more often.

In cooking pasta there are three things to keep in mind: water, salt, and oil. The most important factor is water. There should always be a ratio of six parts boiling water to one part pasta; anything less will produce mushy and clumped pasta. Salt increases the boiling temperature of water, ensuring that it does not stop boiling when the pasta is added. Oil main-tains the boil by forming a "lid" on the surface of the water to seal in the heat. It also prevents clumping.

This recipe practically defines the word rustic. *It will reintroduce you to the concept of pasta, and once you have seen how quick and easy it actually is, you will find the possibilities are endless. B.E.*

2 cups semolina flour, plus more as needed
1/2 teaspoon salt, plus more as needed
1/2 cup water
Olive oil, as needed

To make the pasta dough, in a mixing bowl, hand-sift the flour with the salt. Add the water and knead to form stiff dough, 1 to 2 minutes.

Lay the dough out on a floured surface and roll it flat using a rolling pin. Fold and roll the dough many times, adding flour to prevent sticking; folding helps form a protein structure that will allow the dough to stay together through the cooking process. If using a pasta roller, gradually decrease the thickness of the dough to the desired final thickness. If you don't have a roller, well . . . just wing it! Italian grandmothers do it all the time!

To cook the pasta, bring 6 quarts of water to a boil, with a little salt and oil. For wide, flat noodles, such as pappardelle, cook for 4 minutes, or until al dente. The smaller the noodle, the shorter the cooking time, down to less than 1 minute for capellini. Drain. If you are not serving the noodles right away, stop the cook-ing of the pasta by plunging it in an ice-water bath.

NUTRITIONAL INFORMATION

PER 3 OUNCES PLAIN PASTA: 200 calories (3% from fat), 7.1 g protein, 40 g carbohydrate, 0.6 g fat, 0 mg choles-terol, 158 mg sodium, 2.2 g fiber

MARINATED SEITAN

MAKES 8 PORTIONS

Seitan, or wheat gluten, has been used as a protein-meat substitute in the East for hundreds of years. The traditional procedure for making seitan is a long process that involves making a flour-water dough and then rinsing it under running water to remove the starch components of the flour, leaving behind the high-protein gluten. The dough is then wrapped in cheesecloth, poached to cook until firm, and sliced and marinated. Our version removes the step of rinsing the dough, which saves about 40 minutes. Look for pure gluten flour, also known as vital gluten, in health food stores. E.T.

SEITAN MEDALLIONS

4 cups pure gluten flour

2/3 cup unbleached white flour

2 tablespoons bran flakes

3 1/2 cups water, cool or at room temperature

MARINADE

1 cup dry red wine

2 quarts vegetable stock (page 205) or water

1/2 cup tamari or liquid amino acids

2 cloves garlic, minced

1 rosemary sprig

8 allspice berries (optional)

1 teaspoon dried sage

1 teaspoon dried thyme

1/4 teaspoon crushed red pepper flakes

2 teaspoons pure maple syrup or Sucanat (see page 224)

To make the seitan, combine the gluten flour, white flour, and bran flakes in a large mixing bowl. Slowly add the water, kneading the dough with your hands until the water is absorbed. Continue to knead for 2 minutes, or until the dough is firm and springy.

Slice the dough into 3 equal portions. Knead each portion into a cylindrical bread loaf shape about 5 to 6 inches long. Cut the cheesecloth into 3 by 10-inch pieces, and open up the cheesecloth. Place a seitan loaf, centered lengthwise, at the bottom of each piece of cheesecloth, and roll the seitan in the cheesecloth. The cheesecloth should be snug but not overly tight to allow room for the seitan to expand. Cut the ends of the cheesecloth down to the seitan, and tie each end to seal lengthwise.

Heat 4 to 6 quarts water in a deep pot over medium-high heat. Bring the water to a rolling boil, and carefully immerse the seitan in the water. Decrease the heat slightly, and partially cover. Boil the seitan for 1 1/2 hours, or until very firm. Remove from the water, and let cool to room temperature, or immerse in an ice-water bath until cool. (At this point you can store the seitan, refrigerated, in an airtight container, for up to 2 days.)

Unwrap the seitan. If the cheesecloth sticks, immerse under running warm water to loosen. Slice the seitan into 1/4- to 1/3-inch-thick medallions.

To marinate the seitan, combine all of the marinade ingredients in a deep pot. Place over medium-high heat, and bring to a boil. Add the seitan medallions, and simmer for 40 minutes, or until seitan is dark brown. Let cool to room temperature in the marinade.

Remove the seitan from the marinade with tongs or a slotted spoon. (Store refrigerated, in enough marinade to cover, for up to 4 days.)

NUTRITIONAL INFORMATION

PER SERVING: 164 calories (0% from fat), 31 g protein, 10 g carbohydrate, 0 g fat, 0 mg cholesterol, 590 mg sodium, 1 g fiber

SEITAN SAUSAGE

MAKES 4 SAUSAGES

Throughout the cuisines of many cultures, sausages are used in dishes to provide intense bursts of flavor and a desirable chewy texture—and that's exactly how we like to use this seitan sausage. It has that familiar flavor and texture to make you think it's the real thing. Try smoking the sausage rolled in the traditional shape (see page 219). Lightly brush the finished sausages with oil before smoking to help retain moisture.

This recipe is for our Italian-style sausage, but we've made many variations, which you can find in our first book, The Millennium Cookbook. *For another unique flavor, one that tastes great in Asian stir-fries, add 1 tablespoon of Thai curry paste and ¹/2 cup coarsely ground peanuts or pistachios. E.T.*

SPICY FENNEL SEITAN SAUSAGE

2 cups pure gluten flour

2 to 4 cloves garlic, minced

1 teaspoon whole fennel seeds

1¹/2 teaspoons ground cumin

1 tablespoon mild chile powder, or 2 teaspoons sweet paprika

²/3 teaspoon ground nutmeg

1¹/2 teaspoons dried sage

¹/4 teaspoon crushed red pepper flakes, plus more as needed

2 teaspoons salt

¹/4 cup olive oil

1 tablespoon tamari

1 cup water

BRAISING LIQUID

1 quart water or vegetable stock (page 205)

3 tablespoons tamari

2 cloves garlic (optional)

2 bay leaves (optional)

To make the sausage, combine the flour, garlic, fennel, cumin, chile powder, nutmeg, sage, pepper flakes, and salt together in a medium bowl.

In a separate bowl, combine the olive oil, tamari, and water. Slowly add the wet ingredients to the flour mixture, kneading with your hands as you add the liquid. Continue kneading until all of the liquid is absorbed and the dough has the consistency of firm bread dough.

For a traditional sausage shape, cut the dough into 4 pieces. Roll each piece to 4 inches long. Cut the cheesecloth into 6 by 4-inch pieces, and open up the cheesecloth. Place a seitan loaf, centered lengthwise, at the bottom of each piece of cheesecloth, and roll the seitan in the cheesecloth. The cheesecloth should be snug but not overly tight to allow room for the seitan to expand. Cut the ends of the cheesecloth down to the seitan, and tie each end to seal lengthwise.

To braise the sausages, combine the water, tamari, garlic, and bay leaves in a stockpot large enough to hold the sausages without bending them. Place over medium-high heat, bring the liquid to a boil, and add the sausages. Decrease the heat to medium-low, cover, and simmer for 1 hour, or until firm and plump. Remove from the liquid and let cool to room temperature. (Store refrigerated, in an airtight container with the remaining braising liquid, for up to 1 week.)

Alternatively, for a softer texture, preheat the oven to 400°F. Place the dough in an 8-inch baking dish or casserole. Add the braising liquid and cover with aluminum foil or an airtight lid. Bake for 60 to 75 minutes, until most of the liquid has been absorbed and the sausage is not runny or gummy when sliced but firm and porous, with small air pockets. Remove from the heat and let cool to room temperature before slicing. (At this point you can store the sausages refrigerated, in an airtight container with the remaining braising liquid, for up to 1 week.)

Unwrap the sausages. If the cheesecloth sticks, immerse under running warm water to loosen.

NUTRITIONAL INFORMATION

PER SAUSAGE: 80 calories (47% from fat), 9.2 g protein, 1.6 g carbohydrate, 4 g fat, 0 mg cholesterol, 507 mg sodium, 0.3 g fiber

BAKED MARINATED TEMPEH

MAKES 6 (4-OUNCE) PORTIONS

This is our all-purpose marinade for tempeh. We bake or braise raw tempeh in this marinade for more than 1 hour to infuse the tempeh with the savory flavors and to remove most of the bitterness associated with tempeh. Bake off a double recipe of tempeh and freeze what you will not use in a week. Then just thaw it when you need it—meal planning will be much simpler. E.T.

1 cup dry red wine
1 quart vegetable stock (page 205) or water
1/2 cup tamari
4 cloves garlic, minced
1 tablespoon Dijon mustard
1 teaspoon dried sage
2 teaspoons dried thyme
1/2 teaspoon ground nutmeg
1/4 teaspoon crushed red pepper flakes
2 teaspoons pure maple syrup or Sucanat (see page 224)
6 (4-ounce) pieces tempeh

Preheat the oven to 350°F. Combine the wine, stock, tamari, garlic, mustard, sage, thyme, nutmeg, and pepper flakes together in a bowl. Place the tempeh in a baking pan and pour the marinade over the top. Bake for 1 1/2 hours, or until the tempeh absorbs the marinade.

Remove the tempeh from the remaining marinade for use or freezing. (Store refrigerated, in the marinade, for up to 1 week, or frozen for up to 4 weeks.)

NUTRITIONAL INFORMATION

PER SERVING: 285 calories (28% from fat), 24 g protein, 27 g carbohydrate, 9 g fat, 0 mg cholesterol, 385 mg sodium, 6 g fiber

BAKED TOFU

MAKES 6 (2-OUNCE) PORTIONS

Our baked tofu has a firm texture and a lacquered skin. It is a staple at the restaurant, and it is great for sautéing and adding to salads, stews, and soups because it won't disintegrate like raw tofu does. For smoked baked tofu, smoke the tofu for 30 to 40 minutes after baking it (see page 219). E.T.

1 pound firm tofu
1/4 cup tamari
1 teaspoon pure maple syrup
1/2 teaspoon toasted sesame oil

Preheat the oven to 350°F. Line a baking pan with parchment paper. Slice the tofu in half lengthwise and then in thirds across the widths, making slices about 1/2 to 2/3 inch thick.

Combine the tamari, maple syrup, and sesame oil in a bowl. Dip the tofu in the marinade and place on the baking pan. Repeat, using all of the tofu. Bake in the oven for 20 minutes. Turn the tofu over, brush with any remaining marinade, and bake for another 20 minutes, or until the tofu is caramel brown (it may take longer, depending on the moisture content of the tofu). Remove from the oven and let cool. (Store refrigerated, in an airtight container, for up to 4 days.)

NUTRITIONAL INFORMATION

PER SERVING: 135 calories (47% from fat), 13 g protein, 5 g carbohydrate, 7 g fat, 0 mg cholesterol, 550 mg sodium, 0.1 g fiber

MILLENNIUM OIL-BRAISED GARLIC

MAKES ¹/2 CUP

Keep this garlic on hand to blend into soups, quick pasta sauces, and condiments. E.T.

2 large bulbs garlic, whole cloves peeled
¹/2 cup extra virgin olive oil
1 small rosemary sprig

Preheat the oven to 350°F. Place the garlic, oil, and rosemary in a crock or small deep baking dish. Cover with aluminum foil and bake for 30 to 40 minutes, until the garlic cloves are very soft and just starting to brown. (Store in an airtight container for up to 2 weeks.)

NUTRITIONAL INFORMATION

PER 2 TABLESPOONS: 101 calories (78% from fat), 0.9 g protein, 4.9 g carbohydrate, 9 g fat, 0 mg cholesterol, 3 mg sodium, 0.3 g fiber

CASHEW CREAM

MAKES 1¹/2 CUPS

This is a nice substitute for heavy dairy cream. For a roasted garlic variation, add ¹/4 cup roasted garlic (see page 222). E.T.

¹/2 cup raw cashews
¹/2 teaspoon nutritional yeast (see page 224; optional)
1 cup water

Place the cashews and nutritional yeast in a blender and add enough water just to cover. Blend to a coarse purée. With the blender still running, slowly add the remaining water and blend to a smooth heavy cream. (Store refrigerated, in an airtight container, for up to 3 days.)

NUTRITIONAL INFORMATION

PER TABLESPOON: 16 calories (69% from fat), 0.5 g protein, 0.8 g carbohydrate, 1.3 g fat, 0 mg cholesterol, 20 mg sodium, 0 g fiber

OIL-FREE BRAISED GARLIC

MAKES ¹/2 CUP

This staple is indispensable for our version of oil-free cookery. The soft-braised and slightly caramelized cloves of garlic can add a depth of flavor to your dish and, when puréed, a creamy texture that is often missing from oil-free cookery. E.T.

2 large bulbs garlic, top ¹/2 inch removed or cloves separated and peeled
1 cup vegetable stock (page 205) or dry white wine
¹/2 teaspoon dried thyme
1 teaspoon fresh rosemary

Preheat the oven to 350°F. Place the garlic bulbs or cloves in a crock or small baking dish. Add the stock, thyme, and rosemary. Cover tightly with aluminum foil and bake for 1 hour, or until soft and slightly brown (this may take a little longer with whole bulbs of garlic than with cloves). Let cool before handling.

To remove the cloves from the bulbs, squeeze the garlic out of the sliced-open top, or slice the top of the head again and squeeze to release the cloves. Use immediately. (Store refrigerated, in an airtight container, for up to 1 week.)

NUTRITIONAL INFORMATION

PER 2 TABLESPOONS: 35 calories (3% from fat), 1.3 g protein, 4.5 g carbohydrate, 0.1 g fat, 0 mg cholesterol, 4 mg sodium, 0.3 g fiber

TOFU AÏOLI

MAKES 1 CUP

This basic recipe has gone through numerous incarnations throughout the years, but it has always been a satisfying vegan spread. You can elaborate on the recipe by adding other ingredients to the list: For saffron tofu aïoli, add 1/4 teaspoon saffron threads that have been soaked in 1 tablespoon hot water for 30 minutes. For Dijon tofu aïoli, add 2 tablespoons Dijon mustard. For roasted red pepper tofu aïoli, add 1 peeled and roasted red pepper or pimiento. E.T.

6 ounces silken tofu
1/4 cup Millennium Oil-Braised Garlic (page 212)
1 tablespoon light miso
Juice of 1 lemon
1/2 teaspoon minced lemon zest
1/2 clove garlic, minced
1 teaspoon nutritional yeast (see page 224)
1 teaspoon Dijon mustard
1 tablespoon chopped fresh parsley
2 teaspoons coarsely chopped fresh dill
1/4 teaspoon freshly ground black pepper
4 tablespoons extra virgin olive oil, or 2 tablespoons water (for oil-free)
Salt

In a food processor fitted with the metal blade, purée the tofu, oil-braised garlic, miso, lemon juice and zest, minced fresh garlic, nutritional yeast, mustard, parsley, dill, and pepper. With the machine still running, slowly add the oil and blend until emulsified. Add salt to taste. (Store refrigerated for up to 4 days.)

NUTRITIONAL INFORMATION

PER 2 TABLESPOONS: 20 calories (41% from fat), 2.2 g protein, 2.4 g carbohydrate, 1.4 g fat, 0 mg cholesterol, 159 mg sodium, 0.2 g fiber

THE ULTIMATE VEGAN NOG

MAKES 4 CUPS

This one isn't really a "basic," but we wanted to share our version of vegan nog. Stephanie Hibbert has been our reigning vegan eggnog maker for the past several Thanksgivings. On Thanksgiving morning she comes in at 6 A.M. and prepares 8 gallons of this recipe. Here is the definitive recipe that yields a more manageable quart. We generally prefer the Mori-Nu brand of silken tofu because it blends up perfectly smooth. E.T.

12 ounces silken tofu
1 very ripe banana
1/3 cup pure maple syrup
1 1/2 tablespoons pure vanilla extract
1/4 teaspoon salt
3/4 teaspoon ground cinnamon
1/2 teaspoon ground nutmeg, plus more for garnish
1 cup almond milk, or soy milk or rice milk (for nut-free)
1 cup rice milk
1 1/2 cups soy milk

Combine all of the ingredients in a blender and blend until smooth and frothy. Ladle into cups and sprinkle nutmeg over each serving. (Store refrigerated for up to 2 days.)

NUTRITIONAL INFORMATION

PER CUP: 159 calories (27% from fat), 6 g protein, 28 g carbohydrate, 5 g fat, 0 mg cholesterol, 190 mg sodium, 1 g fiber

CUCUMBER RAITA

MAKES 2 CUPS

Our version of raita, a yogurt-based Indian condiment, uses tofu as its base. E.T.

6 ounces silken tofu
Juice of 2 limes
2 tablespoons light miso
1/2 bunch mint, leaves only
1/2 bunch cilantro, leaves only
Salt
1 cup peeled, seeded, and diced cucumber

In a blender or food processor fitted with the metal blade, combine the tofu, lime juice, miso, mint, and cilantro until smooth. Add salt to taste. Transfer to a bowl and fold in the chopped cucumber. (Store refrigerated for up to 4 days.)

NUTRITIONAL INFORMATION

PER TABLESPOON: 11 calories (41% from fat), 1.1 g protein, 1.4 g carbohydrate, 0.8 g fat, 0 mg cholesterol, 49 mg sodium, 0.4 g fiber

CHIPOTLE PASTE

MAKES 1 1/2 CUPS

Try a little dab of this paste whenever you want to add heat along with a subtle, smoky nuance to a recipe. While you can usually find canned chipotle chiles in adobo (red) sauce in Hispanic markets and some supermarkets, you can easily make your own without the refined sugar and preservatives and adjust it to your tastes using different varieties of chiles. We buy many varieties of the smoked, dried chiles from a local source, Tierra Vegetables in Healdsburg, California. Dried chipotles are available in most Hispanic markets and specialty food stores. E.T.

8 dried chipotle chiles
1 cup mild tomato sauce or tomato purée
1 cup water
1/4 cup champagne vinegar or other light vinegar
3 tablespoons Sucanat (see page 224)

Combine all of the ingredients in a saucepan over medium-high heat and bring to a boil. Decrease the heat to low, cover, and simmer for 30 minutes. Uncover and simmer for 5 minutes, or until thick. Remove from the heat and let cool to room temperature. Transfer the mixture to a blender and purée until smooth. (Store refrigerated, in an airtight container, for up to 2 weeks, or frozen for up to 6 months.)

NUTRITIONAL INFORMATION

PER TABLESPOON: 12 calories (2% from fat), 0.4 g protein, 3 g carbohydrate, 0 g fat, 0 mg cholesterol, 32 mg sodium, 0.5 g fiber

KECAP MANIS

MAKES ¹/₂ CUP

This sweet Indonesian soy sauce can be found in some Asian markets, but we've created our own version, which has star anise and Szechuan peppercorns. E.T.

¹/₂ cup Florida Crystals (see page 224)
1 teaspoon dark molasses
1 star anise
¹/₂ teaspoon Szechuan peppercorns
¹/₂ cup tamari

Combine all of the ingredients in a small saucepan over medium-low heat and simmer for 10 minutes, until reduced by one-third. Strain out the spices. (Store refrigerated for up to 2 months)

NUTRITIONAL INFORMATION
PER TABLESPOON: 38 calories (2% from fat), 2.1 g protein, 8 g carbohydrate, 0.1 g fat, 0 mg cholesterol, 1006 mg sodium, 0.3 g fiber

TARRAGON OIL

MAKES ¹/₂ CUP

¹/₂ bunch tarragon
¹/₄ cup extra virgin olive oil
¹/₄ cup grapeseed oil

Bring 1 quart water to a boil in a saucepan. Plunge the tarragon into the boiling water for 5 seconds. Shock in an ice-water bath. When cool, wrap the tarragon in a clean kitchen towel and squeeze dry. Place the leaves in a blender with the olive oil and grapeseed oil and blend until smooth. Use immediately, or, if storing, let sit for 2 hours and then strain out the darkened solids. (Store refrigerated for up to 2 weeks.)

NUTRITIONAL INFORMATION
PER TABLESPOON: 119 calories (99% from fat), 0 g protein, 0 g carbohydrate, 13 g fat, 0 mg cholesterol, 60 mg sodium, 0 g fiber

BASIL OIL

MAKES 1 CUP

¹/₂ bunch basil
¹/₂ cup extra virgin olive oil
¹/₂ cup grapeseed oil or any light vegetable oil

Bring 1 quart water to a boil in a saucepan. Holding the basil stems, plunge the leaves into the boiling water for 10 seconds. Shock in an ice-water bath. When cool, wrap in a clean kitchen towel and squeeze dry. Place the leaves in a blender with the olive oil and grapeseed oil. Blend until smooth. Use immediately, or, if storing, let sit for 2 hours and then strain out the darkened solids. (Store refrigerated up to 1 week.)

NUTRITIONAL INFORMATION
PER TABLESPOON: 120 calories (99% from fat), 0 g protein, 0.1 g carbohydrate, 13.6 g fat, 0 mg cholesterol, 1 mg sodium, 0.1 g fiber

CILANTRO OIL

MAKES 1 CUP

¹/₂ bunch cilantro
¹/₄ cup extra virgin olive oil
³/₄ cup canola or grapeseed oil
¹/₂ teaspoon salt

Bring 1 quart water to a boil in a saucepan. Plunge the cilantro into the boiling water for 10 seconds. Shock in an ice-water bath. When cool, wrap the cilantro in a clean kitchen towel and squeeze dry. Cut the leaves and the top half of the stem from the remaining stem. Place the leaves in a blender with the olive oil and the canola oil and blend until smooth. Add the salt. Use immediately, or, if storing, let sit for 2 hours and then strain out the darkened solids. (Store refrigerated for up to 1 week.)

NUTRITIONAL INFORMATION
PER TABLESPOON: 161 calories (100% from fat), 0 g protein, 0 g carbohydrate, 18 g fat, 0 mg cholesterol, 79 mg sodium, 0 g fiber

QUICK-PICKLED ORANGES

MAKES 2 CUPS

This quick-pickled version of preserved oranges yields great results in under 1 hour—and it only gets better the longer it sits. E.T.

6 cups water
1/4 cup salt
2 dried chiles de árbol
3 tablespoons champagne vinegar
3 oranges, skin on, cut into small dice

Bring the water to a boil over medium-high heat, and add the salt, chile, 2 tablespoons of the vinegar, and the diced oranges. Decrease the heat to low and simmer for 30 minutes, or until diced oranges are soft. Drain and then toss in a bowl with the remaining 1 tablespoon vinegar. (Store refrigerated indefinitely.)

NUTRITIONAL INFORMATION

PER 2 TABLESPOONS: 11 calories (4% from fat), 0.3 g protein, 3.2 g carbohydrate, 0.1 g fat, 0 mg cholesterol, 236 mg sodium, 0.8 g fiber

MILLENNIUM PRESERVED ORANGES

MAKES 4 CUPS

We came up with this recipe after we had gotten our hands on four cases of the most beautiful organic oranges. With no way to use the oranges quickly enough, we decided to pickle them before they went bad. E.T.

1 quart water
6 tablespoons salt
6 oranges, peel on, sliced into 1/2-inch-thick rounds
6 star anise
6 dried chiles de árbol
2 bay leaves

Bring the water to a boil over high heat and add the salt. Place the oranges into one or two large pickling or Mason jars. Add the star anise, chiles, and bay leaves, and pour the salt water over to cover.

Seal the jars and store at room temperature for a minimum of 2 weeks and up to 1 month before using. The resulting oranges should be both pickle-sour and slightly salty. If desired, rinse the oranges to remove some of the salt. (Refrigerate indefinitely after opening.)

NUTRITIONAL INFORMATION

PER 2 TABLESPOONS: 11 calories (5% from fat), 0.3 g protein, 3.2 g carbohydrate, 0.1 g fat, 0 mg cholesterol, 1254 mg sodium, 0.8 g fiber

MILLENNIUM FOCACCIA

SERVES 10

This recipe has been around in various forms since the early days of Millennium. Real credit for the final version goes to Anne Dunn, a former prep cook, who went on to open the catering company Urban Kitchen. B.E.

3 cups warm water
2 teaspoons active dry yeast
1/3 teaspoon Florida Crystals (see page 224)
5 1/2 cups unbleached bread flour
2 teaspoons salt, plus 1 pinch
1/4 cup Millennium Oil-Braised Garlic (see page 212)
1/4 cup plus 1 teaspoon olive oil, plus more as needed
3 shallots, thinly sliced

Mix together the water, yeast, and Florida Crystals. Let foam for 4 to 5 minutes (do not let the yeast multiply for longer than 10 minutes; a large foamy head should not develop).

In a large mixing bowl, mix together the yeast mixture, flour, 2 teaspoons of the salt, the garlic, and 1/4 cup of the olive oil to form a wet dough. Turn out onto a wooden cutting board. Knead for 5 minutes by folding and turning the dough with a dough knife.

Return the dough to the bowl. Drizzle with olive oil. On a shelf next to the stove, let rise, uncovered, for up to 1 hour, until doubled.

Smack down the dough and let rise for 45 minutes, or until doubled.

Preheat the oven to 450°F. Oil a baking sheet. Spread the dough onto the pan by pulling and stretching, being careful not to tear it. Oil your hands. Poke the dough evenly, using all ten fingers, until uniform in thickness and perforation.

Toss the shallots, the remaining 1 teaspoon olive oil, and the remaining pinch of salt together in a bowl. Spread this mixture evenly across the top of the dough. Poke the dough down again, using all ten fingers, until uniform in thickness and perforation.

Bake the bread on the bottom shelf for 20 minutes. Rotate, and cook for 15 to 20 minutes, until a firm, golden-brown crust has formed all over. Remove the bread from the oven and transfer onto a rack to cool.

NUTRITIONAL INFORMATION

PER SERVING: 341 calories (16% from fat), 8.6 g protein, 61 g carbohydrate, 6.2 g fat, 0 mg cholesterol, 381 mg sodium, 2.6 g fiber

NON-MACHO CORNBREAD

SERVES 12

Why is this cornbread "non-macho"? Every kitchen has its mysteries! I had read about making cornbread in cast-iron skillets for years. I had never tried it, though, because we always make cornbread in quantities larger than a cast-iron skillet can contain. One day I tried making cornbread in our large carbon-steel French sauté pans and it worked just as a cast-iron pan would. You heat the pan over the stove top, get it good and hot, add a little oil, pour in the batter, and place it in the oven. With the heat of the pan and the oil, an immediate crust forms on the cornbread. The heat is distributed throughout the batter, and the crust prevents the cornbread from sticking. In the end, the cornbread tastes great. E.T.

1¹/₂ cups white flour
2 cups fine corn flour
1 cup coarse cornmeal or polenta
¹/₂ teaspoon toasted cumin seeds, coarsely ground
 (see page 223)
2 teaspoons Florida Crystals (see page 224)
2 teaspoons egg replacer (see page 224)
¹/₂ teaspoon baking soda
2 teaspoons salt
¹/₄ teaspoon freshly ground black pepper
¹/₂ cup corn kernels
1¹/₃ cups soy milk, or more as needed
2 scallions, green part only, chopped
¹/₂ jalapeño chile, roasted (see page 222) and chopped
3 tablespoons unrefined corn oil or extra virgin olive oil
1 teaspoon rice vinegar
1 teaspoon canola oil

Preheat the oven to 350°F. Place the white flour, corn flour, cornmeal, cumin, sugar, egg replacer, baking soda, salt, and pepper in a large mixing bowl. Stir or whisk the dry ingredients together.

Put ¹/₄ cup of the corn kernels and the soy milk in a blender. Blend until puréed. Place in a mixing bowl with the scallions, jalapeño, the remaining ¹/₄ cup corn kernels, the corn oil, and vinegar. Whisk together.

Whisk the soy milk mixture into the dry ingredients until just incorporated, adding more soy milk if needed. The resulting batter should be quite a bit thicker than pancake batter.

Heat an 8- or 9-inch ovenproof cast-iron or steel skillet over high heat. When the skillet is hot, add the canola oil, rolling it around the skillet to coat. Pour the batter into the skillet, shaking the skillet to evenly disperse the batter.

Place the skillet in the oven for 25 to 30 minutes, until a knife inserted into the center comes out dry. Remove from the oven. Let cool for 10 to 15 minutes. Run a knife around the edge of the cornbread and invert the skillet onto a baking sheet to remove the cornbread. Let cool until just warm to the touch before slicing. Cut into 12 slices and serve.

NUTRITIONAL INFORMATION

PER SERVING: 223 calories (21% from fat), 4.9 g protein, 39 g carbohydrate, 5 g fat, 0 mg cholesterol, 372 mg sodium, 4.5 g fiber

SMOKING FOODS

Smoked foods have become a signature and an integral part of Millennium's repertoire. We've smoked almost every product in the larder with varying degrees of success. We've smoked reconstituted beans in a perforated pan for sauces and chili. We regularly smoke onions, tomatoes, eggplant, portobello mushrooms, and reconstituted dried chiles for our own chipotles to add to sauces, soups, or stews or to stand alone, as with our grilled smoked portobello mushroom appetizer. We've even smoked plums and cherries for savory sauces. We smoke tofu regularly as a staple for our spinach salad, and we have smoked seitan and tempeh for entrées.

Hot-smoking, which is the process we use, is not the rocket science people often believe it is. All you need is a heat source; a nonflammable, nonmeltable container to hold the smoking chips and to keep them away from direct heat; a rack to hold and suspend the food product above the chips; a cover to contain the smoke; and an outdoor space. I cannot recommend smoking indoors; most exhaust fans are not powerful enough to draw up all of the smoke, creating a potentially dangerous situation.

Our smoker is just an electric heating element, no different from an electric stove: a pan sits over the burner and holds the chips, a rack holds the food in the smoker box, and a vented lid covers the top. We load the smoker with the chips, load the rack with whatever we are going to smoke, put the cover in place, plug the smoker in, and come back an hour later when the smoking process is done. Vegetable products are less dense than meats and absorb plenty of smoky flavor in one round of smoking.

The home cook has a few options for smoking foods. One is to invest in a home smoking unit, available from many sporting goods and outdoor specialty shops. Just follow the manufacturer's instructions.

A second method is to use a charcoal or gas grill. Smoking chips usually come with printed procedures for using a grill as a smoker. Usually you build a small fire in the center and place the chips, presoaked in water or not, in a container over the hot embers. You put the food product around the outside edges, away from the direct heat of the grill and then cover and smoke. A gas grill is used similarly, except that you want the heat only as hot as needed to smolder the smoking chips.

A third method is to use an electric wok outdoors. Place either a baking tin or a homemade aluminum foil container for the chips at the bottom of the wok. Use the steamer tray included with the wok, or find a steamer tray that suspends the food at least 6 inches above the chips. Heat the wok just enough to smolder the chips, creating a light plume of smoke, and place the cover slightly ajar over the wok.

Different varieties of smoking chips are available at sporting goods and outdoor specialty shops. We use a blend of hickory, apple, and cherry wood chips. I find that using mesquite on its own can be too acrid for smoking vegetables. Grape vines are a nice touch if you live near a vineyard; they add an herbaceous quality to the smoke, as do rosemary and thyme stems. We have also used tea, coriander, star anise, and clove in with the chips for various effects.

This table gives approximate smoking times for various smoked ingredients used in this book. *E.T.*

Food	Smoking Time
Apples	15 to 20 minutes
Cherries	15 to 20 minutes
Eggplant	15 to 20 minutes
Mushrooms	15 to 20 minutes
Onions	30 to 40 minutes
Seitan	30 to 40 minutes
Tofu	30 to 40 minutes
Tempeh	30 to 40 minutes

SOAKING *and* COOKING LEGUMES

Most legumes benefit from presoaking before they are cooked; this speeds up cooking time and improves their digestibility. It is not necessary to soak lentils as long as heartier beans, such as garbanzo or black beans. Green and brown lentils, larger French lentils, and green and yellow split peas can be quick-soaked to remove any indigestible impurities. Smaller lentils, such as red lentils, black beluga lentils, and some French lentils, do not warrant presoaking before cooking. Here are instructions for soaking, quick-soaking, and cooking.

To soak beans, use 3 cups water to every cup of beans. Small to medium beans should generally be soaked for a minimum of 4 hours, while larger ones should be soaked for at least 6 hours. With beans of any size, it's often easiest to soak them overnight. After soaking, drain and discard the water.

To quick-soak beans, bring the beans and 3 cups water for every cup of beans to a boil, and boil for 5 minutes. Remove from the heat, cover, and soak for 2 hours. Drain the beans, discarding the soaking water.

To cook beans, use 3 cups of water for every cup of soaked beans, or 4 cups for unsoaked beans. One cup of dried beans will yield 1 1/2 to 2 cups when cooked. Cooking time varies according to length of soaking time and how old the beans are. Properly cooked beans should hold their shape, yet smash between your fingers with little resistance. Following is a table of approximate cooking times for presoaked beans and legumes:

BEAN	COOKING TIME
Aduki	45 minutes to 1 hour
Anasazi	1 to 1 1/2 hours
Black	1 1/2 to 2 hours
Calypso	1 to 1 1/2 hours
Cannellini	1 to 1 1/2 hours
Flageolet	1 to 1 1/2 hours
Garbanzo	1 1/2 to 2 hours
Kidney	1 to 1 1/2 hours
Lima	1 to 1 1/2 hours
Navy	1 1/2 to 2 hours
Pinto	1 to 1 1/2 hours

LENTIL	COOKING TIME
Brown or green	25 to 30 minutes
French or black	25 to 30 minutes
Red	15 minutes

COOKING GRAINS

BARLEY

MAKES 2 1/2 CUPS

Hulled (whole-grain) barley is the most nutritious form of barley. For pearled barley, use 1 1/2 cups of water and cook for 25 to 35 minutes. You can enhance the flavor by toasting the barley first. To toast barley, preheat the oven to 350°F. Toast the barley in a heavy pan or baking sheet for 10 to 12 minutes, until fragrant and nutty.

2 cups water
1 cup hulled barley

In a saucepan over medium-high heat, bring the water to a boil and add the barley. Decrease the heat to medium-low, cover, and simmer for 1 hour, or until cooked through and fluffy. Remove from the heat and let stand for 5 to 10 minutes before serving.

BROWN BASMATI AND OTHER LONG-GRAIN BROWN RICE

MAKES 2 CUPS

Cooking times vary depending on the rice, so check the package's directions. Toasting the rice before you cook it brings out a nice nutty quality.

1 cup brown basmati or other long-grain brown rice
1 1/2 cups water

In a saucepan over medium-high heat, toast the rice for 2 minutes. Add the water and bring to a boil. Decrease the heat to medium-low, cover, and simmer for 30 to 35 minutes, until cooked through and fluffy. Remove from the heat and let stand for 10 minutes before serving.

ISRAELI COUSCOUS

MAKES 2 1/2 CUPS

Israeli couscous resembles pasta more closely than traditional Moroccan couscous. Use it in salads or as a side to a Middle Eastern–inspired dish.

2 quarts water
Pinch of salt
1 cup Israeli couscous

In a saucepan over medium-high heat, bring the water and salt to a boil. Stir in the couscous and decrease the heat to medium-low. Cook for 7 minutes, or until al dente. Drain and cool under cold running water.

QUINOA

MAKES 3 CUPS

Quinoa is a fluffy grain that is high in protein. It can often be used in place of couscous or rice, in salads and in pilafs. Look for it in health food stores. You can also sprout quinoa so that it may be eaten raw (see page 223).

1 1/2 cups water
1 cup quinoa

In a saucepan over medium-high heat, bring the water to a boil and add the quinoa. Decrease the heat to low. Cover and simmer for 5 to 7 minutes, until the water is absorbed. Let stand for 10 minutes before serving.

TECHNIQUES

To prepare artichokes, pull off the tough outer leaves, peel the thorny outer skin from the base, cut off the top ¼ inch of the artichoke, and discard. To keep the artichokes from oxidizing, store in lemon or orange juice water (add the juice of one fruit per every quart of water).

To reduce balsamic vinegar, heat the balsamic vinegar in a saucepan over medium-low heat and simmer for 15 to 20 minutes, until reduced by half. It should be a syrupy consistency that coats the back of a spoon. Let cool to room temperature. (Store, covered, at room temperature for up to 1 week.)

To make breadcrumbs, preheat the oven to 250°F. For 1 cup breadcrumbs, place 12 (¼-inch-thick) slices of French bread in one layer on a baking sheet and bake for 15 minutes, or until crisp and lightly browned (dry bread will be done more quickly). Let cool to room temperature. Pulse the bread in a food processor fitted with the metal blade until reduced to relatively uniform crumbs. (Store at room temperature, in an airtight container, for up to 2 weeks.)

To char and burr cactus, place the cactus pads over a flame to singe the burrs. If you don't have gas burners or a blowtorch, carefully cut off the burrs with a knife. Flip the cactus pads over and repeat on the other side. Roast the cactus pads in a broiler for 2 minutes, or until lightly charred. Transfer the cactus pads to a work surface and scrape off the charred burrs. Make sure to clean your work surface of any remaining burrs.

To rehydrate dried chiles, place the chiles in a bowl and cover with enough lukewarm (below 118°F) water to cover. Let them sit for 1 hour. Drain, reserving the soaking liquid if needed in a recipe.

To toast dried chiles, place the chiles in a dry skillet over high heat. Toast fo 30 seconds per side, or until the chiles darken a couple shades.

To roast fresh chiles or peppers, preheat the broiler. Place the chiles on a baking sheet or directly on the broiler rack and broil for 3 minutes, or until the skin blisters and chars. Turn the chiles and repeat until uniformly charred. Alternatively, you can use a grill or open flame. Place the chiles in a paper bag or a bowl covered with plastic wrap and let steam for 15 minutes. Peel off the charred skin and remove the stems and seeds. (Store refrigerated, drizzled with a little olive oil if desired, in an airtight container for up to 1 week.)

To supreme citrus fruit, using a paring knife, peel the pith away from the fruit until the flesh is exposed. Cut the segments from the connective membrane.

To roast garlic, preheat the oven to 350°F. Place a garlic bulb on a baking sheet and brush with 1 tablespoon olive oil. Cover with aluminum foil and roast for 1 hour, or until soft. Let cool. Snip the ends of the cloves with scissors and squeeze out the garlic.

To make ginger juice, place 1 tablespoon peeled and grated fresh ginger in a cheesecloth and squeeze to make 1 teaspoon ginger juice.

To skin and toast hazelnuts, preheat the oven to 350°F. For unskinned hazelnuts, blanch in boiling water with 1 tablespoon baking soda for 3 minutes to help loosen the skin. Pour the nuts onto a sided baking sheet and bake for 15 minutes, or until toasted and fragrant. Place the hazelnuts in a bowl, cover with plastic wrap, and let steam for a few minutes. Pour the nuts out onto a clean kitchen towel and rub them together or against a fine sieve to scrape off most of the skin.

To toast nuts, for small quantities (under ½ cup), place the nuts in a dry sauté pan over medium heat and toast, shaking the pan constantly to prevent scorching, until aromatic. Almonds and pine nuts should take about 10 minutes to toast. Pecans and pistachios should take 12 to 15 minutes. Some nuts, especially in larger quantities, are best toasted in an oven, as described for hazelnuts (see above) and walnuts (see below).

To soak pumpkin seeds, place the pumpkin seeds in a bowl and cover with lukewarm water (under 118°F). Let the seeds soak for 2 hours. Drain.

To sprout quinoa, place the quinoa in the bottom of a wide bowl or baking dish. Cover with 1/2 inch of room-temperature water. Cover the container with cheesecloth. Let sit for 1 day at room temperature. Drain and rinse the quinoa. Repeat the procedure for a second day. At the end of the second day the quinoa should be sprouted enough to be digestible. If it is not sprouting, start again with new quinoa. Check the quality of your quinoa, and make sure the water is no hotter than room temperature. Rinse the sprouted quinoa before using. (Store refrigerated for up to 2 days.)

To reconstitute sea vegetables, place the dried sea vegetables in a bowl and cover with lukewarm water. Let sit for 40 minutes, or until soft. Drain. The time can vary depending on the type of sea vegetable, so check the package's directions.

To toast seeds, place the seeds in a dry sauté pan over medium heat, and toast, shaking the pan constantly, for 3 to 6 minutes, until the spices darken slightly and give off fragrant wisps of smoke. They can also be toasted in a 350°F oven until the color darkens slightly; the time varies by the type of seed, so check frequently.

To toast spices, place the spices in a dry sauté pan over high heat, and toast, shaking the pan constantly, for up to 1 1/2 minutes, until the spices darken slightly and give off fragrant wisps of smoke. Remove spices from the pan immediately. (Store in an airtight container for up to 1 week.)

To peel and seed tomatoes, cut an X in the bottom of the tomato and blanch in boiling water for 30 seconds. Immerse the tomato in an ice-water bath until cool. Using a paring knife, peel back the skin, starting at the X. Seed tomatoes by cutting them in half and squeezing or scooping out the seeds.

To blanch vegetables or fruits, quickly immerse the vegetable or fruit in boiling water for 30 seconds (or as directed in a recipe), and then shock by immersing in an ice-water bath to arrest the cooking process. This helps prevent loss of color and flavor.

To toast walnuts, soak 1 cup walnuts in 2 cups warm water for 30 minutes to remove some of the bitter tannins and make them crisper. Preheat the oven to 350°F. Drain the nuts. Place on a baking sheet and bake for 30 minutes, or until dry and light brown, rotating the pan every 10 minutes. Let cool to room temperature before using.

GLOSSARY

This glossary provides definitions of a few basic ingredients commonly found in our recipes and much of vegan cooking. For information on other ingredients, such as mushrooms and chiles, consult a food reference guide or our first cookbook, The Millennium Cookbook.

Agar: A tasteless dried seaweed that can be used in place of gelatin and acts as a setting agent. It is widely used in Asia and sold in the form of blocks, flakes, or strands. Agar can be purchased in Asian markets and natural food stores.

Agave nectar: A natural liquid sweetener extracted from the agave plant. The plant's syrup makes a great substitute for honey. It is available in natural food stores. You can also use light maple syrup.

Arrowroot: A starch obtained from the rhizomes or roots of various tropical plants. The finely powdered starch is an excellent natural thickening agent for soups, sauces, and other cooked foods in lieu of flour or cornstarch. Unlike cornstarch, arrowroot does not alter the taste of foods prepared with it. It is tasteless and becomes clear when cooked. Arrowroot can be purchased in supermarkets and natural food stores.

Egg replacer: A powdered, egg-free commercial product made with starches and used as a substitute for eggs in many recipes. Egg replacer can be purchased in natural food stores and in many supermarkets.

Florida Crystals: A brand-name less-refined, granulated cane sugar. We use it for white sugar. It is available in most natural food stores. You can substitute any light, unrefined sugar.

Kudzu powder: The ground root of a common Asian legume, frequently used as a thickening agent. It can be found in most Asian markets.

Miso: A fermented soybean paste that is often used in Japanese cooking to make miso soup or to flavor various dishes. Barley and rice are also sometimes used in miso. Miso comes in several varieties: lighter-colored varieties are used in delicate soups and sauces, and darker-colored varieties are stronger in flavor and used in heavier dishes. In this book, we generally call for light miso. Look for shiro (white) miso, also called sweet white miso, yellow miso, or light barley miso. We use organic chickpea miso from Miso Master.

Nutritional yeast: A seasoning and dietary supplement with a "nutty," cheeselike flavor. It is available in natural food stores, in both flakes and powder form. Do not confuse with brewer's yeast or other active yeasts.

Pomegranate juice: The juice of pomegranates (not to be confused with pomegranate molasses). It is available in natural food stores and Middle Eastern markets.

Seitan: Also called "wheat meat," seitan is a protein-rich food made from gluten (wheat protein). Seitan has a chewy texture and is used as a meat substitute in many vegetarian dishes. It can be prepared in the kitchen or purchased in natural food stores and Asian markets.

Soy sauce: A sauce made from fermented soybeans and wheat or barley. We use tamari (see below) almost exclusively. In raw cooking, we use unpasteurized nama shoyu soy sauce (we prefer Oshawa brand), which is also good in dishes that demand a richer soy sauce.

Sucanat: A brand-name unrefined, granulated cane sugar made from evaporated sugarcane juice. We use it for brown sugar. It can be found in most natural food stores. You can substitute any raw sugar.

Tamari: A dark, thick fermented sauce made from soybeans. Tamari is made without the wheat used in the more commercially common shoyu soy sauce. It is available in natural food stores and Asian markets.

Tempeh: A fermented soybean cake traditionally used in Indonesia. Tempeh is high in quality protein and has a yeasty and nutlike flavor that is popular in vegetarian cooking. Tempeh can be purchased in natural food stores and most supermarkets.

Tofu: A soybean curd made from soy milk. It is available in many textures, such as soft, firm, and extra firm. Silken tofu has a creamy texture. At Millennium, we generally use Mori-Nu brand.

INDEX